SPECIAL FORCES WILDERNESS SURVIVAL

Other books in the series include:

SAS and Special Forces Fitness Training by John 'Lofty' Wiseman
SAS Mental Toughness Training by Chris McNab
How to Pass the SAS Selection Course by Chris McNab
SAS and Special Forces Self-Defence Handbook by John 'Lofty' Wiseman
Extreme Unarmed Combat by Martin J. Dougherty
How to Fight Like a Special Forces Soldier by Steve Crawford
World War II Secret Operations Handbook by Stephen Hart & Chris Mann
SAS and Special Forces in World War II by Michael E. Haskew

SPECIAL FORCES WILDERNESS SURVIVAL

CHRIS McNAB

amber
BOOKS

First published in 2011 as *The Elite Forces Wilderness Survival Guide*

This Amber paperback edition first published in 2021

Published by Amber Books Ltd
United House
North Road
London N7 9DP
United Kingdom
www.amberbooks.co.uk
Instagram: amberbooksltd
Facebook: amberbooks
Twitter: @amberbooks
Pinterest: amberbooksltd

ISBN: 978-1-83886-076-9

Project Editor: Michael Spilling
Designer: Graham Beehag
Picture Research: Terry Forshaw

Printed in United States

CONTENTS

INTRODUCTION

Surviving a wilderness emergency doubtless involves a degree of luck, but having military survival skills can certainly tip the probable outcomes in your favour. These abilities protect you from making poor decisions at critical moments, and focus on the clear goals of preserving health and getting to safety. Protected as our ordinary lives often are by warm homes, good food and a sometimes tedious lack of threats, such skills need to be acquired before an emergency if they are to be genuinely useful. Such is the objective of this book.

Of course, willpower and toughness can also be defining

Global terrain

Military survival skills begin with knowledge, particularly an understanding of the terrain a soldier is likely to face on operations. This map provides an overview of major terrain features across the world, including mountainous and jungle regions.

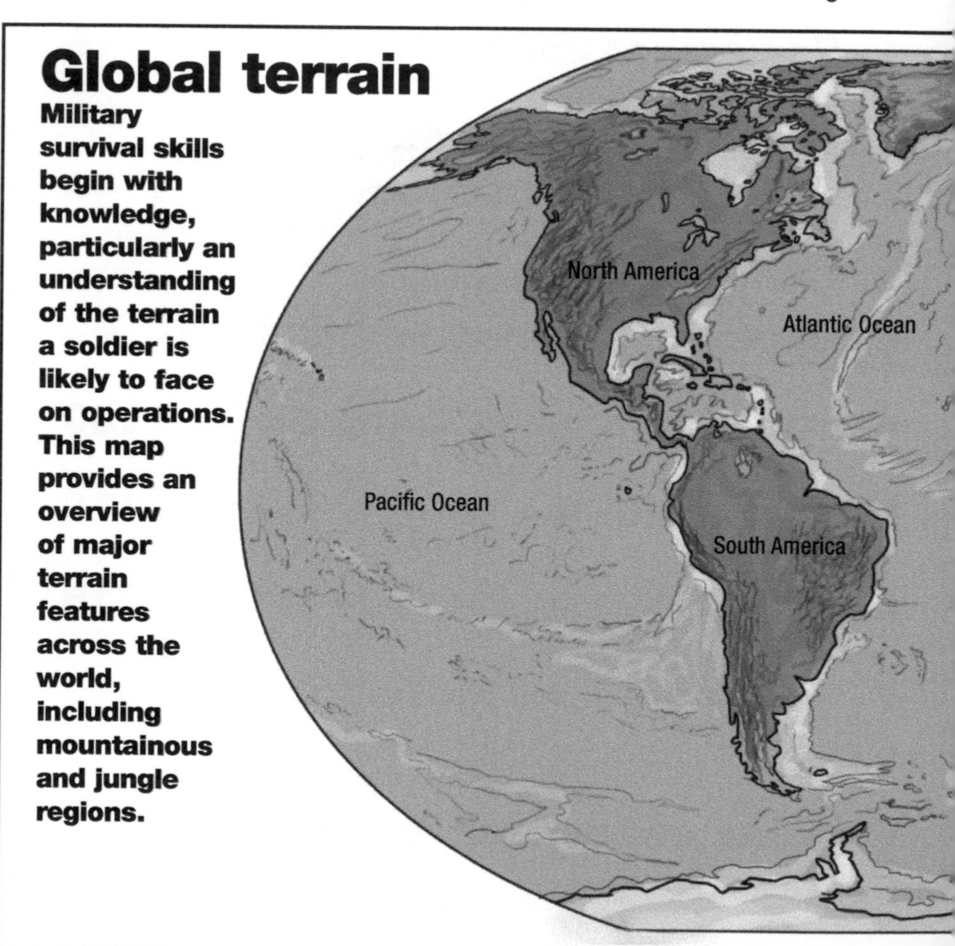

factors in a soldier's survival, ones that will even compensate for a limited knowledge of survival techniques. For perhaps the greatest enemies in any survival situation are fear and loss of control. Mental submission leads to poor judgement, carelessness, apathy and lack of awareness, all factors that can lead you to make an already bad situation that much worse. When faced with any survival emergency, therefore, try to take control of your mental and physical processes from the outset:

- Counter negative thoughts with positive, clear actions.
- Be utterly determined to survive, no matter how hard the situation becomes.

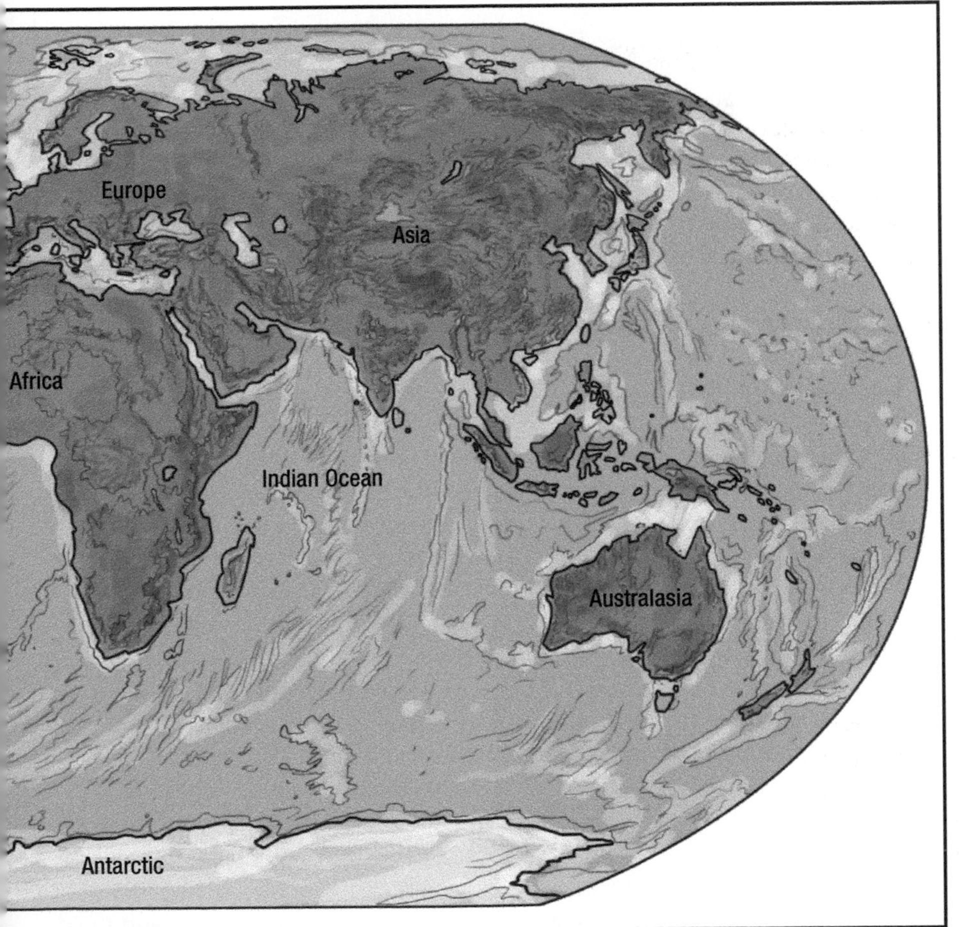

Cooperation

Soldiers rely on their comrades implicitly for mutual protection and survival. For any wilderness expedition, therefore, choose you companions wisely, selecting those with physical and mental toughness plus a good sense of humour.

- Keep busy. Do not aim for unrealistic goals, but set clear survival objectives one at a time and feel a sense of satisfaction and optimism as each is accomplished.
- Control your posture. Soldiers are taught to express confidence with their bodies, not fear. Keep your chin up (literally and figuratively), stand up straight and pull your shoulders back. Breathe deeply from the abdomen. Move decisively and with confidence.

Recognize, however, that negative mental conditions might be the result of insidious environmental factors. Cold, for example, retards blood flow and induces sleepiness, effects that are not only mentally disabling, but can also be a prelude to hypothermia. Equally, high temperatures can lead to dehydration, which has a chronic impact on the brain's efficiency (brain tissue is 85 per cent water). Food deprivation leads to dizziness and blackouts, and an increased vulnerability to cold and thirst. Should you suspect your mental state is caused by environmental factors, tackle those issues first. If cold, seek or make shelter and build a fire. Keep up your intake of water, and if water is scarce cut down on food, as the body uses large amounts of fluids in the process of digestion, particularly of fatty foods. If hungry, naturally make your priority to increase food intake. If fatigue – the primary cause of much depression and anxiety – is at the root of your feelings, schedule 20 minute naps every few hours or so.

PLANNING AND PREPARATION

Survival confidence is often a direct result of how well you prepared

Route planner

Plan any intended wilderness journeys on a route planner, including the stage destinations and intended timetable.

ROUTE PLAN

Date: Time: Starting point reference:

Weather forecast:

Members of party:

Description:

To (grid reference)	Description (of target)	Direction	Distance	Time (for distance)	Height gain	Time (for height)	Total time	Description (of route and terrain)	Possible alternative route	Escape route

Finishing point reference: Estimated pick-up time:

Description: Estimated phone-in time:

Natural threats

Terrain is one of the chief considerations for a commander going to war. In a similar way, you must understand the exact threats and opportunities presented by each different terrain you might encounter.

yourself before going out into the wilderness. As with soldiers, preparation should always begin with intelligence gathering. Research the area to which you are travelling, using every available source, including travel guides, high-quality and recently produced maps and personal contacts who have visited the area. The Internet is another useful tool. Official websites of government foreign departments often contain cultural and political information about world countries, including listings of countries to avoid (the CIA and British Foreign Office both have very comprehensive websites in this regard). The Web also features numerous message boards and news groups where individuals post accounts of their travels. Use their experience to help your own preparation, though try to rely only on reputable websites, as the information is usually not verified by external authorities.

A key research goal should be to find out as much as you can about the climate, geography, and flora and fauna of the country or region you intend to visit. Investigate how the time of year affects weather conditions. Check to see if the area is prone to monsoons, heavy snowfall, forest fires, sandstorms, short daylight hours, excessively low/high temperatures, wildlife problems or any other seasonal events, and try to schedule your trips outside of particularly adverse periods. Nearer to the time of your expedition, monitor the weather conditions of your chosen destination closely. International weather forecasts are readily available over the Internet, and forecasts can even be texted directly to your mobile phone. Listen out for radio weather updates regularly and check national park bulletin boards, but always have the right clothing to cope with any seasonal extreme – weather forecasts are, as the members of any family picnic will tell you, not always correct.

As with elite forces on 'hearts and minds' operations, cultural research should also form a key part of your preparation, especially in today's spiritually and morally complex world. Showing disrespect towards or ignorance of the customs of the indigenous population can land you in serious trouble, if not outright danger in more lawless regions. Watch that you respect any religious sites or artefacts, and dress appropriately for the culture. This latter point is particularly relevant for women, as Western styles of dress can attract at best unwanted sexual advances or at worst severe legal penalties in certain parts of the world, especially in Arab and Muslim cultures. Find out as much as you can about social customs and etiquette, and also about prevalent criminal or political activities that may affect your travel. Learn a few key phrases in the language, including how to make an apology if you cause offence. Do not, however exciting it may seem, go to countries in the throes of conflict. If you get yourself into trouble in such places, someone may ultimately have to risk his or her life to get you out.

PHYSICAL FITNESS

One of the key advantages enjoyed by soldiers in survival situations is that their military training means they are physically strong. Many people, before setting out on an unfamiliar adventure, typically overestimate their level of fitness, particularly if they go on to experience climatic effects such as severe heat/cold, altitude, steep gradients or rough terrain. Also remember that the irregular physical demands of the wilderness can be far more punishing than the controlled exertions of a gym, so always make sure you get fit through a variety of means – weight training for strength; running, swimming or cycling for aerobic endurance; Yoga or stretching for flexibility; and so on.

Try to reform your daily lifestyle to make fitness part of who you are. If you have a diet high in fatty foods, for example, combined with a sedentary job and you smoke, the chances are that you are unfit for any arduous outdoor activity. In terms of general lifestyle changes to improve fitness, try the following:

- Give up smoking and limit alcohol intake to low levels.
- Eat fewer take-out meals.
- Always use stairs, not elevators.
- Walk more. Try not to use the car for any journey under a mile. When you do drive, park the car a decent distance away from your destination so that you have to walk farther.
- Be more active at home. Do your own gardening. Play energetic games with the children. Take them and the dog for long walks.

Press-ups

Press-ups are a key component of military fitness programmes for good reason. They improve upper body strength tremendously, and increase aerobic capacity.

- Limit the amount of television you watch each day, and if you are watching television get up and walk around during the commercials.

Add on to these daily routines a systematic programme of fitness training, and you should be physically ready to tackle a wilderness adventure. However hard you prepare, you can never take the fundamental unpredictability out of nature, but like soldiers you can be in the best condition possible should an emergency strike.

Lunges and parallel bar dips

Use a mix of different physical training exercises to promote all-round fitness. Lunges, for example, develop the thigh and core muscles, while parallel bar dips enhance shoulders and the upper arms.

Seated dumb-bell press

Increasingly, soldiers supplement their PT sessions with weight-training workouts. Learn a variety of free-weight exercises, such as the dumb-bell press here, which enhances shoulders, arms and chest.

1

Equipment and Clothing

What you carry and what you wear can make the crucial difference in a survival emergency.

Special forces soldiers focus a great deal of attention on kit. Every item that they take on operations has to fulfil a valued purpose, and anything extraneous constitutes nothing more than unwanted weight. This being said, many soldiers today also supplement their military issue kit with some of the excellent survival clothing and equipment available on the market. But with so much being on offer, you, like them, should be very strict with what you take with you into the wilderness. A backpack packed with useful contraptions and bulky clothing may feel manageable for a couple of miles, but it can turn into a crushing burden over many days.

Therefore, when choosing the items you need, consider two factors: the type of emergencies that could occur and the climate/terrain you will face. Judge everything in terms of function, and ask yourself one question: does this item directly contribute to my physical welfare? If not, leave it behind.

BACKPACKS

On operations, a soldier virtually carries his home in his backpack. For you, it will carry your shelter, sleeping

Remember that survival equipment and clothing need to be robust, suited to the job and not too complex to use in an emergency.

Military packs

Military-style packs are purposely designed for hard use as well as long-term comfort. Army surplus shops will have a wide variety of items for sale, but check for any damage before you buy, and ensure that equipment fits you properly.

TIP: Packing a backpack

- Keep the contents to an absolute minimum – remove anything of sentimental or luxury value that contributes unnecessarily to weight.
- Pack all the items you will need regularly or suddenly – such as food or a dry pullover or sweater – in the side pockets or top section.
- The top flap of the backpack is ideal for storing wet-weather clothing, as it is quickly accessible.
- Increase waterproof protection for the contents (particularly sleeping bags) by packing them in several separate, strong plastic bags as a precaution in case of a sudden ingress of water, as might occur if you fall into a river.
- Items which are needed infrequently – such as sleeping bags – will go towards the bottom of the pack (unless their bulk requires separate storage in a roll outside the backpack).
- Edges or corners of cans, footwear and hard objects must be kept towards the centre of the pack so that they do not rub against your back.

bag, food and cooking supplies and, ideally, everything you need to survive in the wild. The first issue in selecting a backpack is capacity. Backpacks range from small 20-litre (1220-cubic inch) capacity packs to large 100-litre (6100-cubic inch) military bergens. Be realistic about what you need the pack for, and choose one that is large enough only for your purpose; anything too voluminous will encourage excess weight carriage. A filled backpack should be no more than one-third of the carrier's body weight.

In terms of design, backpacks come in two main varieties – external and internal frame. External frame backpacks tend to work best on lengthy expeditions, as you can strap sleeping bags and tents to the frame without taking up the backpack's internal capacity. Internal frame packs, by contrast, can be more

Packing a backpack

Soldiers become experts at packing backpacks. They work on the simple principle that the items needed most regularly – such as food and wet-weather clothing – are at the top and in side pouches, while items needed less frequently go towards the bottom.

comfortable and manoeuvrable. As always, get the advice of a professional when choosing your backpack, selecting one that offers maximum comfort and strength with the best utility factors.

There are several features you should look for in a good backpack:

- Side pockets – essential for carrying quick-access items.
- A separate base compartment for storing wet or infrequently-accessed items.
- Extendable flaps over the pockets and main openings, which allow you to vary the backpack capacity.
- Double stitching, taped seals, storm flaps over zippers and bar tacks to increase the backpack's strength and waterproofing.

Adjust your backpack so that it fits snugly to your body, with minimal movement when walking, but not so tight that the straps restrict circulation to the limbs – lengthen or shorten the straps accordingly. If the straps are rubbing, do likewise, or pad the straps with foam pieces until the backpack is a perfect fit. Wear the pack high up your back, with the weight centralized. The high position allows your legs to take more of the weight and also reduces the possibility of back strain.

As with clothing, keep backpacks in a good state of repair. Take repair materials with you, particularly strong tape, a tube of superglue, some nylon patches and strong sewing thread. With these materials, you can mend most torn seams or punctured fabric.

SLEEPING BAGS

A good sleeping bag is vital for ensuring rest and warmth during an expedition into the wilds. In terms of shape, close-fitting sarcophagus-shaped or semi-rectangular bags are typical military issue, as they minimize the air space surrounding you, which will require body heat to warm up. They are also less bulky.

For insulation, select a sleeping bag filled with down, one of the best insulating materials, or an equivalent synthetic material such as Thinsulate, Quallofil, Hollowfil or Polarguard. The two have different properties. Natural down (preferably Eider duck or goose) is very light and extremely warm, and down sleeping bags tend to pack up far smaller than synthetic-fill ones. Yet the natural materials tend to lose their insulating properties if they get wet – in wet conditions, therefore, a waterproof cover for a down-filled bag is essential. Synthetic-fill bags, by contrast, are generally bulkier and heavier, but perform better in wet conditions.

Most sleeping bags are graded according to the lowest temperature for which they are suitable, so choose the right bag for your

Horseshoe pack

The horseshoe pack is an expedient method of carrying supplies in the absence of a professional backpack, and was used by insurgent forces such as the Viet Cong. Simply wrap up all the items for carrying in a large sheet (preferably of waterproof material) and tie off the ends, then use further cords to divide the pack into thirds (these stop the contents from sliding around). Finally, sling the pack over one shoulder and tie the two ends at the opposite hip.

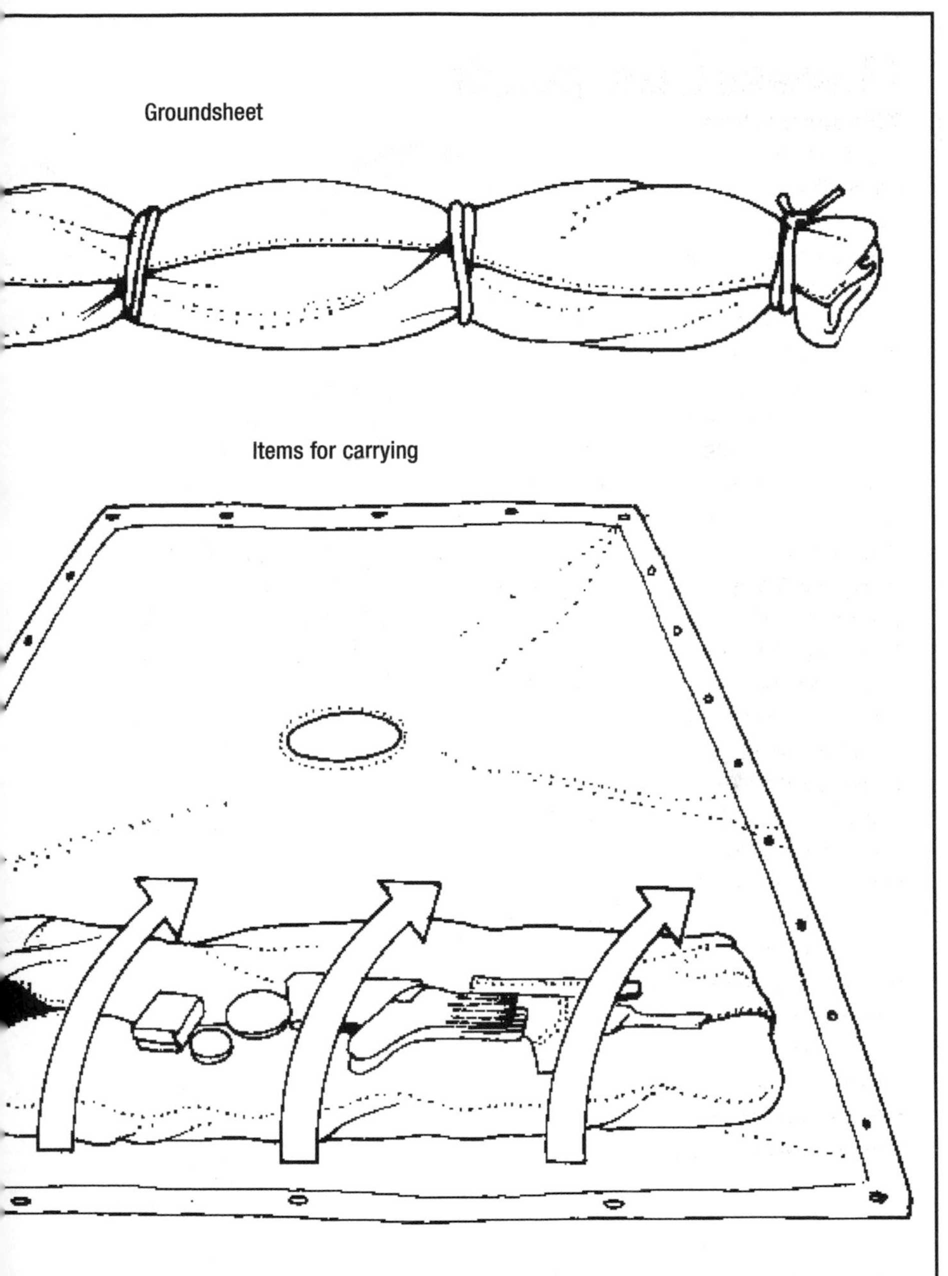
Groundsheet
Items for carrying

intended destination. Alternatively, you could opt for an all-weather sleeping system consisting of a sleeping bag, a fleece liner and a 'bivi-bag' (see below). Whatever you choose, make sure that it fits your height and other dimensions.

Sleeping mats are an important addition if you are planning to sleep out for any length of time, and some modern ones come with self-inflating and deflating functions. Do not sleep directly on cold ground – more heat will be lost through contact with cold ground than with cold air. In fact, remember that if your body is cold you will be cold in the sleeping bag (you warm the bag up, after all). Before getting in, therefore, it could pay off to do some light exercise to raise your body temperature. It's also a good idea to include a couple of lightweight foil survival blankets (such as used by athletes) as back-up if for any reason the sleeping bag is lost.

Note that in tropical climates a hammock may be a better form of bed than a sleeping bag because it is cooler and packs up much smaller. Modern commercial survival hammocks are relatively inexpensive and durable and pack up extremely small. Some also come with their own mosquito nets, useful additions in any tropical or temperate zone.

TENTS

Your tent is a portable home, a primary barrier between you and the

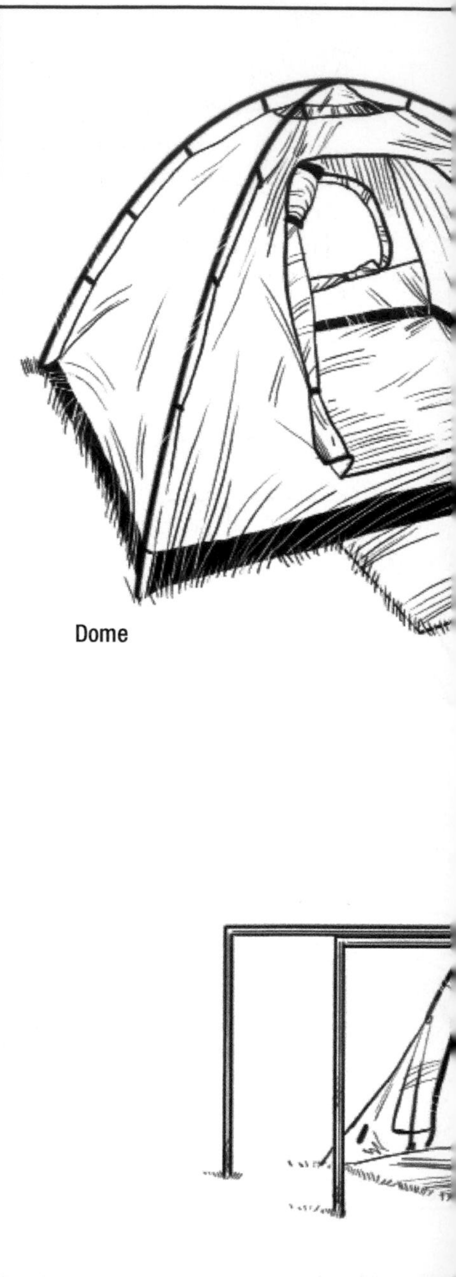

Dome

Types of tent

Your tent should be just big enough to accommodate you and your equipment, while also being resistant to the worst that the weather can throw at you. Tunnel and dome tents are fine for light or moderate conditions, but geodesic tents offer greater stability in high winds. The British Army's own pop-up tent, for example, is of geodesic design.

elements. The huge variety of tent types on the market makes buying a tent a complicated experience, hence expert advice from shop staff is imperative. As with any other survival equipment, however, you should buy one suited to your needs, not to your desires.

The first criterion in tent selection is obviously space, but for backpacking and hiking purposes the tent should rarely exceed two-person capacity. Generally, avoid traditional canvas tents, which have decent durability but are heavy to transport. Instead, look for tents that have strong polyester flysheets, with a heavier polyurethane-coated nylon groundsheet and GRP/fibreglass or aircraft aluminium poles. (Many modern tent fabrics also offer UV treatments to protect you from penetrating sunlight.)

With any basic wilderness tent, ensure that it has the following:

- Full waterproofing, with seams that are taped and lap-felled (meaning that the layers of fabric interlock). Choose a waterproofing standard of 1500HH or higher, depending on the climate you will endure, and ensure that all fabrics are treated with fire retardants.
- An inner cotton wall, which helps reduce condensation and improves the tent's 'breathability'. If you go for a single-sheet tent, choose one made of a breathable material such as Gore-Tex. (Because of weight considerations, single-sheet tents may be the best option.)
- Poles linked together with shock-cords for easy construction.
- Mosquito nets, for zipping over the entrances – especially important if you are travelling to a tropical or summertime location.
- Light weight – no more than 2.72kg (6lb) for a two-person tent.

Of course, if you want to be far more minimalist, you can always choose a simple tarp shelter or a bivi-bag. The latter is a portable shelter constructed using hoops, which erects into a low-profile, one-man tunnel tent. Their use is not ideal for extended pursuits, as you cannot cook or even store any significant equipment inside.

They are, however, windproof and waterproof, and weigh only about 540g (1.19lb), so they are easily packed as a back-up to the main tent or for use during one- or two-day activities in temperate conditions.

For more extreme climates, you need a proper winter tent, which carries its own set of specific requirements. It should have a weight of 3.63–4.54kg (8–10lb) – the extra weight provides the tent with greater sturdiness in winter conditions – and needs extra capacity to handle the larger amounts of equipment carried in winter expeditions.

Regarding tent shape, geodesic (dome-shaped) tents are a good choice, with an ideal shape for resisting high winds.

SURVIVAL TIN

The survival tin is a portable container for carrying the basic tools of survival. Essentially the tin is a last resort, the

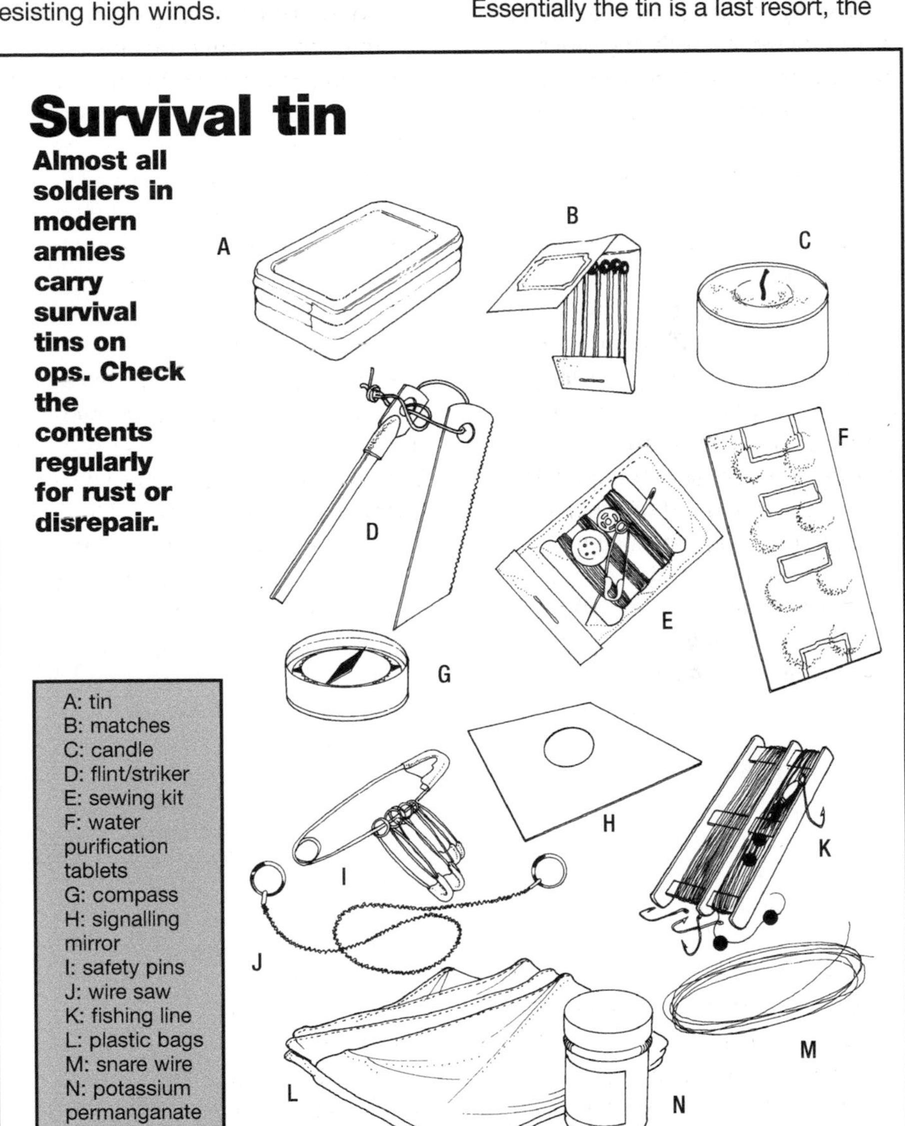

contents of which can be used when more substantial pieces of kit have been lost or are unavailable. For this reason, do not put it in your backpack, in case that is lost or stolen; instead, tuck it away safely in a buttoned or zipped jacket or trouser pocket.

The basic contents of a good military survival tin are as follows:

- Matches – dip the heads in melted candle wax and let them dry to give a waterproof coating. (Commercial waterproof matches are available.)
- Small candle – not only for light and fire, but also because tallow wax is edible in an emergency.
- Flint and striker for firestarting – some of the best types include a magnesium section; small flakes of magnesium can be scraped onto tinder before spark ignition, the resulting hot flame increasing the chances of lighting damp tinder.
- Water purification tablets – pack enough to provide a week's supply of clean drinking water.
- Small hand mirror – used for signalling by flashing sunlight. Purpose-designed commercial types are available.
- Safety pins – can repair clothing and be used as improvised fishing hooks.
- Sewing kit – for stitching damaged clothing or making clothing out of animal skins.
- Fish hooks, line and split-lead weights – the fishing line can also be used to catch birds.
- Clear, strong plastic bag – ideal for storage solutions or for use as a solar still.
- Brass snare wire – use for animal traps or lashings.
- Wire saw – insert pieces of wood through the end loops to create an ideal saw for cutting logs.
- A small whistle – used for auditory signalling.
- Button compass – carried as a back-up to your main compass.

Survival knife

Special forces survival knives can be obtained from military surplus stores. Good versions include, in the handle, a button compass, flint and striker and fishing line/weights, plus other features on the blade such as wire cutters.

That last item, the button compass, is a vital element of your survival tin/survival pack. Check both it and your main compass regularly for leaks (the needle is usually floated on oil), and learn basic methods of compass navigation before venturing into the wilderness.

Regularly check the contents of your survival tin for signs of deterioration. Prevent damage from shaking by packing the contents with cotton balls or cotton wool, which can also be used for making fire. Coat any metal objects in a thin film of grease to protect them against rust.

KNIVES

Knives are critical pieces of a soldier's kit, being employed for everything from skinning animals to making shelters. The best type of knife is one that has a single, strong blade sharpened on one side only, with a broad opposite edge and a wooden handle securely fitted with rivets that pass right through the tang. Military survival knives, though expensive, are also useful, as the handles contain basic survival tools, such as fishing line and weights, a button compass and water purification tablets.

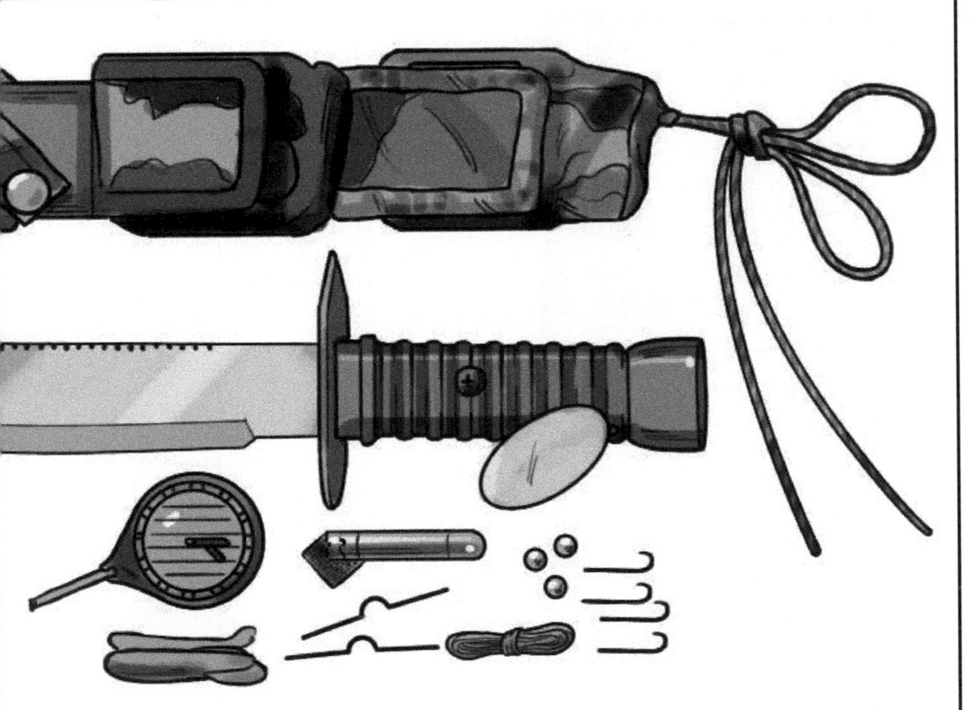

Survival telephone

Many soldiers often carry satellite and mobile phones to supplement their military-issue comms. Satellite phones differ from mobiles in that they have greater coverage, the best models being configured to work reliably in any environment.

As a back-up, carry a small but sturdy lock knife. A multi-blade knife such as a Swiss Army Knife is useful, but the absence of a locking system can make it dangerous to the fingers when cutting tough materials. Having said that, the Swiss Army Knife contains a highly practical range of blades, some including decent saws plus tweezers and fish hook removers.

Just as they take care of their firearms, soldiers also look after their knives. Keep your knife clean and sharp, and always carry it within a scabbard (to protect both you and the blade), especially when travelling. Never stick or throw it into tree-trunks or branches, or even soft ground; the hard wood and grit in the soil will damage and blunt the blade.

Survival axe

This survival axe features a folding haft, which enables you to store the axe conveniently in a small pouch. Axes are excellent tools for shelter/raft building and for collecting firewood, speeding up the process of gathering materials.

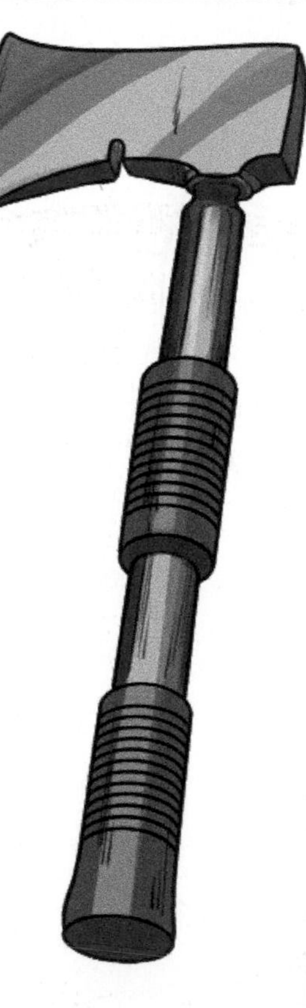

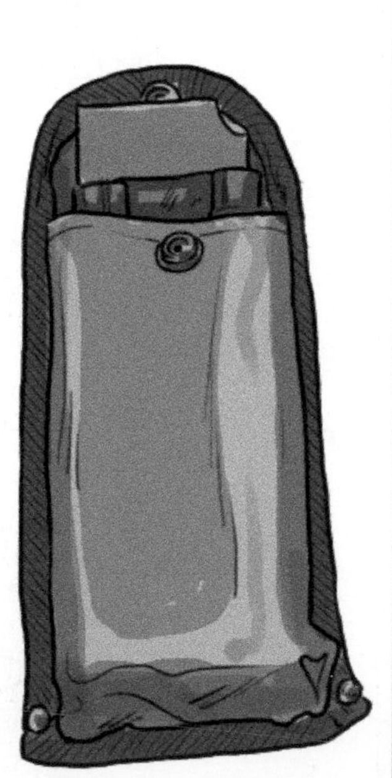

COOKING EQUIPMENT

The most important item of cooking equipment is a portable stove. This should be lightweight – 500–700g (1.1–1.54lb) – and also compact, without too many loose attachments. Your choice of fuel – butane/propane, methylated spirits (denatured alcohol), paraffin (kerosene) or petrol (gasoline) – depends on how the stove will be used. For instance, when used in a tent, paraffin stoves require a lot of ventilation to disperse toxic gases. Never use hexamine blocks (small blocks of inflammable material that burn with a hot flame for around 10 minutes) or petrol within a tent. Note also that cooking gas can freeze in subzero temperatures.

When it comes to cookware, you can buy compact cooking sets made of stainless steel, and with four or

Survival stove

Portable gas stoves are light and convenient to use, and provide the simplest route to heating small amounts of water and food.

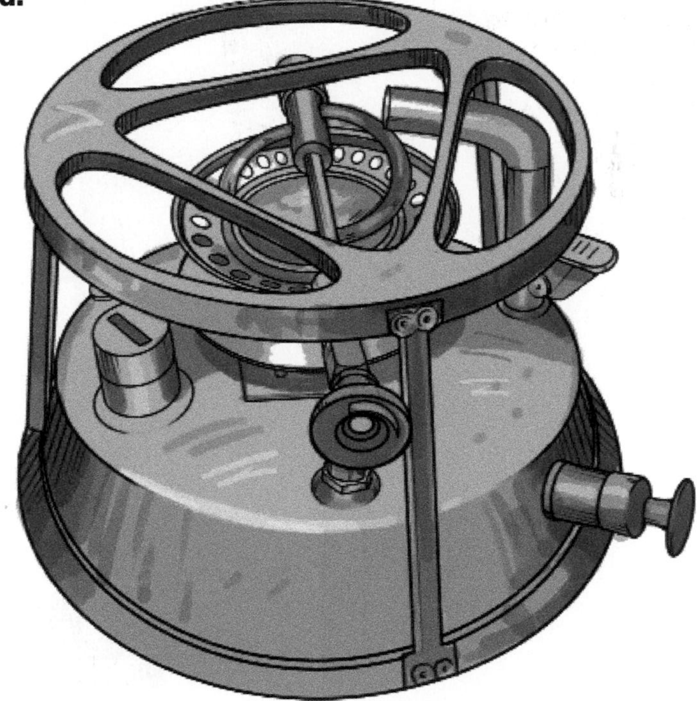

Hydration bladder

Instead of, or as a supplement to, water bottles, many special forces soldiers will wear hydration bladders such as this one for convenient access to water. A typical bladder will have a 2-litre (3.5-pint) capacity.

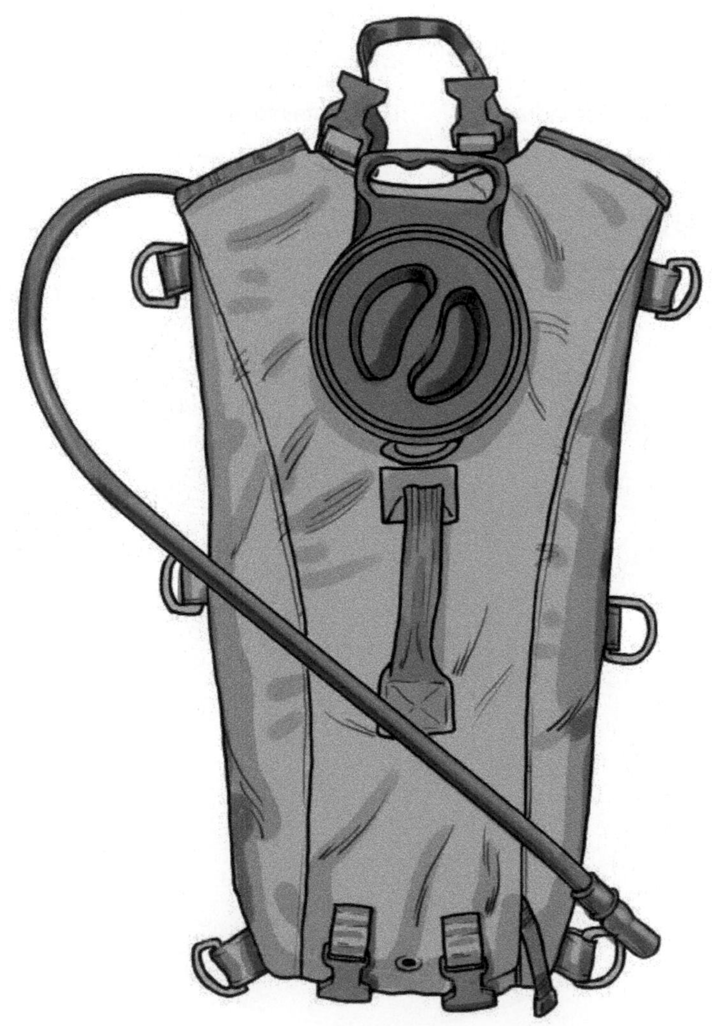

Storm kettle

Storm kettles are a traditional soldier's friend. They are a simple method of heating, with no complex parts to go wrong, and they keep working in the toughest environments.

Fishing equipment

The advantage about packing fishing equipment is that a few weights, hooks and sinkers, plus a length or two of line, fill up almost no space in your pack. Ideally, take a variety of hook sizes and line weights to enable you to go after different varieties of fish.

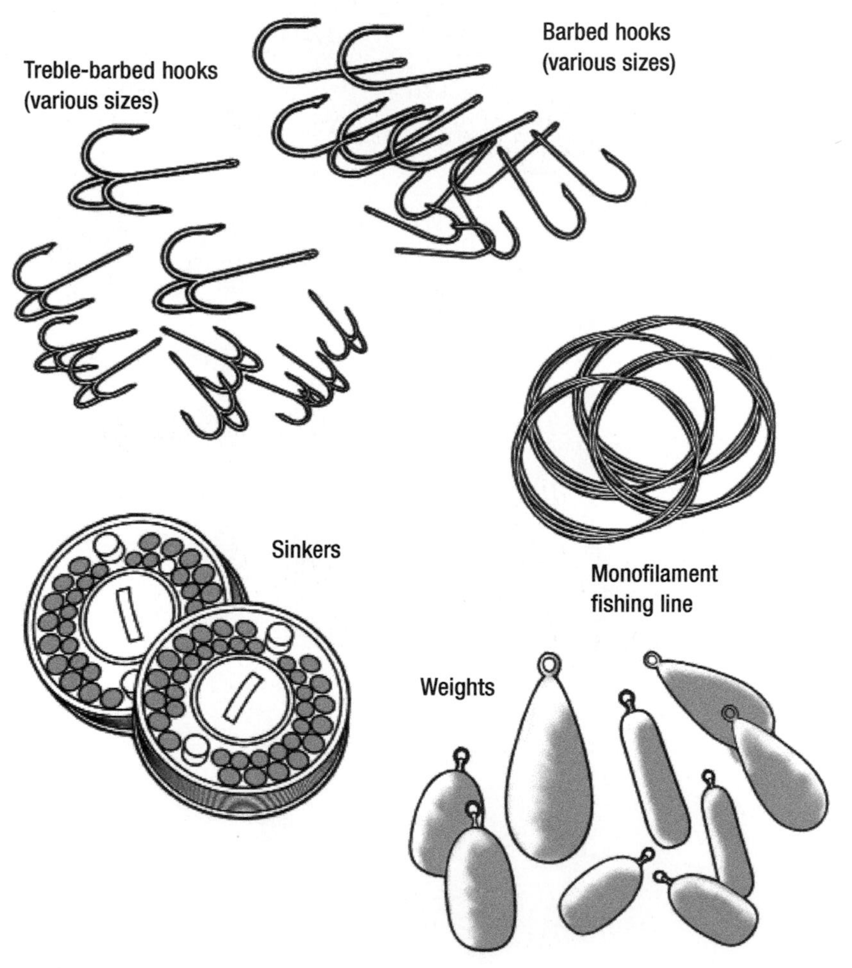

Wire saw

The NATO-issue wire saw is often part of special forces escape-and-evasion and survival kit. It will cut through wood, plastic and bone, and packs up into a convenient pouch.

Vacuum-packed food

In the field, soldiers often survive on little more than Meal, Ready to Eat (MRE) pouches, plus durably packaged energy foods like dried fruit, nuts and chocolate. Waterproof food packaging is recommended to guard against contamination, damp and decay.

five items each stored inside one another. For short trips, however, two vessels may suffice. For crockery, use lightweight plastic plates and bowls. As always, don't take more than you actually need.

CLOTHING

Military survival clothing has to meet multiple demanding requirements, keeping the soldier warm/cool (depending on the climate) while protecting against everything that the weather and environment can throw at him – rain, snow, harsh sunlight, insects etc. Technological advances in survival clothing over the last 20 years, however, have been exceptional, particularly in the science of fabrics.

A core problem faced by survival clothing is that when the wearer exerts himself, he sweats. The sweat can be trapped in inner clothing, soaking it through. In cold climates, when the wearer stops moving, the sweat-soaked clothing then draws away body temperature as it dries, increasing the wearer's danger from hypothermia and other cold-related conditions.

Thankfully, modern 'breathable' fabrics have gone a long way to addressing this problem. Gore-Tex is the best known of these materials – other brands include Ultrex and Extreme. The micro-porous membrane allows perspiration to evaporate through it, limiting sweat build-up inside the clothing. Critically, however, the material remains fully waterproof to external water. It achieves this by having nine billion pores per square inch, each pore being 20,000 times smaller than a water droplet, but 700 times bigger than a molecule of water evaporation. You can also choose survival fabrics that offer an ultraviolet protection factor (UPF) of 40+, significantly reducing your chances of sunburn.

Layering

The fundamental principle of survival clothing is layering, working on the thinking that several light layers provide better insulation than a few heavy layers. In essence it involves trapping still air between numerous layers of clothing, to reduce the temperature gradient between the body and its surrounding environment. Each band of air is warmed by the body and produces multiple layers of insulation. You can readily add or take away layers as a method of temperature control.

The most important layer is that which you wear next to the skin. It should be light and of breathable fabric – for this reason avoid pure cotton T-shirts as these are easily soaked by sweat. In cold climates, the 'base layer' should also have thermal properties, and cover the legs and the arms.

Depending on the climate, the subsequent layers might be as follows:

- A woollen or wool-mixture shirt.
- An insulating layer, typically consisting of a thermal fleece, which has a very high warmth to weight ratio.
- Finally, light windproof and waterproof trousers. This layer must pull easily over other clothing (including boots) without being tight-fitting.

Note that many modern survival jackets combine multiple layers in one item, typically fleece and outer layers; these are often zipped together to allow you to separate them if need be. Exercise some caution about breathability claims, however. Modern fabrics are indeed excellent at 'wicking' away sweat,

TIP: Maintaining survival clothing

Soldiers are taught in basic training to take responsibility for their clothing, knowing that it will lose its protective properties if it is allowed to fall into disrepair. Here are some soldier's tips about maintaining your clothing:

- Keep it clean. Dirt reduces both waterproofing and heat retention, so if your clothing becomes dirty clean off the dirt with a non-abrasive method, such as wiping down with a damp cloth.
- Keep it repaired. Sew up any tears in clothing as soon as you get the opportunity, before the tear has a chance to widen. Waterproof glues are available to repair tears in waterproof seams.
- Keep it dry. Dry your clothing out at every opportunity, either by hanging it up in the open air or by suspending it near – but not over – an open fire. Never crumple up wet clothing and leave it in a pouch or backpack – it will develop mildew and may begin to rot.

but sweat build-up is always likely if you are working your body hard. For this reason, carry duplicate items of all clothing up to the final jacket and waterproof layer. This enables you to change out of sweat-soaked inner clothing when you break from exercise.

Jackets

The principal quality of an outer jacket is that it should be windproof and waterproof, and be made from a breathable fabric. Make sure that it's big enough to accommodate several layers of clothing underneath without being tight, and it should be knee-length with drawstrings at the waist and hem. All zippers, particularly the main zip, should feature storm flaps sealed by both stud fastenings and Velcro to prevent the wind and wet from entering. Adjustable wrist fastenings are useful – tight elasticated versions can be good in wet or cold weather, but they can also cause you to overheat should the weather warm up. (Some more

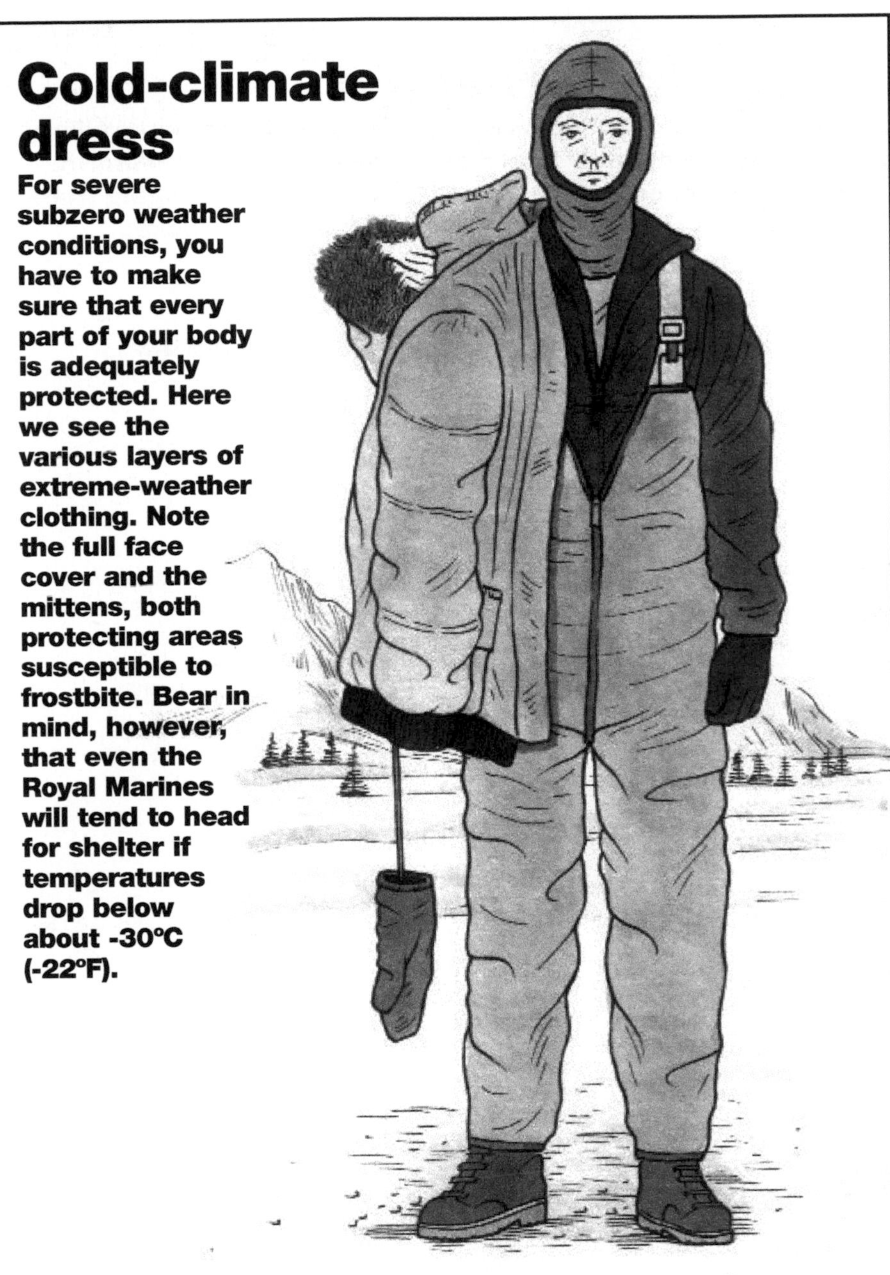

Cold-climate dress

For severe subzero weather conditions, you have to make sure that every part of your body is adequately protected. Here we see the various layers of extreme-weather clothing. Note the full face cover and the mittens, both protecting areas susceptible to frostbite. Bear in mind, however, that even the Royal Marines will tend to head for shelter if temperatures drop below about -30°C (-22°F).

Layering principle

The layering principle offers you the best way of controlling and preserving body heat. The British Army CS95 uniform, for example, consists of seven different items, ranging from a thermal vest base layer to an outer Gore-Tex jacket.

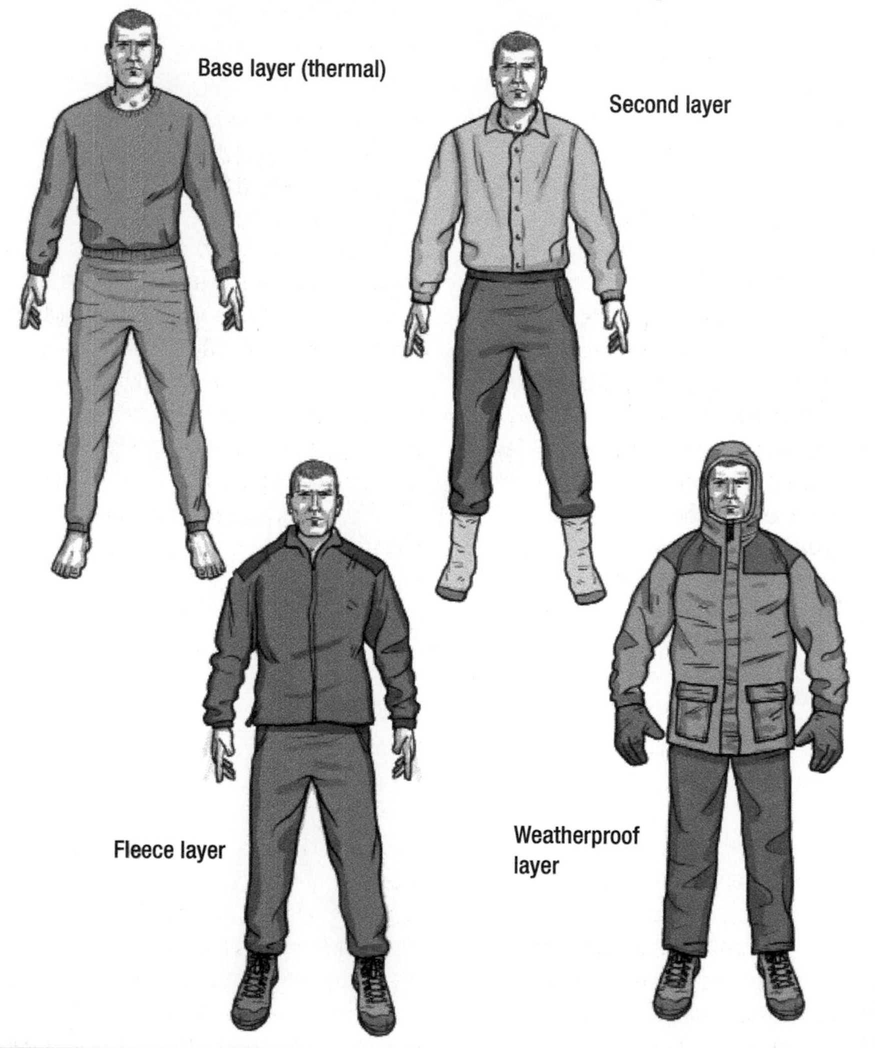

expensive jackets feature one-handed adjusters, which can be useful if you are wearing gloves or carrying items.) The jacket's hood must have enough space for a hat to be worn underneath, and it should also fasten up to cover the lower part of the face. A wire stiffener and drawstrings will allow you to pull the hood close around the face, preventing both heat loss and the wind blowing the hood off your head.

For practicality, the jacket needs at least two large outside pockets with waterproof flaps, and it is best to have a large inside pocket that can hold a map. Sleeve pockets can also be useful for storing smaller items for quick access. Regarding colours, choose something that makes you easier to see in an emergency. Bright colours stand out and increase the chances of a rescue patrol spotting you. The only exception to this rule might be if you are doing any hunting, in which case camouflage is the best choice. The ideal in this situation would be a light camouflage waterproof layer over a bright jacket – the waterproof layer can be removed if conditions are dry.

Note that a useful additional, or even alternative, outer layer can be a waterproof poncho. When fitted with a hood, a poncho provides excellent general protection and is large enough to drape over your backpack, protecting that item as well. In emergencies, it can also double up as a groundsheet or improvised shelter.

Trousers

As with all other survival clothing, trousers should be of breathable material and also have quick-drying properties (look for trousers with drying loops fitted, so you can easily hang them up). They also need to be strong, as they come into regular contact with foliage, trees and rocky surfaces. Polycottons and polyamides are good trouser fabrics, particularly for general trekking or hot climate use. Make sure that the trousers allow free leg movement and are not too tight, otherwise your legs will sweat more. All pockets should be large and fastened with zippers covered by storm flaps. Reinforced knee-covers are useful, particularly if you are heading for mountainous terrain. In addition to your standard trousers, you should have a pair of windproof and waterproof trousers. These are worn over your regular trousers and feature a zipper at the side around the ankle to allow you to put them on while wearing boots.

Headgear

Always take warm headgear with you into the wild. Even on summer days, temperatures can vary significantly depending on factors such as time of day, altitude and cloud cover. At night particularly, temperatures even in desert areas can plunge dramatically.

Waterproof clothing

Waterproofing is critical, as even the warmest fleece or woollen clothing will lose much of its insulation when wet.

Furthermore, a simple woolly hat can make you more comfortable as you sleep, a time in which body heat is lost rapidly if not conserved.

In general, woollen or synthetic thermal hats are good for temperate and cold-weather conditions. For more severe cold, you need an insulated hat with neck, ear and cheek protection, possibly worn over a thin balaclava for full face coverage.

In hot climates, increasingly popular leather or canvas Australian-type 'sheepherders' hats are excellent, providing a wide all-round brim to give shade, while being waterproof and ventilated. They also have a near-miraculous resistance to being blown off in high winds. Alternatively, you can wear an Arab head-dress, known as a keffiyeh or shemagh. SAS soldiers donned these during operations in Iraq, and they are relatively easy to make. Take a piece of light, sun-reflective cloth, ideally white in colour, about 1m (3ft 3in) square, and fold it over the head, neck and shoulders. Secure in place with a cord around the top of the head. When completed, there should be enough excess material to be wrapped around the face when necessary (such as in a sandstorm). Avoid baseball caps – the brim only provides limited shade.

Footwear

Anyone who visits a modern adventure store is confronted by a huge variety of outdoor footwear. This includes hiking sandals, hiking shoes, walking and climbing boots and mountaineering boots. Each has its merits, but the general principle to follow is that the harder the terrain you will tackle, the more substantial the footwear needs to be. Above all, choose boots that are suitable for your activity. A mountain boot, for example, is more rigid than a standard walking boot, and will make for tough going over flat land. Do not wear athletics shoes for any wilderness activities, however, as their soft construction will not provide adequate protection against twisting and impact, or cope with cold and rough terrain.

Whatever boot you choose, certain properties are always desirable. Flexibility is important to ensure comfort, although the boot or shoe needs to be strong enough to provide good support to the structures of the leg and ankle. The exception to flexibility is if you need a mountaineering boot with regular use of crampons – these boots require more rigid toes, soles and heels. The sole of the boot should have a deep tread, and you can also buy boots with shock-absorbing features to reduce the risk of injuries such as tendonitis. Boots with waterproof, breathable membranes will help to keep your feet dry in wet conditions. In terms of materials for the uppers, there are many to choose from, with

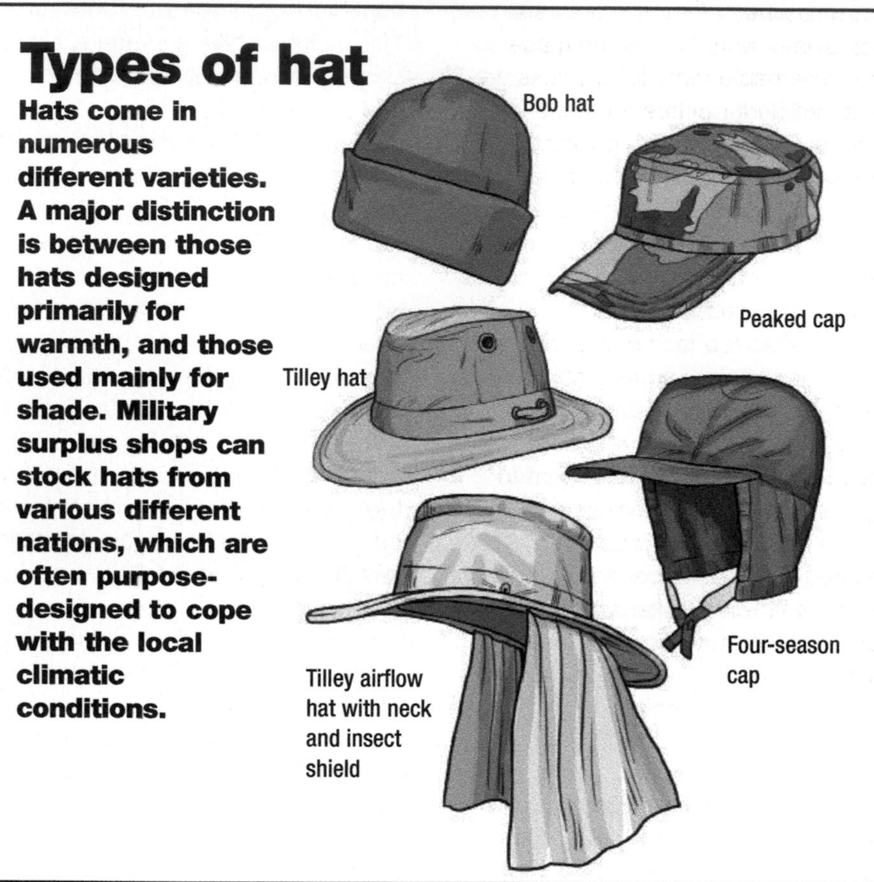

lighter footwear often made from synthetic materials such as Gore-Tex while more traditional leathers are used for the heavier boots.

It is impossible to be prescriptive about which boot to choose, as the selection depends on many factors. Whatever you do choose, however, purchase the boots long before you plan to put them to heavy use, and wear them around the house to increase their flexibility and so avoid blisters. Break them in further with a few short test hikes. When buying boots, put on the layers of socks you will need to wear, and always try them on in the afternoon when your feet are warm and expanded.

Socks and gloves

Hiking socks not only insulate the feet from cold, they also reduce the friction between foot and boot and wick away sweat (if they are made from breathable materials). Socks are classified under different categories, such as for walking and climbing, so choose a type appropriate to your activity. A woollen or cotton-blend sock is good, with Lycra grip sections around the ankle and instep to prevent the sock slipping.

Try various types of socks before embarking on your activity to make sure they are suitable. Avoid socks that are too tight, as these restrict the circulation and can promote frozen feet. Take plenty of spare socks so you can put on a dry pair when necessary. Wearing wet socks for any length of time puts you at risk of developing trench foot, so change them regularly.

An old soldier's trick is to wrap damp socks around the neck or stomach to dry them out. Some socks are impregnated with antibacterial agents to maintain the health of the garment; if not, wash out old socks on a regular basis.

Choosing the right gloves is just as important as choosing the right socks. There are many woollen and ski gloves available, but in severely cold climates mittens provide better insulation. Wearing a pair of thin thermal gloves under your mittens allows you to use your fingers when you need to, but make sure the mittens are attached to the jacket by a cord or they can be easily lost.

TIP: Insect repellent

On tropical ops, insect repellent is an essential precaution for soldiers, particularly against mosquitoes and ticks. The US Center for Disease Control recommends repellents with the following chemical composition, based on the length of time between applications:

- 1–2 hours
<10 per cent DEET
<10 per cent picaridin

- 2–4 hours
~15 per cent DEET
~15 per cent picaridin/KBR 3023
~30 per cent oil of lemon eucalyptus/PMD

- 5–8 hours
~20 per cent–50 per cent DEET*

*This composition is also best used in areas where both ticks and mosquitoes are prevalent.

2

Living Off the Land: Water and Plant Food

Of all the survival priorities, finding adequate supplies of water comes at the top of the list.

For soldiers, hydration is one of the most important planning considerations. Combat operations, particularly in tropical or arid zones, deplete body fluids at an alarming rate. If the losses aren't matched by fluid intake, then problems range from mild dehydration through to death from heat exhaustion. For this reason, US Army units often have strict hydration schedules, each soldier having to drink a specific amount of fluid at a dedicated time. When supplies of bottled water are not available, however, soldiers need to look elsewhere.

Here we will explain some of the tried and tested methods used by elite forces to obtain water in the wilderness. We will then go on to consider plants as a primary source of survival food, while the next chapter will consider animal foods. Note that your travel preparations should include a detailed study of the edible and poisonous flora and fauna of your destination, using reputable field guides for identification. As we shall see, there are some ways in which you can compensate for uncertainty, but as always it is far, far better to be properly prepared.

Finding water is an active pursuit, not a passive hope. Think not only about how to find water, but also how to catch it and store it for later consumption.

WATER

Finding water is undoubtedly a soldier's most important priority in any survival situation, ranking well above the need for food. The reason for this is quite simple – our bodies can typically endure on little or no food for prolonged periods before we succumb to starvation. Without water, by contrast, we stand a high chance of dying within just a few days. Dehydration begins if only 1–5 per cent of body fluid is lost and not replaced, producing symptoms such as thirst, confusion, nausea and fatigue. Serious medical problems accrue as dehydration increases and affects blood pressure, kidney function, digestion, brain processes and waste disposal. Losing one-tenth of the total body water content results in severe illness, including headaches, dizziness, shaky limbs, blurred vision and difficulty breathing. Continue to lose fluids without replacing them, and you will eventually go into circulatory shock and are likely to die if the fluid equation is not quickly restored.

Water supplies

Obviously the most accessible sources of water in the wilderness are those that you have brought with you. Fluids should be kept in impact-resistant containers with leak-proof tops. There are a variety of containers available, from traditional military-style water bottles through to large collapsible water bags that hold up to 15–20 litres (26–35 pints), but which conveniently fold down into a small pack when not filled.

Water is heavy stuff, so you have to strike a balance between taking plenty of fluids with you and managing your weight loads. Also, establish a strict drinking regime. Follow the 'little but often' rule for fluid intake, but should an emergency survival situation strike, immediately ration the remaining water to last as many days as possible with a reasonable supply. Do not break the ration unless there is a significant increase in air temperature or levels of exertion.

An excellent modern survival tool is the water filter pump. These hand-held machines contain a cylinder full of purifying chemicals – water is pumped through the cylinder out of an outlet tube into a waiting container, the machine extracting dirt, debris and bacteria (not viruses) as it passes through. Filtration pumps are available from good outdoor activity suppliers, but make sure that you choose appropriately. They vary in the size of the filter pores; generally speaking, you need smaller filtration pores (with higher levels of filtration) for use in tropical or developing countries than you do in temperate climates.

In a true, unexpected survival situation, however, you are unlikely to have plentiful supplies of fresh water

Water storage

There are many different types of water storage vessel available, from vacuum flasks through to high-capacity military hydration bladders. Remember that water adds considerably to weight, so increases in fluid weight may mean you have to reduce other elements of pack.

Water-carrying frame

A water-carrying frame can be made by cutting a Y-shaped wooden bough, leaving forks on the uppermost branches of the Y. Using cord, you can strap a water container to the bough, tying the whole structure to your body in the manner of a backpack.

Water filter pump

Portable water purification pumps were first developed by the US military during the 1980s. Their advantage is that they instantly clean natural water, rendering it drinkable as it passes through in-built filters, without the need for boiling.

TIP: Fluid loss

Special forces soldiers are taught that our bodies are in a constant process of losing body fluids:

- Urine output – approximately 1.5 litres (2.6 pints) per day.
- Defecation – approximately 0.2 litres (0.4 pints) per day.
- Sweat/skin diffusion – approximately 0.5 litres (0.9 pints) per day.
- Daily average loss in temperate climate, normal levels of exertion – 2–3 litres (3.5–5.3 pints).
- Tropical/desert conditions, heavy exertion – water replacement should be around 19 litres (33.4 pints) per day.

or filtration pumps. In those circumstances, you need to look for safe water in the natural world.

Open water

Streams, rivers and ponds are by far the most conspicuous sources of water. However, many natural watercourses, particularly those in the tropics, contain all manner of bacteria, animal and plant matter, parasites and diseases. Drinking such water untreated is likely to lead to diarrhoea, worsening your body fluid situation rather than improving it. With few exceptions, you should always filter and purify any water, no matter how crystal clear it looks.

In flat, agricultural land, water sources may not be obvious, but inspect irrigation ditches between fields, and look in gullies or culverts. Also, don't disregard dew as a source of open water. A field of grass or plants – unless in the most arid regions – is covered with literally gallons of dew in the early morning (remember that many large grazing animals thrive almost exclusively on dew water). Collect dew by simply running a cloth over the grass or plants to soak it, then wringing out the water into a container. Do this at first light, before the sun has had time to dry out the landscape.

Remembering that water flows from high ground to low ground will help you in your hunt for water in the wilderness. Any high ground that receives rain or snow is likely to have water in the valley below, or at least in the cracks and channels that scar its face. In any rocky terrain, even flat ground at sea level, look for springs and seepage bubbling up through the rock. Limestone and lava rocks often have underground water sources beneath, and can feature substantial

Dew collector

Dew collectors can be improvised from sheets of plastic, although commercial versions like the one seen here are far more efficient. Condensation gathers on the sides of the collector, eventually running down into the central reservoir. Such fluids can be drunk without filtering or purifying.

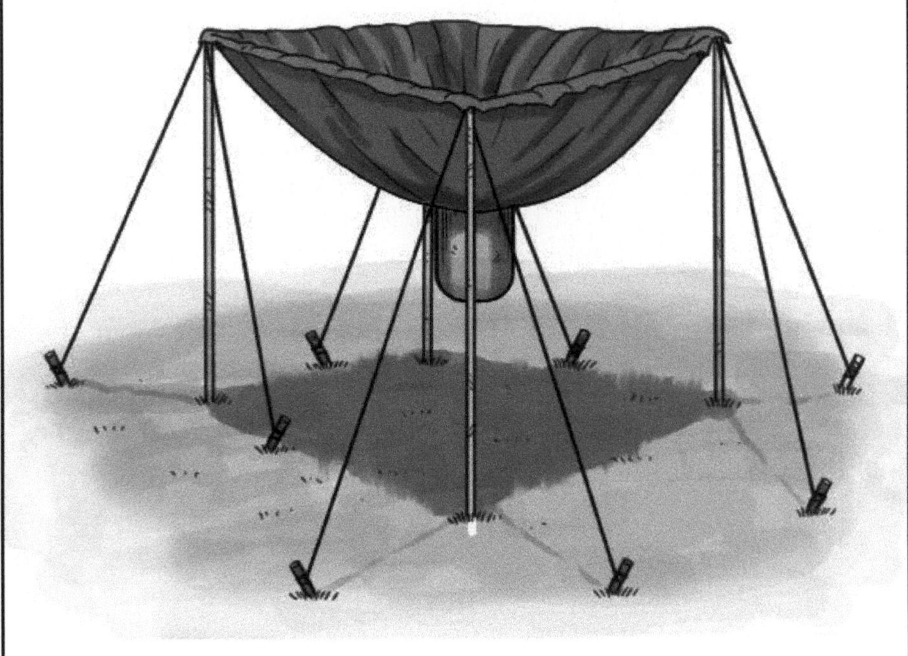

springs that often can be drunk from unfiltered at their source.

In arid terrain, underground water may indeed be your only source of fluids. Although a riverbed, ditch or culvert may have apparently dried up on the surface, water could still persist below – muddy textures to the earth or fresh patches of green vegetation are good indicators. If the plants only extend to around 1.5–1.8m (5–6ft) in height (any higher, and the water table is likely to be too deep), you may be able to tap into underground water directly around the root system. Dig straight down to

Digging for water

Digging down into damp earth can often lead to significant finds of water. Create a hole several feet deep and about 30cm (1ft) wide and allow the water to seep through the earth and collect in the hole. Always filter and purify such fluids before you drink them.

Sediment hole

Soldiers learn to read the terrain for water indicators. For example, water from a river can seep through the earth banks into a sediment hole, this process partially filtering the water as it passes through the earth.

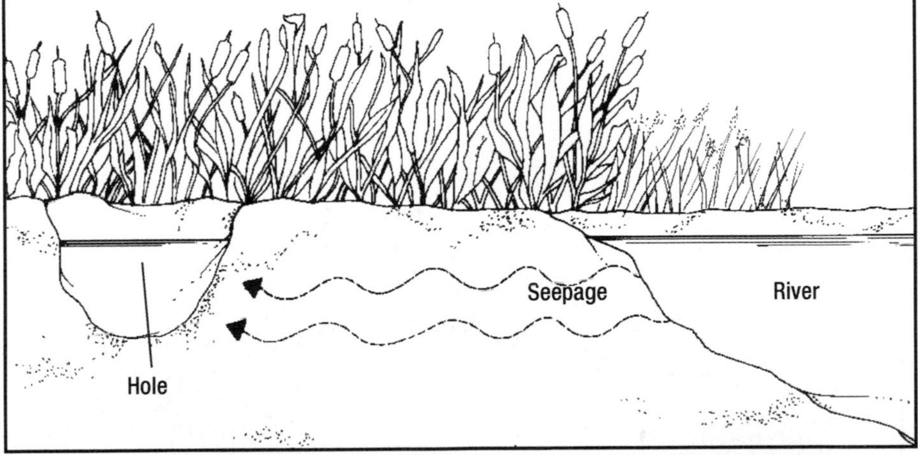

TIP: Water to avoid drinking

- Pools of water with strong smells.
- Water with powder or foam deposits on the surface or edges, both of which can indicate chemical pollutants. (If you suspect water is polluted by chemicals, boil a small amount dry – a chemical residue will be left in the bottom of the vessel if the water is polluted.)
- Water with gaseous bubbles or green slime on the surface.
- Water surrounded by dead plants or animals.
- Stagnant water with no inlets or outlets.
- Rivers or streams choked with algae and weeds – agricultural chemicals are the probable pollutants.

Water from a dry riverbed

The US Army's 'Survival' manual lists 'the foot of concave banks of dry rivers' as a key place to look for water in arid regions. A trick of African tribesmen is to use a long reed to suck up water from the earth – target the outside bend of the river, which is usually the last place from which the surface water evaporated. Alternatively, dig down into the earth until you strike water.

the roots (as long as this action does not expend too much valuable energy) and collect water where you find it. Tribesmen often dig for water in dried riverbeds, probing beneath the outside edge of a bend, which is usually the last place from which surface water evaporated, or beneath a section heavily shaded by trees.

In sandy environments, target the trough between two sand dunes, and on a beach dig above the high-tide mark – the sand filters out the brine and the hole will steadily fill up with fresh water. Regardless of the terrain,

Rain trap

SAS jungle training includes how to build this simple but effective rain trap. Using a wooden frame and a large, glossy, waterproof leaf as a gutter, you can direct rainfall straight into a container for purification-free drinking.

TIP: Collecting water

As soon as rain begins put out as many open receptacles as possible. Use waterproof fabric, large leaves or pieces of bark to act as gutters directing water into the containers.

- Make your own rain reservoir by digging a deep hollow into the ground and lining it with a single piece of waterproof material, such as a camping groundsheet, securely weighted with stones around the edges.
- Keep stored water covered over at all times and in the dark if possible, as direct sunlight encourages the growth of green algae.
- Filter and purify rainwater that has been stored for more than two days, to remove foreign bodies, parasites and germs.

dig for water by going straight down until the earth becomes wet and water seeps into the hole. At first the water will be dirty and full of silt, but will become clearer with time. Collect it, then filter and purify for drinking.

In polar or winter conditions, water is readily available in the form of snow and ice. Always melt frozen water before drinking it, as eating snow or ice directly can accelerate hypothermia, cause tissue damage to the mouth and lips and create stomach disorders. Water from clean snow and ice does not usually need to be filtered and purified, though do so if the snow or ice is taken from coastal areas – it may contain harmful marine micro-organisms. In freezing conditions, store any water you collect in plastic rather than metal bottles, as metal containers can split should the water inside freeze and expand. Whatever the container used, allow forming ice room to expand by not filling it to the top.

Water indicators

Any landscape, even in the desert, will contain water indicators. As suggested, fresh green vegetation always denotes water, either as an open source or underground. On an arid mountain, for example, clumps of fresh grasses or bushes are likely to indicate water pooling in a rock shelf or running down a natural gully.

Certain plants predict future rain, and such advance warning is useful

Rain collector

If rainfall is scarce, you want to maximize the amount of water you collect every time there is a downpour. This simple rain collector will channel large volumes of rainwater down into a container, although it will usually need constructing in advance of rainfall beginning (keep your eye on the skies).

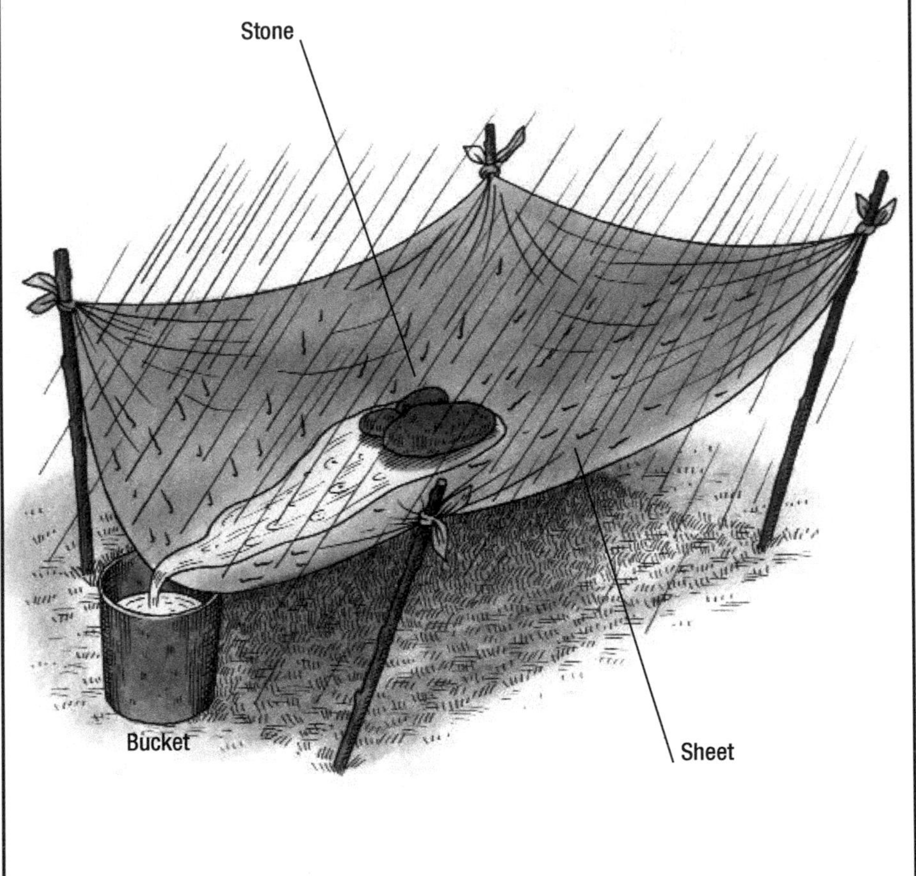

Water soak

A water soak is simply a piece of water-absorbent cloth, wrapped around a tree, that becomes soaked from rainwater. The water eventually drips from the hanging end of the cloth, into a container.

Melting ice

The US Army's 'Survival' manual instructs soldiers never to consume ice without melting it first, as this increases the risk of hypothermia and tissue damage to the face. The improvised melting device below is good for turning large blocks of ice into drinking water.

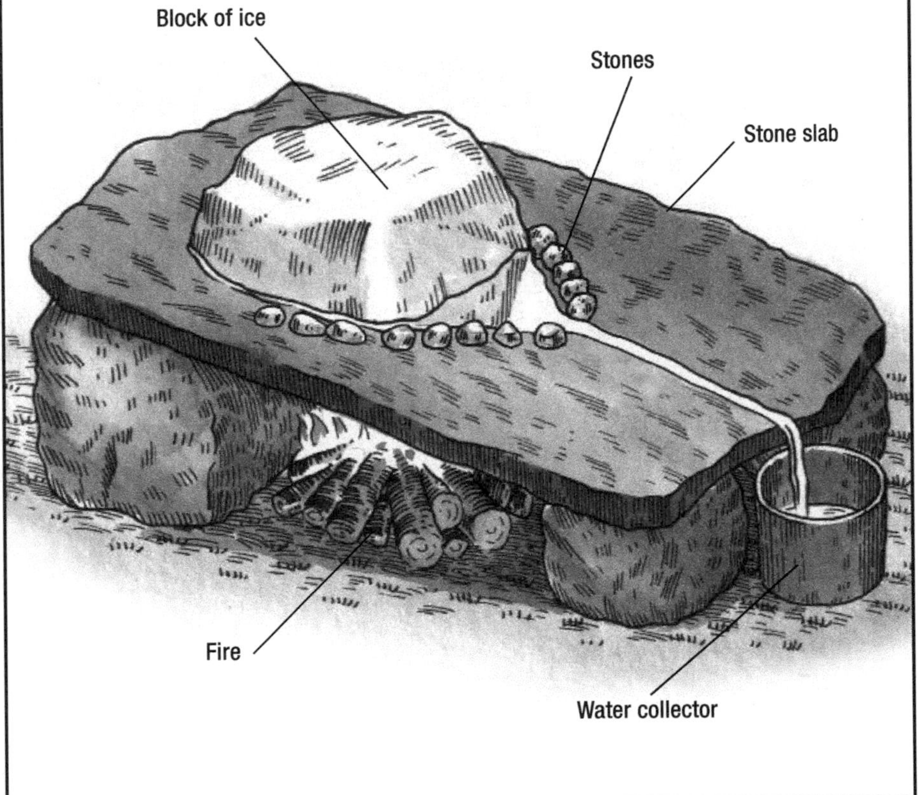

for preparing rain-collecting vessels. When rain is coming, all plants release stronger scents, usually an earthy, musty or perfumed smell. Pine cones expand with the increased air moisture indicative of approaching rain, and close in dry weather.

Some plants also contain water within themselves, either internally

Water from a banana tree

Banana trees are a good source of drinkable water. Cut down the tree at the point shown, and water will fill up the stump. The first three fillings will taste unpleasant, but subsequent water should be drinkable. A banana tree stump can supply water for up to four days.

Water from a vine

US special forces survival training includes how to extract water from a vine. Cut a notch in the vine as high up as you can, then slice through the vine close to the ground. The open, lower end will now drip fresh, drinkable water.

or in any cup-shaped structures. The inner flesh of the barrel cactus, for example, is rich in fluid – cut into the middle and squeeze the fluid out of the mashed pulp. Date palms and the baobab tree have water in the trunk (the baobab only collects it in the rainy season), which will ooze out when the trunk or a branch near its base is cut. The lobes and fruit of the prickly pear plant contain water, as does the bark of the saxaul tree. In the arid Australian outback, the bloodwood desert oak and water tree have water-rich roots that can be cut open and sucked.

Rainwater can be licked directly off leaves, or at least directed down the

Pitcher plant

As its name suggests, the pitcher plant is a useful repository for water in tropical areas.

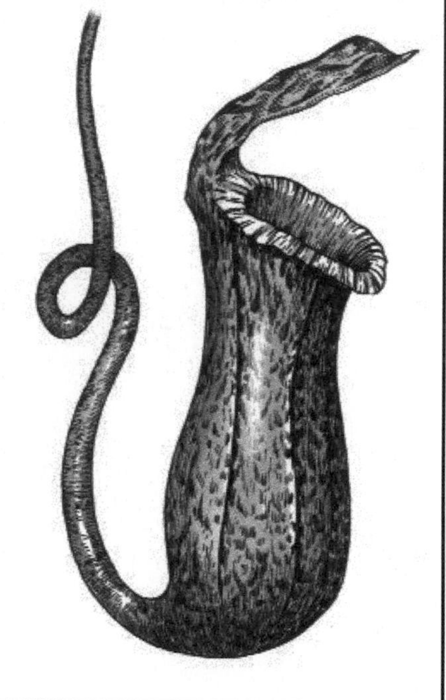

leaf into a container, and trees also hold water in holes and forks, although some filtering is likely to be required. Do not, however, take water from a plant that you know or suspect might be dangerous, or which has any suspicious coloration.

Animals are also efficient water indicators. Grazing animals, for example, usually head for watering holes around dawn and dusk; if you can't see the animals themselves, look for large numbers of tracks gathering at a single point. (Don't follow carnivorous animals, as they derive much of their essential fluid from prey rather than open water.) Grain-eating birds do likewise, flying low and straight when heading out to water, but stopping more frequently on their way back. Flies and mosquitoes tend to keep water sources within 100m (328ft) distance, their numbers often increasing the closer you get to water. Ants march to water sources in column; you might see them ascending a tree to visit a water reservoir in the trunk.

Transpiration

The very air that surrounds us contains moisture, in varying degrees according to the climate and the location. There are a handful of techniques for converting some of this moisture into a drinkable form. Note, however, that these techniques are unlikely to provide you with significant volumes of fluids, but alongside other water sources they could make the difference between life and death.

The transpiration bag involves tying a preferably clear plastic bag (avoid bags with moulding holes in their surfaces) over a large bundle of green foliage – dead foliage will

Transpiration bag

A transpiration bag will typically only produce small amounts of water, but they can be life-saving. Make sure that the plastic bag is tied tight at the neck, and that the bag contains no holes. Any gaps will result in water vapour escaping to the outside rather than condensing inside. Also, never use poisonous vegetation, as it will produce poisonous water.

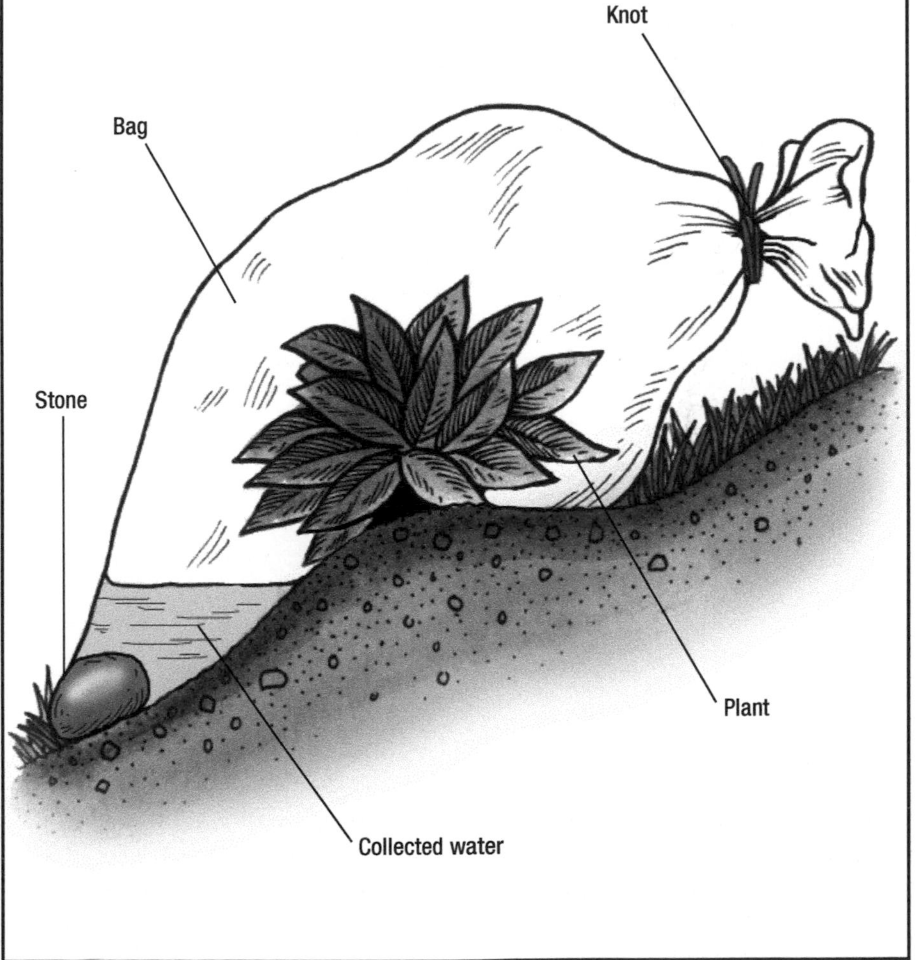

not work – or you can simply tie the bag over the end of a bushy branch. The condensation produced by the plant during photosynthesis condenses against the inside of the bag and then runs down to the lowest corner, ready for you to drink. Make sure that the neck of the bag is tied very tightly, so as not to allow the water vapour to escape, and ensure the water-collection point is free from foliage, to avoid the condensed water soaking back into wood and leaves.

The solar still is a more advanced option than the transpiration bag.

Solar still

The solar still works best if placed in damp ground containing moisture. The hole should be about 1m (3ft 3in) across and 60cm (2ft) deep to produce useful volumes of water.

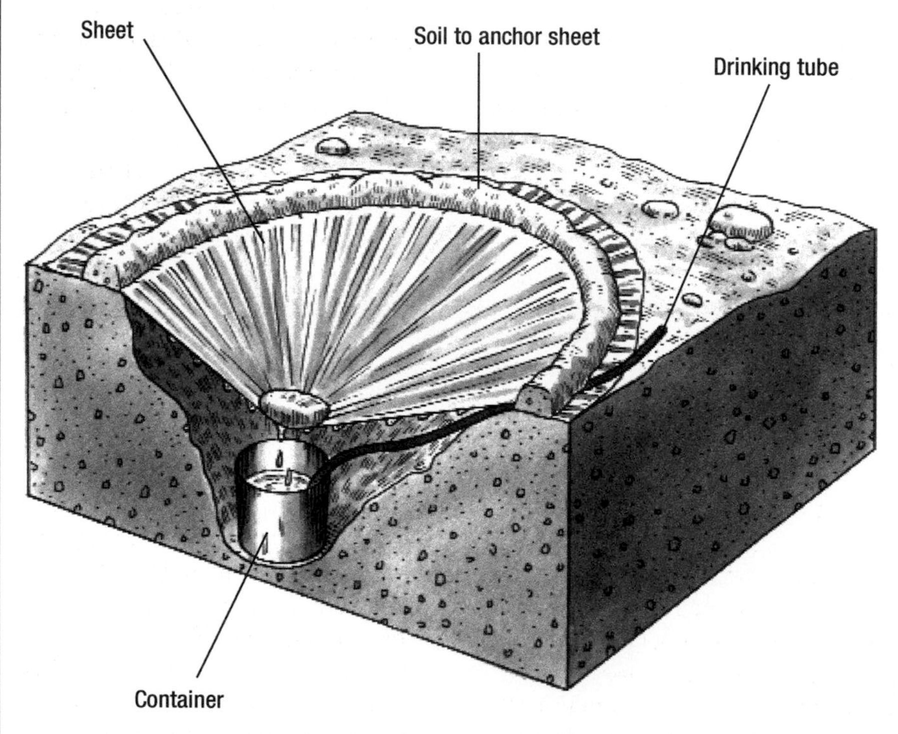

First take a sheet of plastic, ideally 1m (3ft 3in) long on each side. Dig a hole in the ground of a diameter several inches less than the diameter of your sheet, and place a container in the bottom – this will act as a water catcher. Spread the plastic over the hole, and weight down the perimeter with plenty of heavy rocks and stones, leaving no gaps. Put another stone in the middle of the sheet, causing the sheet to dip down directly over the container.

Now leave the solar still for 24 hours. During the day, sunlight will heat up the soil, and the soil will release water vapour into the hole. The vapour condenses on the cooler underside of the plastic, and the condensation runs down the plastic to the central dip and then drips into the container. The solar still also works at night when the sheet is cooled but the trapped air in the hole remains warm. Insert a tube, if available, underneath the plastic into the container so that you can drink without having to dismantle the still. However, make sure the plastic is sealed tight around the tube or the water inside the still will evaporate into the outside air.

Filtering and purifying

Once you have collected water, it needs filtering and purifying. The process of filtering serves to clean the water of animal and plant matter, while purification hopefully destroys bacteria. Filtering can be as simple as pouring the water several times through a close-woven piece of fabric – such as cotton – into a container. This removes most of the larger particles of dirt and vegetation, and renders the water clear enough for purification. A more advanced approach is to create a filter system out of several layers of contrasting material – such as sand and rocks – with each layer stripping out different-sized particles. (See the accompanying artworks on page 70.)

In terms of purification, the most elementary but still effective method is boiling. Boiling water for a minimum of 10 minutes will kill off bacteria and all germs, though will not negate chemical contamination.

Another option is to use purification chemicals. There are three main chemical additives for water purification: iodine, potassium permanganate and chlorine. Iodine and potassium permanganate come as liquid and granules respectively. When added to water (follow instructions closely), these chemicals turn the water slightly pink and give it a chemical taste, but render it safe to drink. Chlorine tends to come in tablet form, and usually one tablet is added to 0.5 litres (0.9 pints) of water to make it safe to drink. Again there is a distinct chemical aftertaste. Adding charcoal to the purified water removes some of the chemical taste.

Water filter

A water filter frame uses pouches of contrasting natural materials to remove unwanted particles from natural water. Pour the water into the uppermost pouch, and allow it to filter slowly down into the container at the bottom.

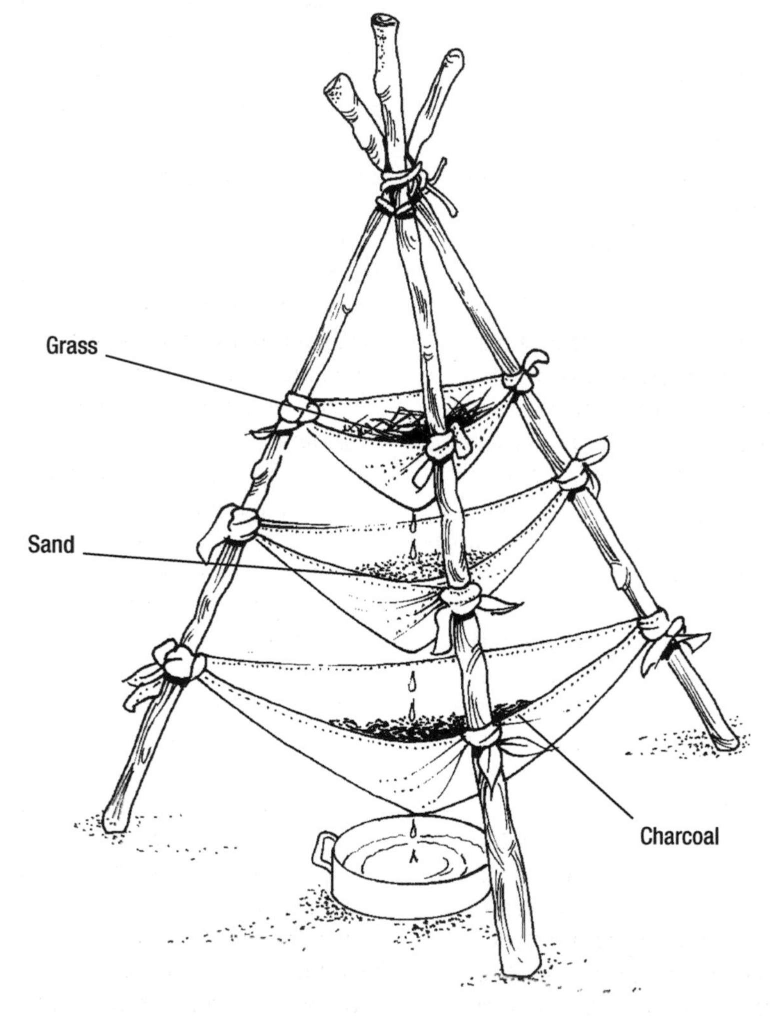

However, you must only do this once the purifying chemical has stopped working.

PLANT FOOD

In any prolonged survival emergency, remember that a balanced diet is just as important in the wild as in domestic life. If you eat one food source alone, even a good one, you leave yourself open to a variety of illnesses resulting from technical malnutrition. For example, wilderness hunters of the past have died by relying purely on rabbit meat for sustenance, the conditions of 'rabbit starvation' resulting from the meat taking out more nutrients from their bodies than the food supplied.

Plant foods are amongst the most accessible survival foods, primarily because they do not involve the strenuous activities of hunting and killing. One important initial note, however, is that not all plants are safe to eat. Some will induce illness, while a select group of other plants will kill within hours or days if ingested. Furthermore, do not think that a plant is safe to eat because an animal is seen eating it. Many animals have digestive systems resistant to toxins that would make humans severely ill.

As noted earlier, therefore, research into edible and poisonous plant types is vital. Compensating for the fact that you will be unlikely to know all of the world's millions of plant species, observe the following rules. Generally speaking, blue and black berries are usually safe to eat (there are exemptions, such as the highly poisonous black berries of deadly nightshade), as are single pieces of fruit hanging on a stem, or aggregated fruits. Yet if you cannot positively identify a plant, you can always perform what soldiers know as the Universal Edibility Test (UET). Reject the plant as a food if you experience an adverse body reaction at any point during the following test:

The UET

- Avoid eating, if possible, for eight hours before the test to guarantee the accuracy of the results, and during the test drink only water and eat only the plant sample.
- Divide the plant into its basic constituents – leaves, stems, roots and so on – and test only one part of the plant at a time.
- Smell the plant for strong acid or almond-like scents, and crush some of the plant to release potentially hidden smells. If you detect unpleasant smells, reject the plant.
- Rub a sample of the plant on the inside of your elbow or wrist. Wait 15 minutes and see if there is any adverse reaction such as blistering or irritation.
- If there is no skin reaction, place a small piece of the plant on the outer surface of the lip to test for

TIP: Fungi

The US Army's *Survival* manual states 'Do not eat mushrooms in a survival situation! The only way to tell if a mushroom is edible is by positive identification.' This is good advice. Edible fungi are high in vitamins, minerals, proteins, and even contain fats, and so are a first-rate survival food. However, there are numerous inedible varieties, some with positively lethal poisonous content. The poisons in fungi are not killed by cooking, nor can the Universal Edibility Test be used with fungi (the dangers are too great and some fungi poisons operate over long time periods). If you can, with absolute certainty, identify a fungus as edible, it can be prepared in a variety of ways. It can be simply eaten raw, or boiled in soups or stews (soak tough fungi in water to soften for cooking). Fungi are a long-term storage food when air-dried. Place the separated caps and stems on a rock in the sun until they are dehydrated, then store them in an airtight container. Soak them in water to rehydrate them before eating.

burning or itching. Leave for three minutes.
- Put the piece of plant onto your tongue; hold it there for 15 minutes without chewing.
- Now chew the material, but do not swallow. Hold the chewed plant in your mouth for another 15 minutes.
- Swallow the food and wait for eight hours. Should you start to feel ill, induce vomiting and drink plenty of water. If there is no adverse reaction, eat a handful of the plant and wait another eight hours. If there is no sign of illness, the plant is safe to eat when prepared in the same manner as during the test.

Besides the UET, there are other rules to follow for acquiring plant foods, although these are more negative:

Plants to avoid eating

- Any type of bulb.
- White and yellow berries. About half of red berries are safe, so eat only if you can make a positive identification.
- Red plants.
- Overripe fruit.
- Fruit marred by mildew or fungus.
- Any plant with an almond-like scent, indicating a cyanide compound (crush up some of the leaves to release the smell).
- Plants with a white, milky sap, unless you know the plant is safe.
- Five-segmented fruits.
- Plants with three-leaved structures.
- Uncooked legumes (beans and peas). These absorb minerals from the soil and cause digestive problems.
- Plants with tiny barbed hairs on the stem and leaves; these can be laced with irritant chemicals.
- Any plant which irritates the skin on contact.
- Any dead or diseased plant.
- Plants with umbrella-shaped flowers, though carrots, celery and parsley (all edible) are members of this family.
- Grain heads with pink, purplish or black spurs.

Edible plant types

There are thousands of edible plant types, far more than can be explored here. When you research edible plants, however, be aware of all the different parts of the plant that can be consumed (and, of course, those that should be avoided). Edible plant parts can include nuts, berries, fruit, leaves, roots and even bark. Blackberry and raspberry fruits, for example, can be eaten raw, but the leaves can also be boiled to make a tea. Beech tree nuts can be eaten or crushed down to produce a useful oil, while bistort roots are edible after soaking and cooking. The common dandelion is completely edible and nutritious – boil or roast

Poisonous plants

Water hemlock and foxglove are just two of thousands of poisonous plant types in the wild. Wherever you travel, learn about the most common poisonous and edible plants in the region. Use multiple identifying characteristics – leaf shape, flower colour, height etc. – to identify a plant.

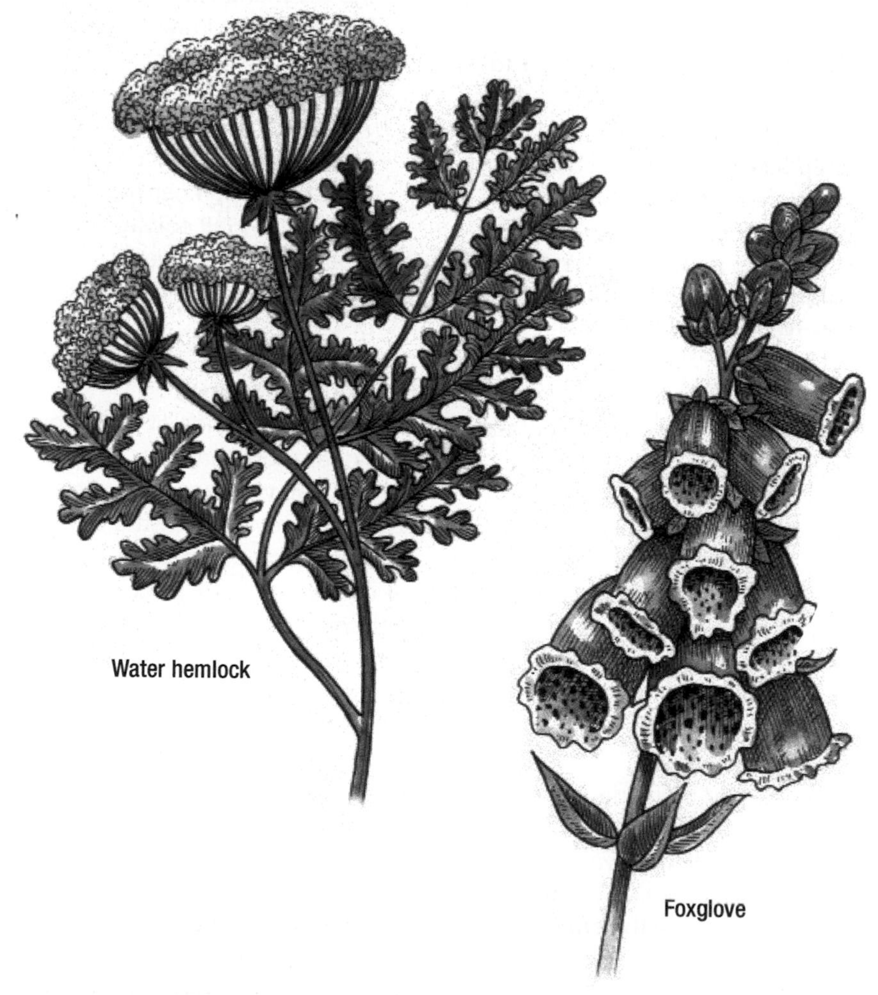

the roots, or eat the young leaves raw (older leaves require boiling). Nettle leaves require around 15 minutes of boiling to cook and kill the stinging parts of the plant, after which the leaves are edible. Nettle tea also forms a healthy drink, as does boiled pine needles.

The plants named above are common to temperate zones, regions in which the availability of plant foods varies considerably between the seasons. (In the autumn and winter, for example, meat is an essential component of any survival diet, there typically being insufficient

Strychnine plant

The strychnine plant occurs in tropical areas of Asia. It contains a lethal poison that attacks the nervous, muscular and respiratory systems, the effects increasing cumulatively over time.

TIP: Poisonous plant types

The following is a US Army list of some of the most common types of poisonous plant in temperate zones. Spend time with a reputable botanical reference work and learn to identify these plants with total confidence – your life could depend on it.

- Baneberry
- Buttercups
- Deadly nightshade
- Death camas
- Foxgloves
- Hemlock
- Larkspur
- Lupins
- Monk's-hood
- Oleander
- Poison ivy
- Poison sumacs
- Vetches or locoweeds
- Water hemlock

edible plants.) In the tropical jungles, by contrast, there is a dramatic proliferation of edible plant types all year round. Fruit trees are common, including passion fruit, guava, rambutan, banana, breadfruit, papaya and mango. Coconuts are available along coastal areas – eat the white flesh inside the coconut and drink its nutritious milk (although not too much, as an excess can induce diarrhoea). The section from which the leaves protrude, known as the 'cabbage', can be cooked and eaten. The young shoots of bamboo are edible raw or cooked, although avoid or cut off the fine black hairs along the edge of the leaves, and bamboo seeds can be eaten when boiled. Other common tropical plants with edible parts include Nipa palm, yams, rattan palm, sago palm, taro and water lily.

In desert landscapes, plant life is sparse and frequently inedible, with notable exceptions. Fig trees and date palms produce well-known and delicious fruit, for example, and carob contains an edible pulp, extracted from its seed pods. (The seeds can also be ground and cooked as porridge.) Acacia provides edible (once they are cooked) seeds, young leaves and shoots, and the roots contain water.

The fruit and seeds of the massive baobab tree can be eaten raw, the young leaves can be eaten after boiling, and the roots also provide water. Conveniently, most desert grasses are edible. Cook and eat the white stem that is exposed when the grass is pulled from the ground. Wild gourds yield edible fruit (although unripe fruit needs boiling), young

Edible plants

When foraging for edible plants, try to collect as many varieties as possible for balanced nutrition. Plant foods can include leaves, roots, flowers, bark, fruit, berries and nuts, although access to such foods varies according to locale, season and climate.

Raspberries and blackberries

Beech nut

Almond

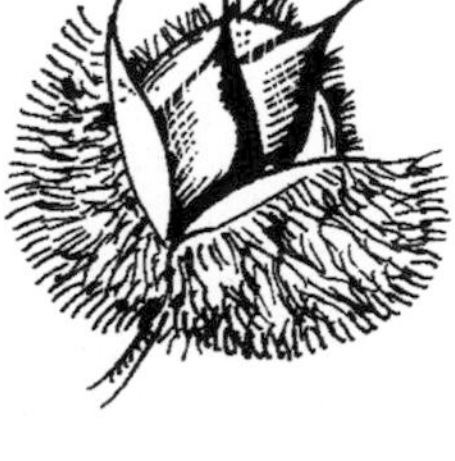

Sweet chestnut

Walnut

leaves and seeds (use boiling and roasting respectively), with water in the stems and shoots.

As this incomplete list shows, even the austere desert environment can offer significant plant food sources. Things become a bit more challenging in polar environments, in which only the hardiest of plants can survive. Several mosses and rock-dwelling plants are edible, however. All parts of Iceland moss, bearberry,

Making drinks from plants

Pine needles can be converted into a simple, nutritious tea. Crush up fresh, green needles and add them to boiling water, leaving them to steep for about 20 minutes. Drain through a cloth to serve.

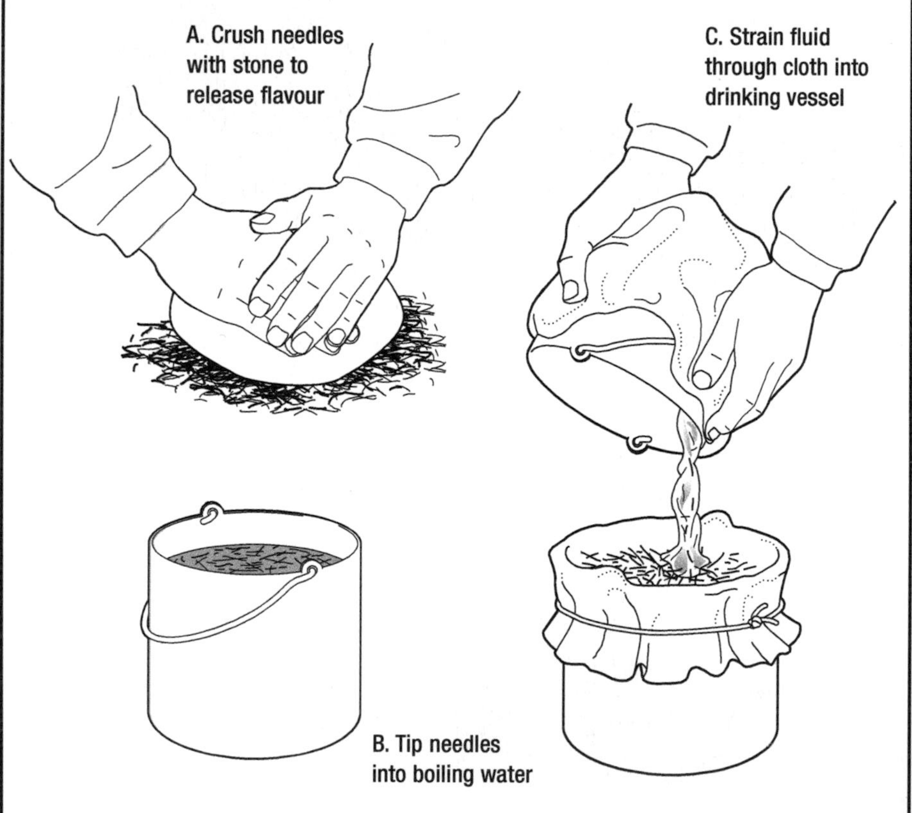

rock tripes and reindeer moss, for example, can be eaten after several hours of soaking and then boiling. Trees offer several other opportunities for acquiring food. The arctic willow has edible young shoots, leaves, inner bark and roots (when peeled), and both the black and red spruce provide edible young shoots, as well as needles for making a nutritious tea. The fruits of the salmonberry can be eaten raw.

Tropical plant food

Here are three common tropical plants that all special forces soldiers should be able to identify for survival food.

Digging up edible roots

Roots can be extremely hard to remove from the ground. You can dig up shallow roots by sharpening a stick into a flat, blade-like end. Dig down the sides of the roots, and use the stick to lever them out.

Palm climbing

To climb a palm tree, wrap your hands around the opposite side at chest level, then jump both feet onto the trunk, keeping your knees perpendicular to your body. Work up the tree in a series of similar jumps.

3

Living Off the Land: Hunting, Trapping and Fishing

Animals are one of your most important sources of survival food, but are also amongst the most difficult to acquire.

Killing animals for food is something most soldiers, but particularly special forces soldiers, become acquainted with in their training. When food supplies run out or are low, they are taught that all the Earth's creatures, from insects to antelope, can be potential sources of food.

On a mission, the rewards of hunting are quite simply the food itself, which is nutritious and sustaining, plus ancillary benefits such as bones, skin and fur, which can be turned into various survival resources such as clothing or tools. The risks are twofold. First, there is the risk from the animals themselves, some of which can be extremely dangerous.

Second, hunting can be a physically intensive activity, and possibly end up burning more calories and energy than the eventual meal provides.

Animals have vastly superior senses when compared to human beings, and have evolved to sense and survive threats. To hunt and kill them, therefore, requires tactics, knowledge, intelligence and stealth. It also requires weapons.

Using animals for survival food not only requires knowledge of weapons and hunting, but also of related issues such as safe preparation and cooking of meat.

Shooting posture

If you are able to hunt with a rifle, make sure that you adopt a stable, solid posture before squeezing off the shot. A front brace, made out of little more than a forked stick, is useful for providing a rest for the fore-end of the gun.

WEAPONS

When it comes to hunting, soldiers have the natural advantage of being armed with high-quality professional firearms. Yet sometimes issues of noise discipline, limited ammunition or loss of weapon mean that firearms can't be used to acquire meat. Knowing how to improvise hunting tools, therefore, is essential for soldiers as much as it is for you when surviving in the wilderness.

The most elementary of weapons is a wooden club, which with the right weight and dimensions can even be used to kill larger mammals such as sheep and goats. Make a club from a branch about 5–6cm (2–2.5in) in diameter, preferably widening towards what will be the

TIP: Diseased animals

Soldiers must stay healthy in the field, hence they avoid eating any diseased animal. Signs of illness include problems in movement, disturbed behaviour, poor-quality fur or skin, a distorted or discoloured head, isolation from a herd or pack and enlarged lymph nodes in the cheeks (relevant only to larger animals, such as deer). If you are forced to eat such animals, boil the meat thoroughly and cover any cut or sore on your own body when preparing the meat.

Hunting crossbow

Modern crossbows are excellent hunting tools, being virtually silent but with effective ranges of up to and beyond 100m (328ft). Note that in many countries, however, crossbow hunting is illegal.

striking end, and about 75cm (2ft 6in) long. Clubs are generally best for dispatching animals that are already caught or wounded, while a throwing stick can be used to bring down small animals from a distance. Ideally, the throwing stick should be slightly bent in shape – think about the shape of a boomerang – and about 90cm (3ft) long. It needs to be light enough to throw with speed, but heavy enough to deliver a stunning impact. Skim the stick in a horizontal plane to maximize the chances of hitting the target.

Still on the theme of sticks, spears can made for either throwing or stabbing, and can be as simple as a hardwood pole or branch sharpened at one end, the point hardened by scorching it over a fire. A decent spear can be up to 1.8m (6ft) long, the length giving you some protective distance from your prey. You can make more durable and lethal points by partially splitting the shaft at one end and inserting a piece of sharp metal or bone in the split before lashing it securely into place. (Put lashings beneath the split as well, to prevent it working down the shaft.) When throwing a spear, put your full body weight into the cast and follow right through with the throwing arm,

Spear thrower

The ancient device, seen here carved from a single piece of wood, increases the acceleration of a spear throw, and therefore gives the spear greater velocity and range. Put your whole body weight into the action, and flick the thrower from the wrist at the end of the throw.

Types of spearhead

Multi-pointed spearheads are best suited to light prey such as fish and rabbits, while for heavier creatures you need robust, single points that achieve deep penetration.

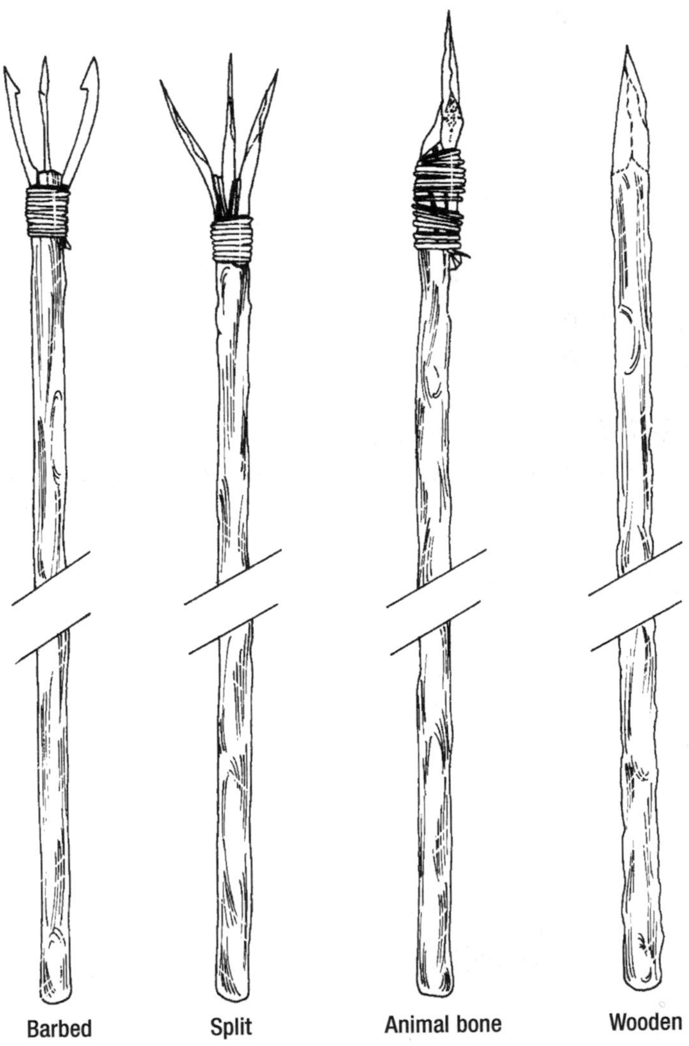

Spiked harpoon

This fishing harpoon is made from multiple long thorns tied to the end of a long shaft of wood. Prior to use, you can protect the thorn points by sticking a pad of thick leaves onto them.

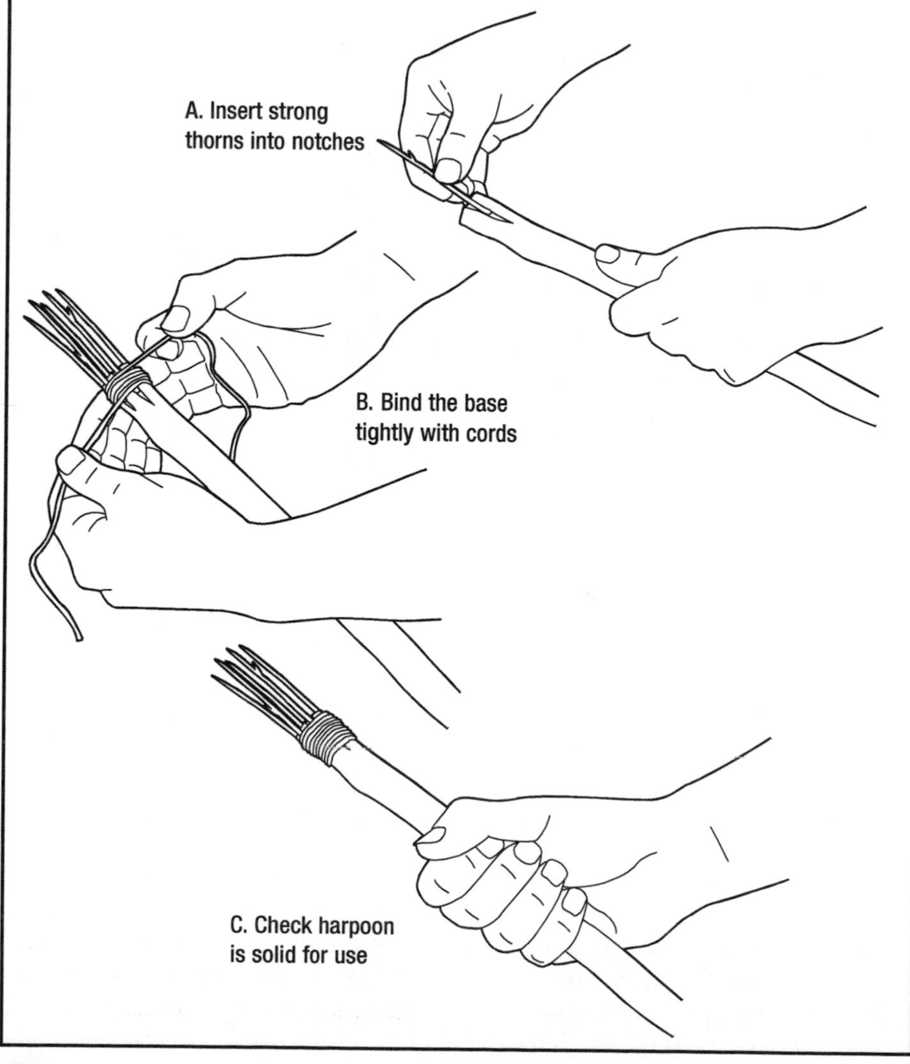

Modern slingshot

Modern slingshots are extremely powerful, and often feature sighting devices. They can kill animals up to rabbit size.

keeping your eyes focused hard on your target. When stabbing, lean into the thrust to supply weight and power, but not so far forward that you will fall if the spear snaps.

Spears introduce us to the use of missile weaponry. There are a range of survival weapons in this category that take us beyond mere muscle power, using leverage and physics to provide an at-distance killing capability. A classic childhood weapon is the catapult, which has the advantage that many of us know how to use one. For the Y frame, choose a piece of wood that retains some flexibility, such as hazel. Elastic from clothes will work reasonably for the sling part, but it is far better to use high-quality elastics such as surgical tubing or even rubber cut from a tyre inner tube. Put a leather or cloth pouch in the centre to hold the projectiles. A catapult is highly accurate in practised hands, and will easily kill small mammals and birds.

TIP: Bola missile

SAS survival training includes instruction on how to make a bola missile, a traditional weapon used to kill flying birds or bring down running animals. Take three to six stones, each about 5cm (2in) in diameter, and wrap them in individual pouches of material. Then tie each pouch to a piece of string about 1m (3ft 3in) long. Gather all the ends of the strings and knot them together very firmly – this point is where you grip the missile to throw it. To launch it, swing it above your head for several revolutions before throwing it at your prey – keeping your eyes glued to the target at all times will help to improve the accuracy of the throw. A good bola will wrap itself around the prey, while the stones will stun or kill it.

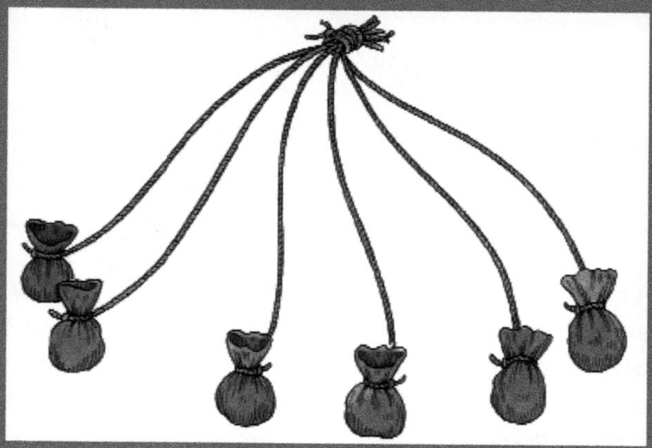

Traditional slingshots (of the David and Goliath kind) take a bit more skill to use. Make a slingshot with a length of string or cord about 1.2m (4ft) long, with a patch of leather or cloth in the centre. To fire, place a stone securely in the patch, hold both ends of the string and swing the sling around in a fast circle above your head, or to the side of your body. After a few revolutions to build up speed, as the projectile swings

Improvised slingshot

This ancient weapon requires a lot of practice to master, but can be used to kill birds and small mammals.

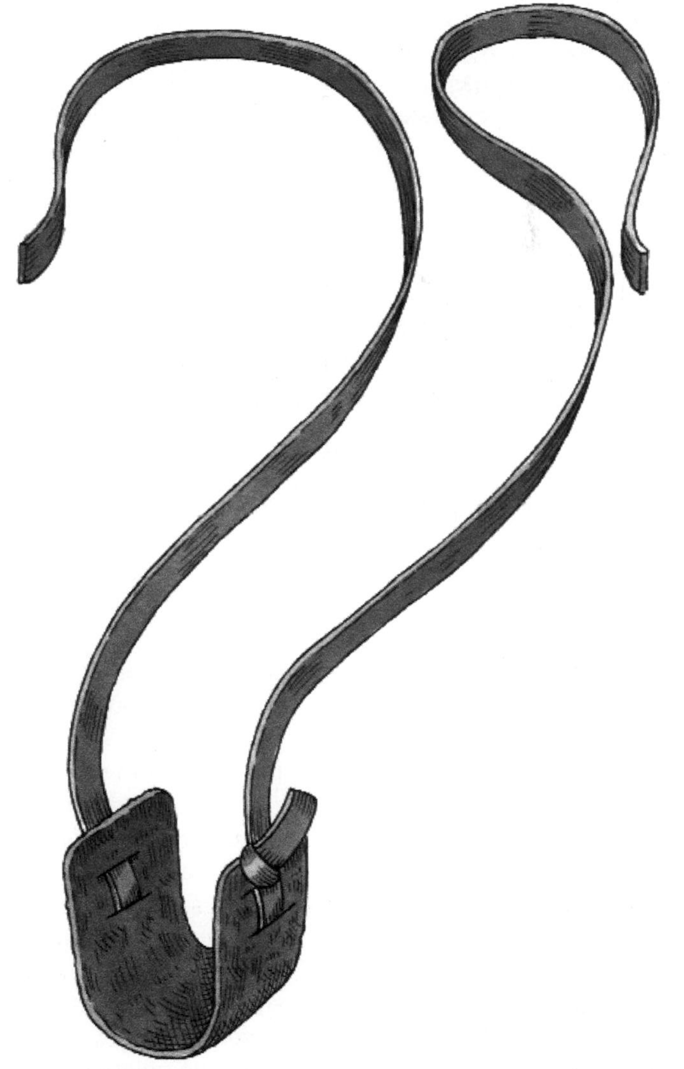

Hunting bows

Hunting bows are available in many degrees of sophistication. Self-bows (left) are the simplest, but compound bows (right) deliver far greater power.

towards the target, let go of one end of the string to project the stone.

A bow is one of the more sophisticated survival weapons, capable of killing prey such as deer and goats at distances of up to 100m (328ft). Improvising one of unseasoned wood will mean it is never as powerful as a commercially produced bow made from seasoned materials, but by choosing an appropriate hardwood, such as yew, hickory, oak or cedar, both its power and serviceability will be acceptable in the short term.

The bow should be about 1.2m (4ft) long, and shaped from a solid branch. It needs to be evenly weighted at both ends and should widen in the centre to form a comfortable handpiece. Cut notches about 1.25cm (0.5in) from the bow tips to hold a string, which can be made from rawhide or any other durable but slender cord. Sling the bow securely, but do not put it under too much tension or the bow will have limited pull and reduced range. Rub the wood with animal fat or oil to prevent it from drying out.

Make arrows from hardwood shafts about 60cm (2ft) long and 6mm (0.25in) across, with any irregularities on the surface of the wood smoothed out with a knife or rough stone. The point can be nothing more than sharpened wood, though better penetration will be achieved by attaching pointed pieces of stone,

Improvised bow

An improvised bow of green wood will have limited range and durability, but does mean you can tackle large mammal prey.

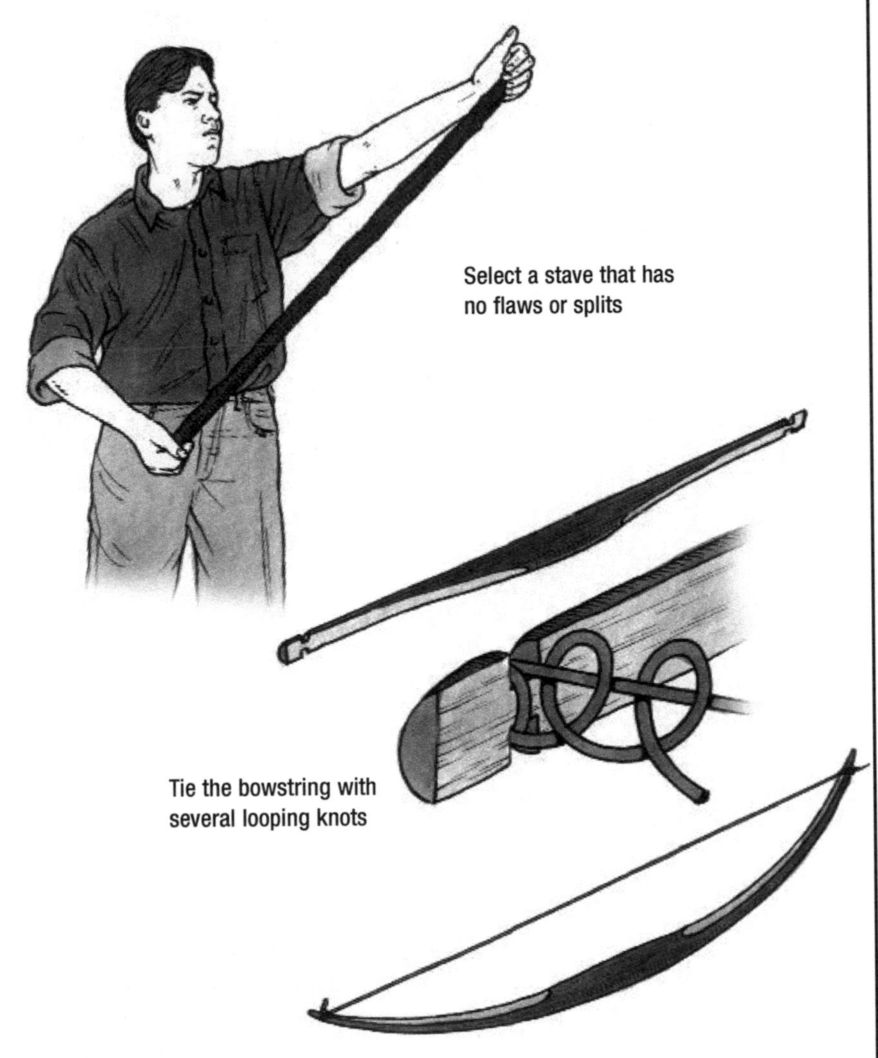

bone, metal or glass. Use feathers, paper, cloth or even leaves to make flights – three equally-spaced flights are optimum – and notch the blunt end of the arrow to fit into the bow string.

Firing a bow takes concentration and correct targeting. Make sure you are close enough to the prey for the arrow to penetrate deeply – practise before you go hunting so that you have a realistic understanding of the weapon's range and trajectory. For large animals, aim at the torso, ideally the area just behind the shoulder, where the heart and other vital organs are located. Fix your eyes on the target area, and smoothly pull and release the bow. Note that it is unlikely that the animal will drop dead on the spot. Instead, watch the direction in which it runs, wait a good few minutes, then follow the blood trail until, hopefully, you arrive at an incapacitated creature.

TRACKING AND HUNTING

In many ways, special forces soldiers can apply similar principles to hunting animals as they do to hunting people. They track both using the 'sign' left by their passage – in the case of animals: footprints, droppings, signs of feeding (animal bones, shelled nuts, etc.), fur or feathers, burrows and nests, broken or bent vegetation, chewed bark or roots and scratch marks on trees.

A combination of several pieces of sign can let you know an animal's direction of travel, its territorial area, its dietary preferences, and even its species (if a print is clear). If following tracks, use droppings, broken vegetation and other sign to fill in gaps. Three pieces of linked sign will give you a direction of travel, probably a route of travel regularly used by the animal. Remember, however, that sign is affected by the passage of time, so only follow sign that has a fresh appearance.

Having spotted potential prey, now you have to close to striking distance. When stalking, keep downwind of the prey and move silently and smoothly behind cover. Avoid silhouetting parts of your body against the skyline. If the animal is moving, it may well be best just to stay still out of sight and let it come towards you. Obviously, don't wear anything brightly coloured when stalking, and observe 'noise discipline' – remove anything that might rattle or make any other noise.

For those not used to killing, the actual moment of violence can be distressing, but it must be done with commitment. Remember that you are trying to kill the animal, not hit it. If you wound the creature, finish it off immediately. Birds and small mammals can be dispatched with a sharp downward blow from a club or fist to the back of the neck and head; for a larger animal, especially if it is

Tracking

Special forces trackers connect multiple pieces of 'sign' – such as the footprints and droppings here – to deduce an animal's direction of travel, and its regular trails.

Tracking a kill

Deer will often wander a long distance from the point at which they are shot. Follow the blood trail, and if it doesn't terminate in a dead animal adopt a zig-zag search pattern until the creature is discovered.

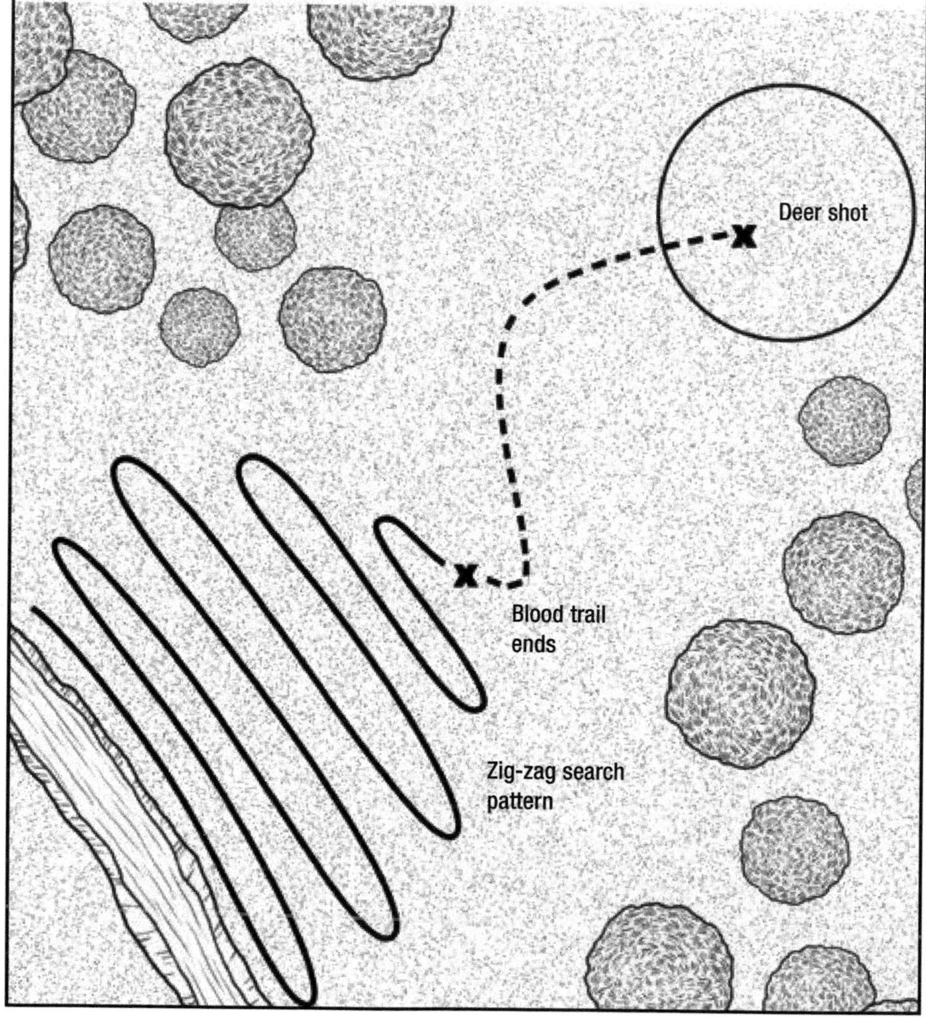

Dispatching a rabbit

Royal Marines are taught this technique for dispatching a rabbit in their basic training. Hang the injured animal downwards, gripping its back legs. Then chop hard with the edge of the free hand down onto the rabbit's neck. If performed swiftly, the blow kills the animal instantly.

still active, kill it by using the weapon again from a distance.

TRAPPING

Survival trapping involves constructing an automatically released mechanism that will either hold or kill a passing animal. The commonest types of trap are snares, deadfall traps and spear traps, and all offer the advantage of effectively hunting for you while you do other things. Some of the most basic traps can be constructed in a few minutes and still yield decent results.

One caution – remember that traps can be just as dangerous to people as to animals. Special forces soldiers never leave a trap in place when they move on to another area, in case they 'catch' a local child or village livestock. Also, when setting a trap – particularly a spear or deadfall trap – don't put yourself in the impact area. Make sure that you check your traps relatively regularly. Not only is it cruel to leave a trapped animal suffering for long periods of time, but other prey animals might come and take it before you get there.

Snares

A snare works by catching an animal with a slip-knot loop, strangling the creature or holding it until you return to finish it off. Professional snare kits are good, but you can make a basic trap out of the wire in your survival tin, string or thin rope and even tough plant material or animal sinew. (Remember, if the trapped animal is not lifted from the ground by the snare or otherwise immobilized, it will often frantically bite at the wire, so for those traps use only inedible wire.)

This chapter has several illustrations of useful snare types. When setting up the snare loop, place it a few centimetres off the ground, and ensure that no surrounding vegetation will prevent it from closing properly. You can construct, however, a 'tunnel' out of surrounding vegetation, slightly wider than the animal's body, on the approach to the snare to channel the animal's head into the loop, or use a baited 'trigger' to catch the animal when it feeds. Don't bother placing a snare directly outside an animal's hole or den – the animal will more easily notice disturbances and unfamiliar smells around its home.

There are several variations on the standard snare, but 'spring snares' are one of your best options. These work by attaching the snare wire to a 'trigger' – a release mechanism that is in turn attached by a string to a branch held under tension. When the animal pulls on the snare wire, the trigger is released and the branch whips into the air, lifting the trapped animal off its feet. Spring snares not only prevent an animal from making effective efforts to free itself, they also keep it off the ground and away from predators.

Animal footprints

Learn a wide range of animal footprints, to help with your recognition skills when tracking.

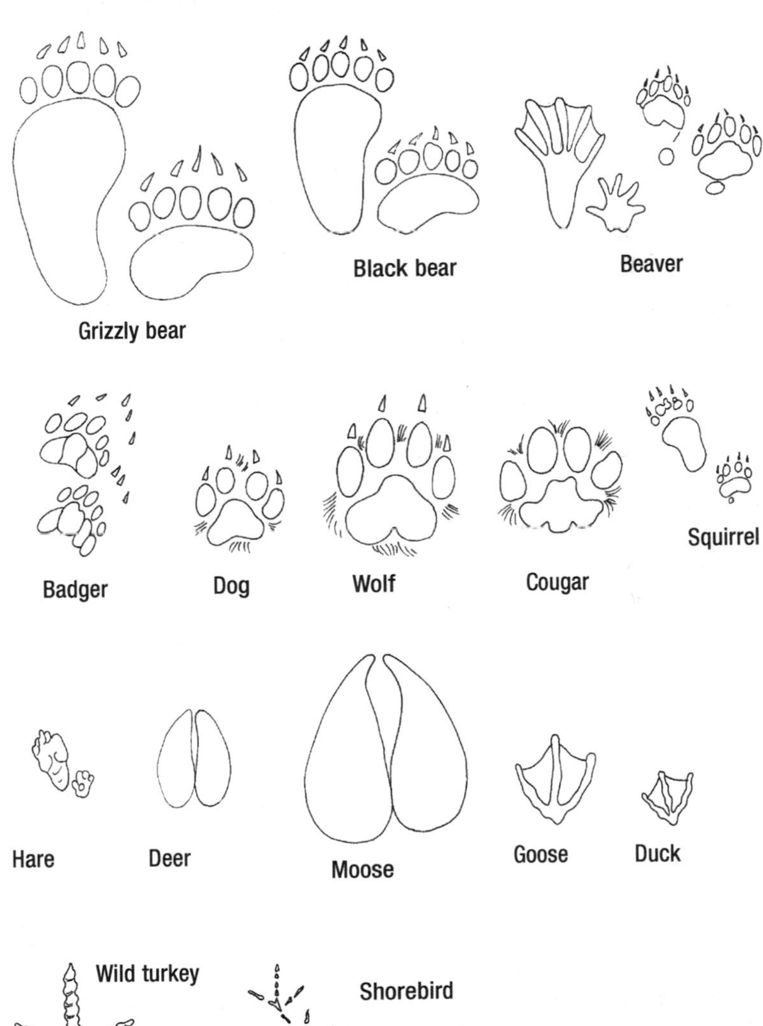

Snare wire

Commercially bought snare wires often feature self-locking mechanisms that tighten efficiently around an animal as it struggles to break free. A spool of 20-gauge snare wire will be available at a good military surplus store for very low cost.

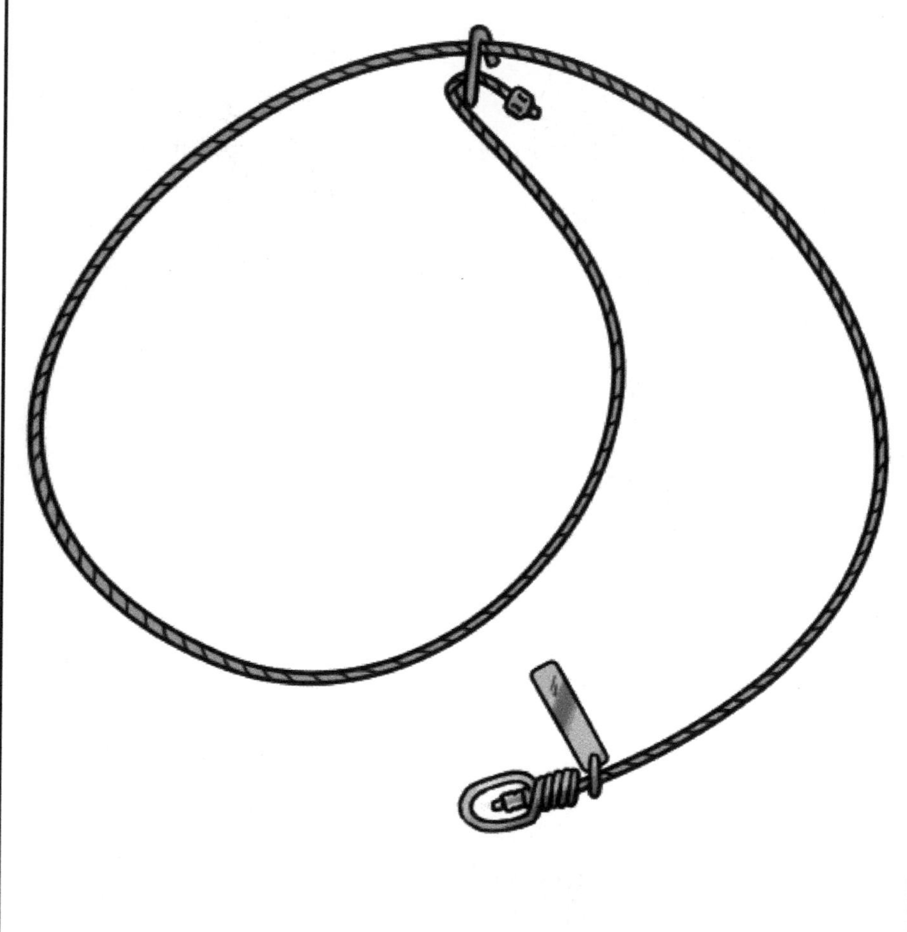

Spring snare

Here the overhead branch provides tension on the notched trigger, holding it in place until a passing animal is snared by the noose. The branch will then whip the trapped animal into the air, holding it there for your return.

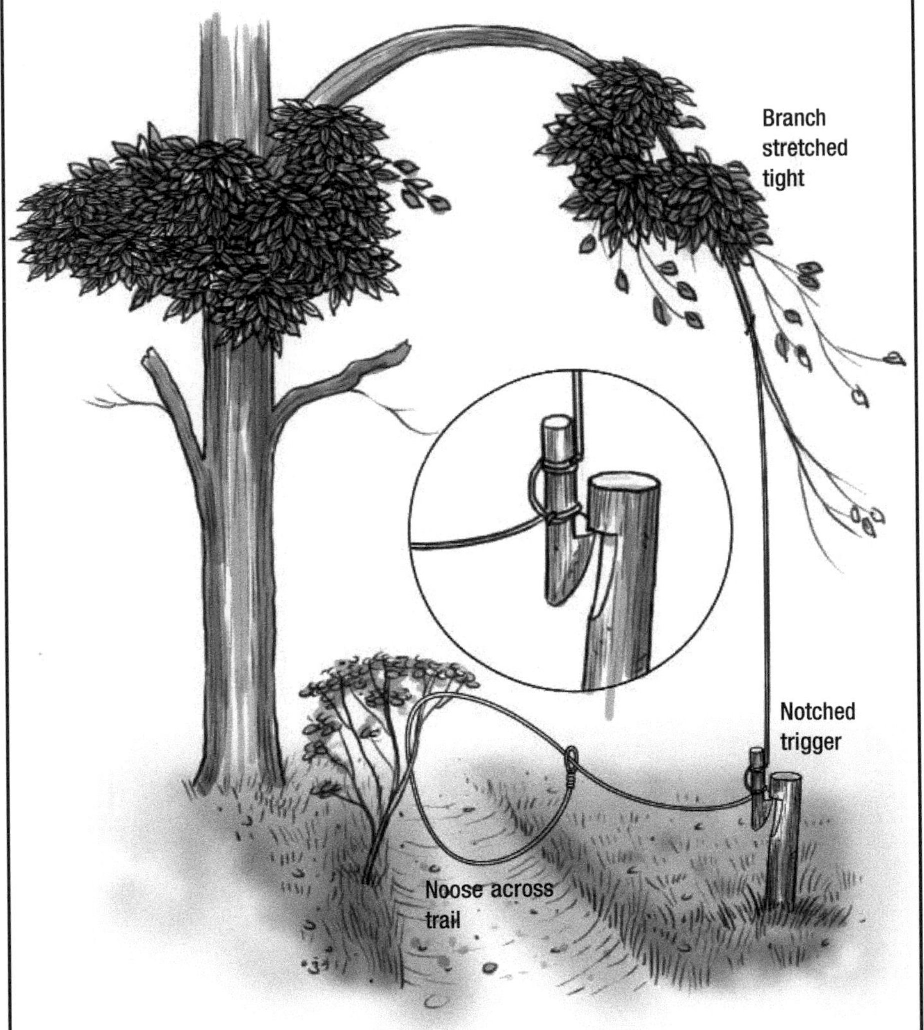

Spring spear trap

Spring spear traps like this one were used by the Viet Cong as anti-personnel booby traps during the Vietnam War. For hunting, they are perfectly suited to large mammals, such as wild boar and deer.

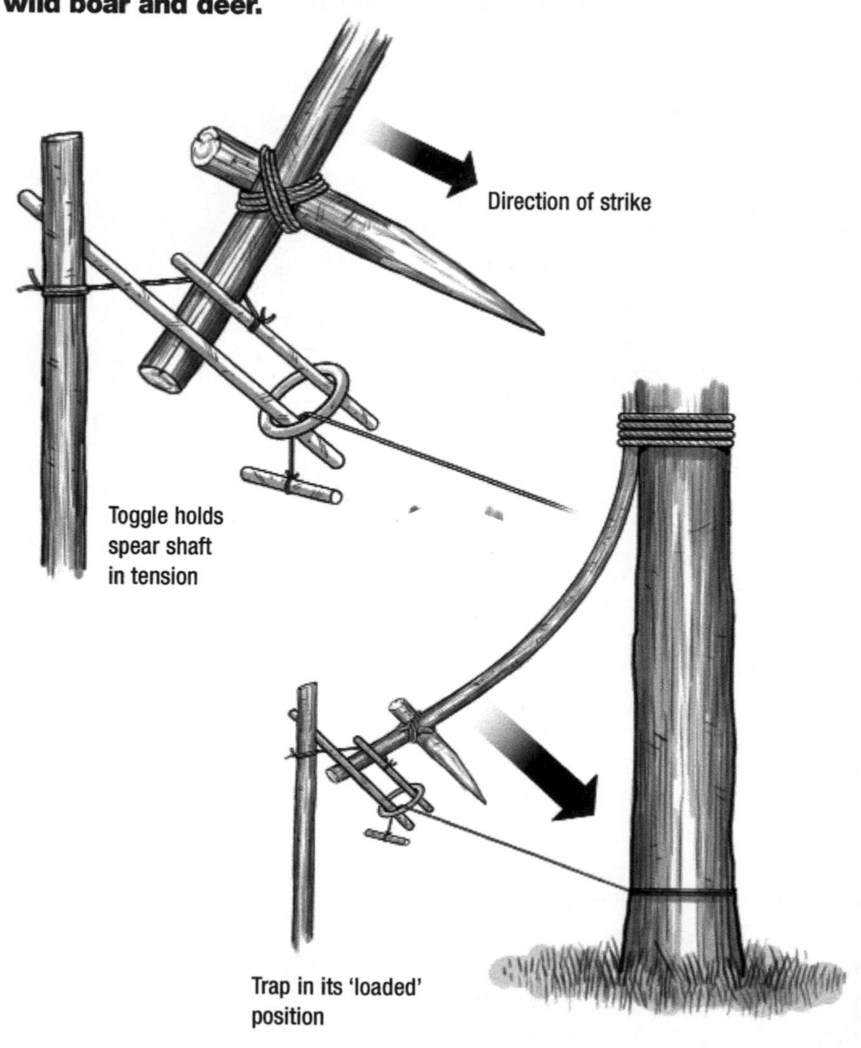

Spear traps

Unlike snares, spear traps are designed to kill their prey outright, and quickly. In their basic form, they consist of a branch held under tension with sharpened stakes attached to it. A wire runs from the end of the branch to the bait, restraining the branch against the tension and usually held in place by a stick embedded in the ground or by two interlocked notched sticks. When the animal takes the bait, it trips the wire, releases the branch, and is killed by the stakes.

Spear traps should be used to kill medium-sized to large mammals. Adjust the length of the sharpened stakes according to the prey type; for killing a goat the penetrating portion of the stake should be at least 15cm (6in) long. The stakes should sweep across the exact location of the bait, and having multiple stakes increases your chances of hitting the prey. Experiment with the plane of sweep, either horizontal or vertical according to the surroundings.

Note that spear traps can and have been used by guerrilla forces as anti-personnel weapons. For this reason, elite forces – always mindful of 'hearts and minds' – always dismantle their traps when not in use, so as not to endanger local people.

Deadfall traps

Deadfalls kill using a falling weight – usually a heavy log or stone – activated either by trip wires or by

TIP: SAS advices when making traps

- Avoid excessive handling of the trap, as this will leave your scent on it, and keep the trap away from campfires and foods for the same reason. Smear your hand with mud to mask your scent.
- Mark the direction to a trap with tall branches or markings on trees to avoid losing the device, something especially important in snowy conditions.
- Don't stand or work on the animal trail you are trapping. Instead keep to one side to make minimal disturbance.
- If you have to break branches, smear the white exposed wood with mud to camouflage your work.
- Try placing some bait in a potential trapping site; if it disappears the location is suitable for the trap.

Spring deadfall trap

This elaborate deadfall trap uses a bent branch, held under tension between two sticks, as the power behind a rapid-release trigger mechanism. When an animal takes the bait, it pulls the peg from the loop, releasing the branch, which in turn snaps out the attached support stick under the rock.

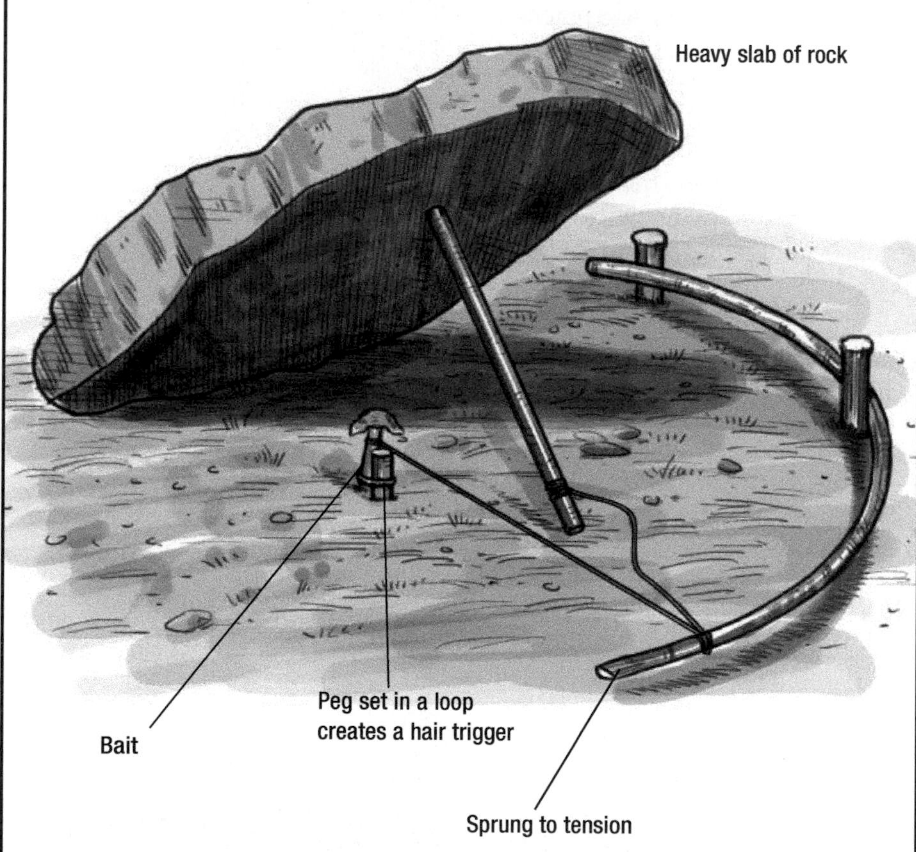

Deadfall traps

Deadfall traps need to be strong enough to resist wind and rain, but sensitive enough to be triggered easily by an animal. The trap at the top here uses multiple logs to increase the impact area.

TIP: Trapping birds

The following are some useful special forces methods for catching birds.

- Bird lime – boil holly leaves and grain in water to produce a glue-like substance. Spread the bird lime along branches commonly used by birds for perching; when the birds land here they will become stuck.
- Put fish hooks into pieces of bird food – remember to secure the fish hook to a branch or other anchor using fishing line.
- Tie straight lengths of fishing line across flight paths commonly taken by birds – flying birds may hit the lines and fall injured to the ground for you to collect.

baited triggers. These traps are best used for medium-sized mammals such as foxes, badgers and small deer and larger ground-feeding birds such as ducks and geese. Don't use heavy deadfalls for small prey, as the weight will crush the meat and bones too severely and render them unusable. When baiting deadfalls, keep the bait well back towards the hinge of the trap – as the deadfall drops, the animal will flinch and attempt to run, so putting the bait near the hinge means it is likely to be caught within the impact area.

Note that for large deadfall traps you will need the assistance of another person – never put yourself under a large deadfall weight while setting a delicate trigger.

BUTCHERING

Once you have killed an animal, bleed, gut, skin and cook it as soon as possible to prevent the meat from spoiling. Bleeding essentially involves slitting the animal's throat and letting the blood run out. Catch and retain this blood – it can make a nutritious addition to a stew or soup.

When it comes to gutting and skinning, the procedures vary slightly according to the animal, but follow a general pattern. First, cut around the anus and, in male animals, the penis. Insert the first two fingers between the skin and the membrane enclosing the entrails, then run the knife, blade up, from between the fingers up to the chin, taking care to cut only the skin, not the membrane. Having split the animal open, roll it on its side and remove the entrails. To skin the animal, make an incision up the inside of each leg from the knee to the crotch, then

Bird traps

Simple bird traps can be made by stringing wires and nooses made of of fishing line across bird flight paths or around roosting areas.

Skinning a rabbit

This basic technique for skinning a rabbit can be applied in general principle to many other small, four-limbed mammals.

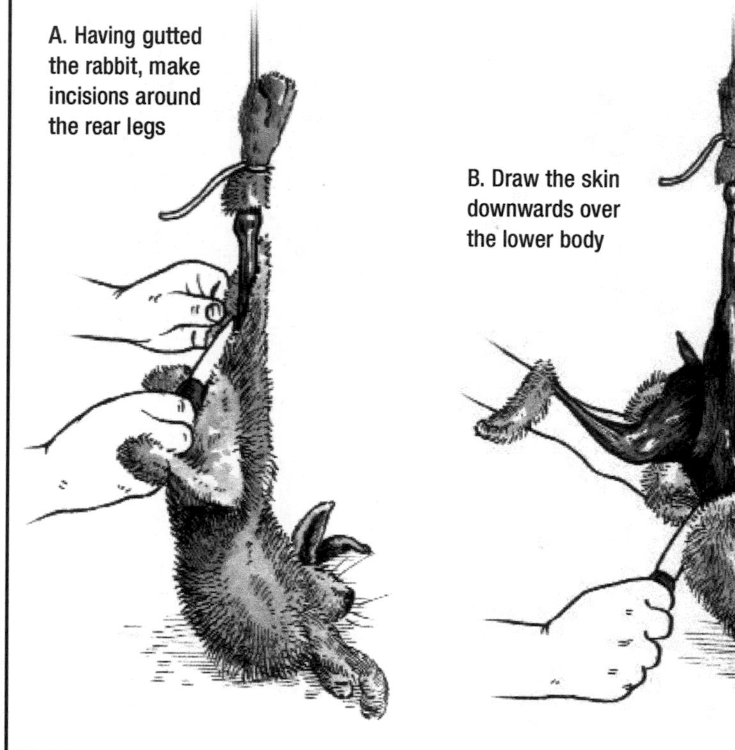

cut off the legs at the knee. Next work your hands around the carcass between the skin and the meat, systematically loosening all the skin and then drawing it off over the head.

Now the animal is ready for butchering. Split it at any natural joint and make steaks out of thick muscular sections of meat. Remember that survival nutrition is very different to your daily diet. Waste absolutely nothing about the carcass. Keep the organ meats (offal), for example, especially the kidneys, liver and heart – all are good to eat – and the feet, tail and

bones for making stock (clean them well before use). The fat can be used for cooking, or simply added to other dishes to make them more nutritious.

If you catch and kill a bird, first bleed it by cutting its throat beneath the tongue. Pluck the feathers out with a quick snapping motion, beginning from the chest. (If you are purely after breast meat, you can just pluck the chest and then slice out the individual breasts.) Submerging the bird in hot water first will make plucking easier, except in the case of water birds.

TIP: Finding fish

A basic understanding of fish behaviour will help guide you on where to fish. Look for bubbles and ripples on the water's surface, indicating a fish feeding just beneath. In inland waterways, fish are attracted to shaded places, whereas in colder weather they can head for shallow sunny patches. Fish generally prefer the still waters found immediately downstream of objects like large rocks or gravel banks or on the inside of bends, which have a slower current than the outside of the bend, although this behaviour can change for migratory fish such as salmon.

Now gut the bird, first cutting from the neck to the tail.

FISHING

Fishing is probably a soldier's best method of acquiring meat foods in a survival situation, as it places low demands on energy for potentially excellent yields. Decent amounts of fish can be caught with little more than a fishing hook, some weights and a fishing line. Bait the hook with worms, insects, minnows, berries, maggots or scraps of food. You can also fashion your own lures out of pieces of tinfoil, metal, feathers or colourful (and still wriggling) insects. When fishing with a line, keep yourself well back from the bank edge if possible, and stay low. Movement on the bank scares off fish and the refraction of light through the water enables them to see the bank side at a shallow angle. Don't let your shadow fall on the water.

Setting up a nightline enables you to continue fishing at night. Take a length of fishing line, and attach further hooked lines to it at regular intervals along its length. Picking a narrow, manageable stretch of a river or stream, stretch the main length of fishing line from one bank to the opposite bank (tie it between trees, or set stakes in the ground), at a height that allows the subsidiary lines to dangle into the water. Then simply leave it out for the entire night and draw it in at dawn to check for fish. Remember to change the bait regularly and do not leave the line out past daybreak – predators will steal your catch.

Note that if you don't have professional fishing tackle, you can make your own substitutes. Grasses

Making fishing hooks

Basic fishing hooks can be improvised by following the instructions below. Note that the size of the hook will limit the size of the fish you are likely to catch.

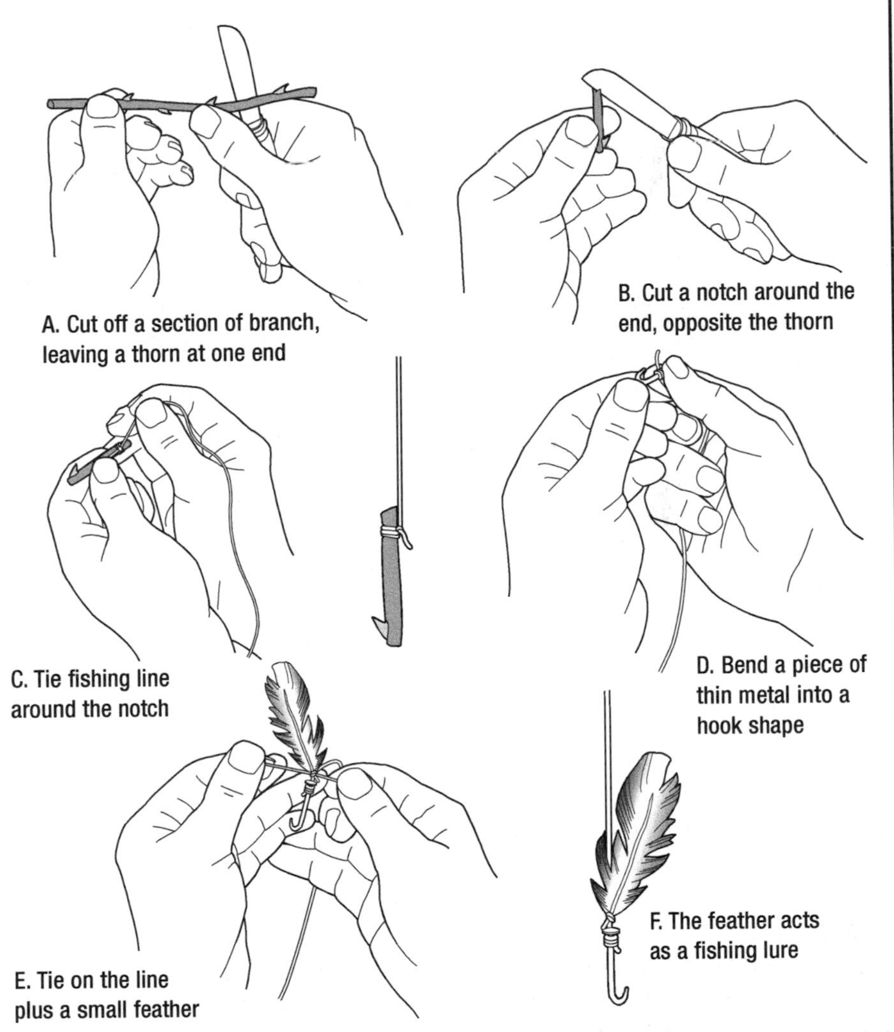

A. Cut off a section of branch, leaving a thorn at one end

B. Cut a notch around the end, opposite the thorn

C. Tie fishing line around the notch

D. Bend a piece of thin metal into a hook shape

E. Tie on the line plus a small feather

F. The feather acts as a fishing lure

Keeping out of sight

The refraction of light through water means that fish can see objects beyond direct line of sight. For this reason, when fishing try to stay well down on the bank, and avoid letting your shadow fall on the water, which will act as another warning sign to the fish.

or thin strands of animal sinew can be used for fishing line, and improvised fish hooks can be made out of thorns, bent nails, pins or pieces of sharp wood. (Note that any wooden hook will need to be replaced as it softens in the water after several hours.)

A rudimentary fishing rod can be created from nothing more than a branch (choose young branches, as they combine strength with flexibility). Create floats from buoyant material, such as cork, pieces of wood and rose hips, and set these along the line to adjust the depth to which the hook descends. For fishing weights, professional split-lead weights are obviously the best, but buttons, small stones, pieces of metal and any small heavier-than-water object will suffice.

Drop the line into places where fish are likely to be, and watch the float diligently. If the float suddenly dips below the surface, draw the rod in steadily but firmly. Another way of fishing with a rod is fly-fishing. Make a brightly-coloured lure out of feathers and pieces of cloth, or use a live beetle or grasshopper, and attach it to a hook without a weight. Flick the fly, as it is known, onto the surface of the water upstream and allow it to float downstream. During the summer season, fish will attempt to grab the lure, thinking that it is an insect.

Another traditional fishing technique is spear-fishing. Instead of making a standard single-point spear, as described above, tie several long, sharp thorns (bones or splinters of wood will also work) to the end of the stick, the thorns splayed in different directions to create a trident-like structure. To spear fish effectively, stand in the water or on the bank with your shadow behind you. (Do not enter the water barefoot, especially in the tropics or coastal waters.) Dip the end of the spear into the water – if you strike from above the water, the splash will scare the

TIP: Shellfish

Shellfish can be found in abundance along coastal areas, even in polar waters, but require caution as a source of food. Do not eat:

- Dead shellfish (live mussels should close when touched or tapped).
- Shellfish that are tightly shut and do not open after they have been boiled for 5–15 minutes.
- Shellfish that are not covered at high tide.

Running line

A running line across a stream is a great way to acquire food while you are doing something else. Set the fishing hooks on lines of various lengths, to maximize your chances of a successful catch.

fish away. When you spot a fish, gently move the spear over it, then drive the spear swiftly downwards to skewer it on the end.

Fish trapping and netting

Fish trapping and netting are two techniques that can catch large amounts of fish in a short space of time. Indeed, properly trained soldiers always resist overfishing a small stretch of river. Not only will it deplete fish stocks – which will make them unpopular with the locals – but they might also catch more fish than they can either eat or store, creating a health hazard through rotting meat.

Both trapping and netting involve some initial labour. Netting, for example, requires you to make a large gill net – tie multiple lengths of rope horizontally between two trees, then weave in the vertical lines to make a grid pattern. The mesh size should be about 4cm (1.5in). Once you have a decent net, you can stretch it across the entire width of a river, weighting it along the bottom so

Bottle trap

Bottle traps are among the simplest fishing devices covered in US Army survival training, requiring nothing but a plastic bottle. The fish swims in through the inverted bottle neck to get at the bait, but finds itself trapped inside.

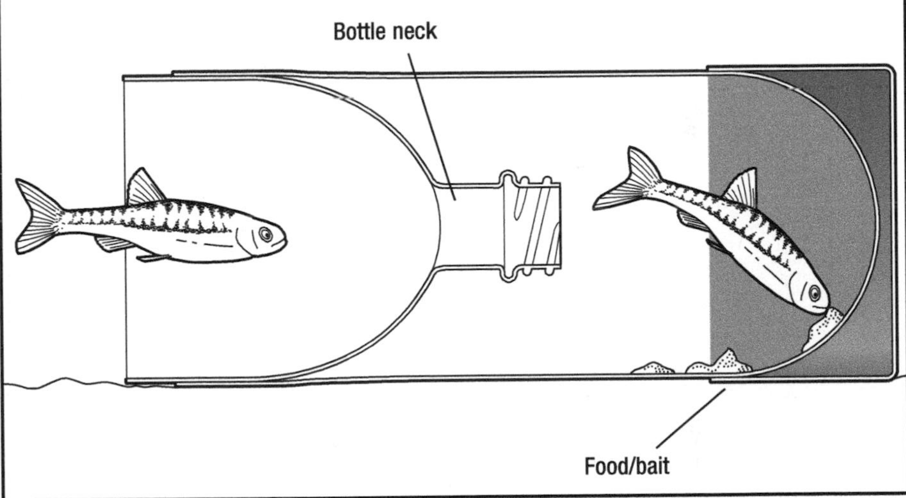

it hangs vertically in the water. (Set it at a 45-degree angle to the current to avoid damage to the net from drifting objects.) Leave it in the water for about one hour only, to produce a large but manageable catch.

The classic trapping device is a funnel trap. Make a lozenge-shaped basket from saplings with one end closed, the other open. At the open end, shape a funnel with its narrow end pointing into the basket, and then cover the body of the trap with twine or net to stop fish from escaping once caught. Place some bait at the back of the basket and submerge the whole construction under water. The principle of the funnel trap is that the fish can swim into the basket easily through the funnel, but cannot swim back out through the narrow inner spout. A similar, more basic, trap can be made by cutting a plastic bottle off at the head, then turning the head round and inserting it into the bottle (make sure you leave the cap off, or the trap is useless). Damming or funnelling techniques

Corralling fish

By strategically embedding sticks into the bed of a stream or river, you can trap fish in a confined space. The 'entrance' to this trap is formed by two inward-curving rows of sticks, narrowing like a funnel. Note that the mouth of the funnel should face into the current.

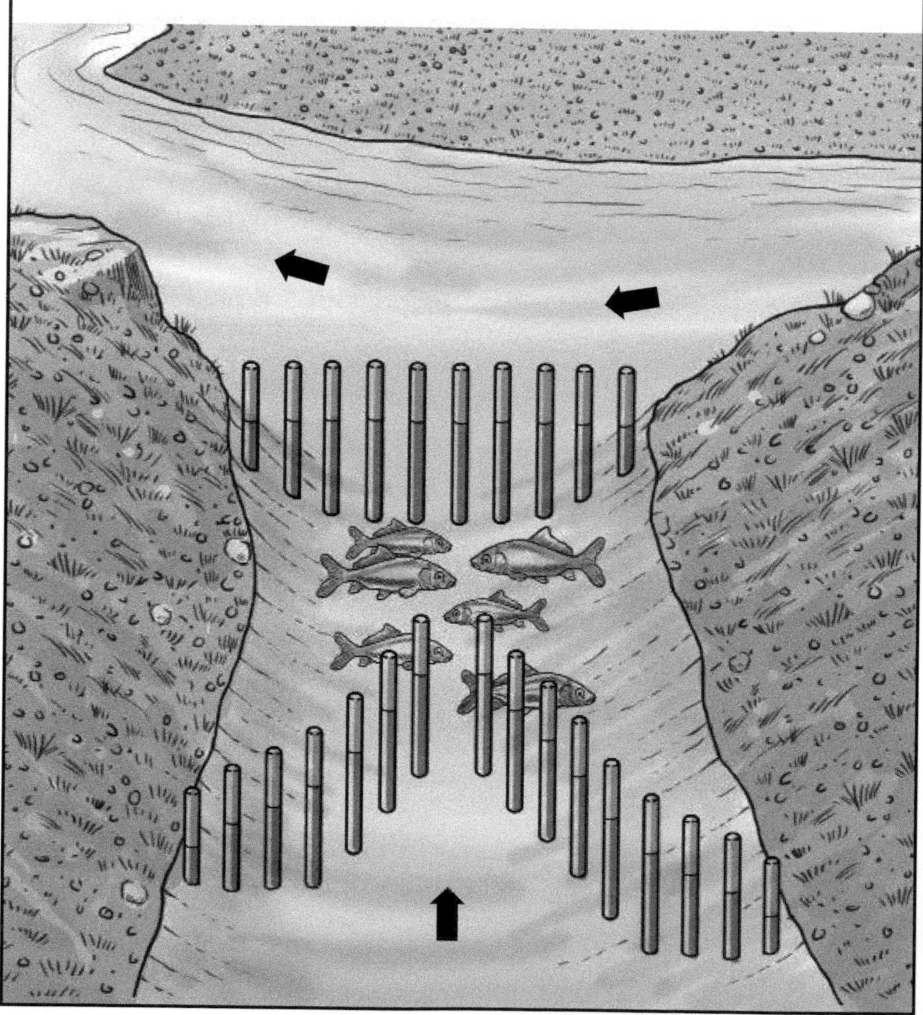

Gutting and filleting fish

All but the tiniest fish need to be gutted before cooking. Gutting is performed simply by slitting from the anus to behind the gills and then pulling out the innards.

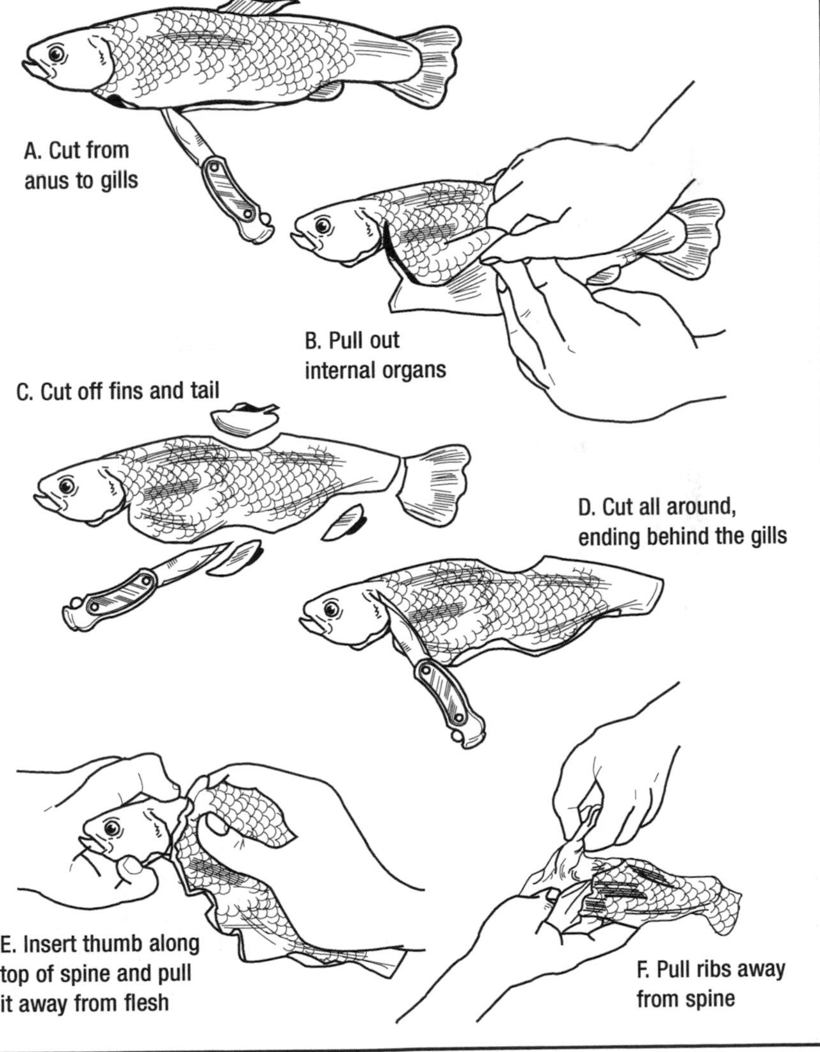

TIP: Ice-fishing

For Arctic ops, special forces soldiers are trained to fish frozen lakes using the following technique. First cut a hole in the ice, making sure that the ice can take your weight. Make a pennant from cloth or paper and tie it to a light stick (the flagpole) that is shorter than the diameter of the hole. Now tie another stick, which should be longer than the hole diameter, at a right angle onto the first stick. Fasten the fishing line to the other end of the flagpole and rest the long stick across the hole. When a fish takes the bait the flagpole will be jerked upright.

will improve catch yields from both netting and trapping, and can also serve to corral fish for line-fishing or spearing. A basic funnel can be built by constructing two rock walls in the water, the wide part of the funnel facing into the current and the narrow part of the funnel leading directly into a net, trap or a basin of still water. In tidal rivers and estuaries, another method of concentrating fish is to construct a semicircular wall against the riverbank that is lower than the water level at high tide, but higher than the water level at low tide. When the tide goes out, fish will be trapped in the enclosure, to be caught by netting, line-fishing or spearing.

FOOD FROM INSECTS AND MOLLUSCS

As unpalatable as they sound, insects and molluscs can make excellent survival foods, being particularly high in protein. They also have the advantage of being present in large numbers, especially in tropical or summertime temperate climates. Ants, crickets and grasshoppers, for instance, are all edible. Large numbers of ants are required to provide sustenance, admittedly, and they should be boiled for around six minutes to kill off any stings or poisons. Crickets and grasshoppers are a far better food source. Kill by swatting with a leafy branch, pull off the wings, antennae and legs, then roast or boil.

Bees and wasps are also edible, as are their pupae, larvae and honey, but they come with risks. Obviously, don't go straight for a bee or wasp nest – instead make a very smoky fire using grasses directly beneath the nest (the smoke will kill the bees) and do this only at night when all the bees will be in the nest. When it is

Termite nest

Termites are edible creatures, and one method of gathering is to push a long stick into a termite nest. The termites clamp onto the stick, and can then be scraped off the stick directly into a pan.

Insect food

Here we see three types of termite, all edible, and a grasshopper. All provide decent levels of protein, and the larger termites also offer high levels of fat for their size.

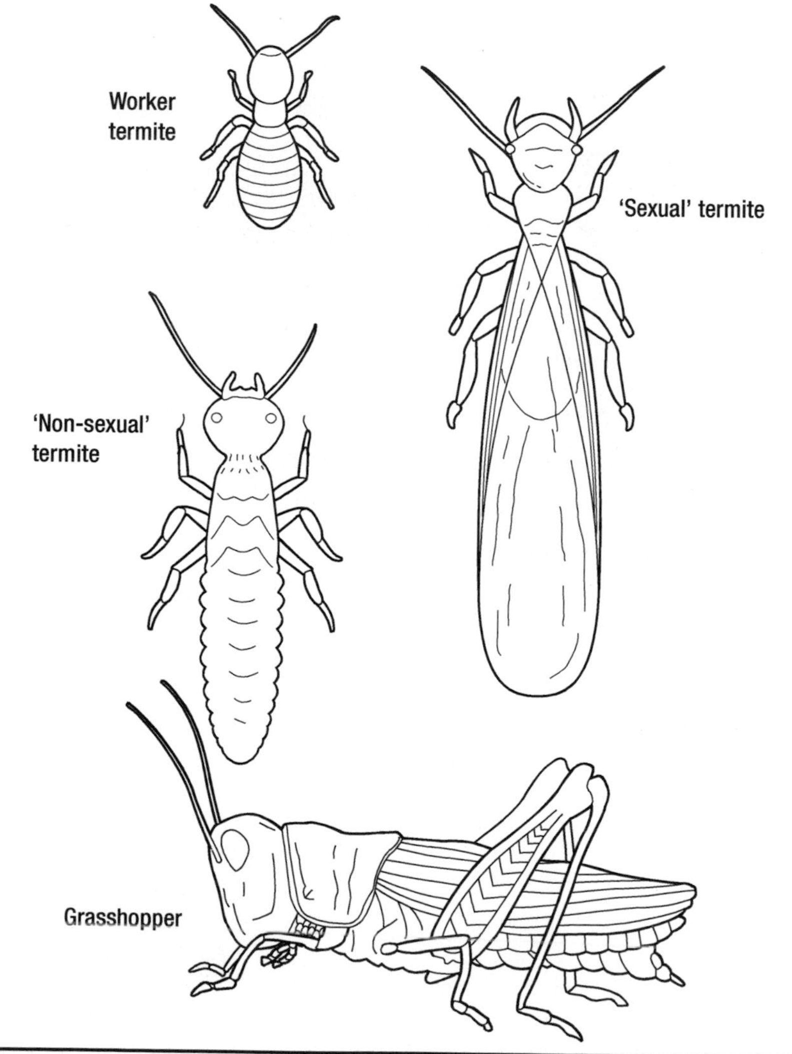

safe to do so, extract the honey from the nest (keep the honeycombs to provide a waterproofing wax) and prepare the bees for cooking by removing the poison sting and sac, the wings and the legs. Cook by boiling or roasting. Never assault a hornet's nest, as hornets are extremely aggressive and possess far more powerful stings than bees or wasps.

Slugs and snails make excellent food, but first starve the creatures for 24 hours before eating, to ensure that they excrete their internal poisons. To cook, drop them live into boiling water and cook them for 10 minutes. Do not eat snails with highly colourful shells, as they might be poisonous, and steer clear of tropical sea snails, some of which have lethal stings.

TIP: Eating termites

Termites can be collected in quite large volumes by pushing a long, thin stick into the side of a mud termite nest, and withdrawing it – aggressive termites will have their jaws clamped on the stick. Alternatively, smash off a piece of the nest with a stone and drop it into water, letting the termites float out to the surface for collection. They are tasty and nutritious creatures and can be eaten cooked by almost any method. To eat them, remove the wings and legs.

SURVIVAL COOKING

The next chapter will address the techniques of making fire and constructing cooking utensils, but here we need to explore the issue of survival cooking itself. Cooking the foods you catch or gather has several purposes, not least making foods taste good, which is in turn a morale booster. Cooking also makes some foods edible, killing off poisons, germs and parasites and softening tough fibres. Remember that all cooking methods kill off some of the vitamin content of food. While it might be tasty to fry up some berries to provide a sauce for some meat, nutritionally it is far better to eat the berries raw (if safe).

Almost any type of hot fire can be used for cooking. For example, a trench fire can be used as a grill by making a wire mesh or a grid of green sticks (mature wood will catch light) over the trench on which to place food. Make sure that any fire is up to temperature before starting to

Hobo stove

The hobo stove is a classic special forces method of improvised cooking. As well as cutting an opening in the side of the can for making the fire, cut multiple vents around the bottom to ensure air flow.

cook. The hottest point is usually when large flames die down and the wood forms itself into hot coals. Don't position food too close to a fire as it may simply char on the outside while remaining uncooked on the inside. You can check whether meat is properly cooked by driving a knife or wooden skewer into the middle of the meat and withdrawing it. If the juices run out red, it is not yet cooked. If they run clear, the food is OK to eat. Also, tentatively touch the end of a skewer. If it is hot, that means the central part of the food has been cooking.

Boiling is an ideal form of survival cooking, in that it cooks foodstuffs thoroughly and it is especially useful for breaking down tough plant matter. Roasting food skewered and held over an open fire, by contrast, is probably the most accessible cooking technique, although as we have just noted, you must ensure that the food is turned continually over the heat to avoid uncooked spots. The meat should be set just off to one side of the fire over a receptacle to catch any dripping fat, which can be used later for frying and eating. An improvised 'frying pan' might consist of nothing more than a sheet of metal or a flat, dry rock.

If you are in one location for any length of time, it might be useful to construct more advanced cooking facilities. The hobo stove, for example, requires a large metal tin or drum, washed out thoroughly and scraped clean of any unpleasant or flammable residues. Cut out a rectangular port in the side of the drum through which you can make and stoke a fire, and punch one or two rows of ventilation holes around the bottom circumference. To use the hobo stove, stand it securely on the earth and light a fire inside the drum. Place a top plate over the opening at the top as a frying and heating surface.

An alternative to the hobo stove is the Yukon stove. Dig a circular hole in the ground about 24cm (9in) across and about 30cm (1ft) deep. Then cut a channel leading down into the hole. Here is the place for starting and feeding the fire; the fire itself is made at the base of the stove's body. To create this body, stack up rocks around the edge of the hole in a funnel shape, but ensure that you do not close up the fire channel. If possible, try to make the funnel narrow towards the middle and flare out slightly at the top. Finally, pack the funnel with clay and earth to seal it and stabilize it.

Yukon stoves generate considerable heat, but you can partially control the temperature by altering the aperture of the vent at the top with pieces of wood or stone and thereby restricting the oxygen supply. To cook with the stove, place food on skewers or a grill and position them over the vent, or you can wrap food in parcels of leaves and put them just inside the fire channel.

COOKING TECHNIQUES

Although boiling, frying and roasting are your basic survival cooking methods, there are a variety of other techniques available that produce

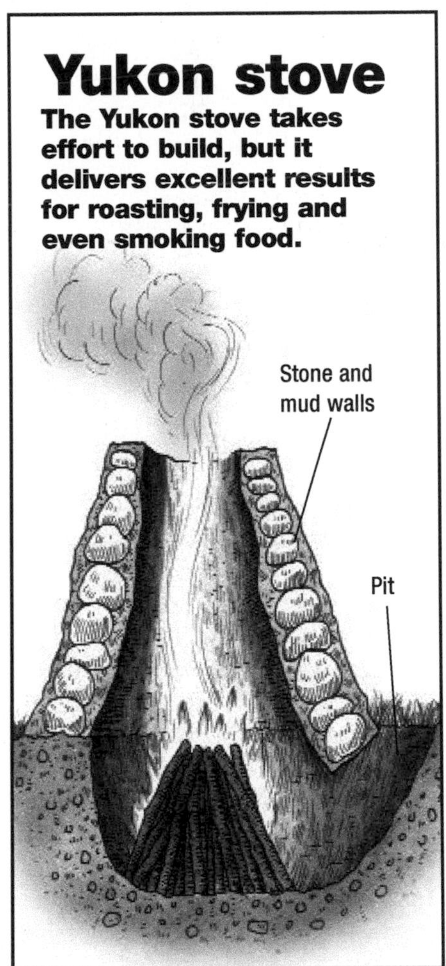

Rock oven

Rock ovens are primarily for roasting, and their temperature can be controlled by altering the width of the aperture at the front. Include a vent on the top to release smoke.

delicious results. For example, animals that feature scales, spines or feathers can be cooked in a wrap of mud or clay. To do this, encase a piece of meat or fish in clay then wrap the clay in a 'parcel' of green leaves and grass. Place the parcel directly within a glowing fire, making sure that it is covered with embers. The mud or clay serves to prevent the meat from burning, while the external heat cooks the contents inside with an even temperature. After an hour or so, remove the parcel and pull off the clay, which should lift off the inedible outer parts, leaving you with a ready-to-eat meal.

One excellent cooking technique utilizes a bed of hot rocks. Make your usual campfire on a bed of rocks. When the fire has died down entirely, brush away the ash and embers with some leafy sticks to expose the hot rocks. Place meat or vegetables

Baking in mud

Mud baking is a very gentle form of cooking, and is particularly suited to cooking fish without charring the meat.

A. Lay prepared fish on leaves

B. Wrap in plant material, tying with twine

C. Cover in mud

D. Cook over a fire

Cooking on hot rocks

Hot rocks are another good method for cooking meats. Never heat up very wet rocks, however, as they could explode as their water content expands.

straight onto the stones, turning the food frequently to prevent it burning. Keep the pieces of food small so that they cook thoroughly on the rocks' residual heat.

An advanced and extremely gentle special forces cooking method is the steam pit. Dig a trench and make a platform of rocks in the bottom. Now make a fire on the platform. When the fire has died down, clear away the glowing embers and push a long stick into the middle of the pit. Cover the rocks with a thick layer of green grass, and place meat, wrapped tightly in a binding of leaves, into the middle. Cover the parcel of meat with another layer of grass and then spread a layer of earth, filling the entire pit.

Pull out the protruding stick and pour a small quantity of water into the hole. Seal the hole left by the stick. The water will turn to steam underground and cook the food to tender perfection in about an hour with minimal loss of nutrients.

FOOD PRESERVATION

In a survival situation, you must try to preserve any excess food for later, as you do not know where the next meal is coming from. Keep the food as cool and as dry as possible, preferably in an airtight container – moulds and bacteria thrive on moisture. Also keep it out of direct sunlight, and away from insects and other hungry creatures.

To preserve food for more than a few days, however, it needs to be dried. Drying reduces the water content of foods to below five per cent of mass, so the moulds and bacteria then struggle to develop and the food is preserved longer. The technique works best on lean foods such as fish and poultry, vegetables and fungi, not fattier meats.

The most basic, and difficult, drying technique is simply to expose the food to warm, dry air preferably assisted by warm winds, which also serve to keep away insects. Place vegetables on warm rocks in the sun, and hang thin, trimmed fillets of meat over a wooden frame or simply over tree branches, but watch out for crawling insects. Your goal is food that is desiccated and stiff, a process that can take several days in some instances. Note that berries cannot be dried by the above method because they have watertight skins. Cut open non-segmented berries and expose the inner flesh to the air for drying. Mash segmented berries before drying and spread them on a hot surface until dry. The food is finished when it is dry and brittle to the touch. To rehydrate, soak the food in water for a few hours or boil for between 30 and 60 minutes.

Drying food just using the air is a difficult process to control, and there is a strong likelihood of the food being either stolen or contaminated by creatures, or simply beginning to rot. A faster and better method of drying, therefore, is smoking. Smoke absorbs the moisture from food, and leaves a waxy coating on the food's surface, which resists the absorption of moisture. An easy method of smoking is to drape or skewer strips of meat over a smoky fire – make sure that the fire is generating little heat but lots of smoke, otherwise you will end up cooking the food. Alternatively, you can build a smoke tepee. Take three long, straight branches and tie them together at one end to form a standing tepee. Make a platform of green branches halfway up the inside of the structure and start a fire beneath it. When the fire is smouldering, throw on piles of leaves (preferably green). The fire will now produce a heavy smoke. Place pieces of food on the smoking platform and cover the entire tepee over with a cloth, branches or turf while leaving a small air gap for the fire. The food should be dried out after about 18 hours inside the tepee.

Drying/smoking frame

This basic lattice drying frame can be used for air-drying thin strips of meat or, if set over a smoky fire, for smoking foods.

Drying a skin

An animal skin can be air-dried by stretching it between a rectangular frame, as shown here. Large hides, however, will need salting as part of the drying process to ensure that all the moisture is removed.

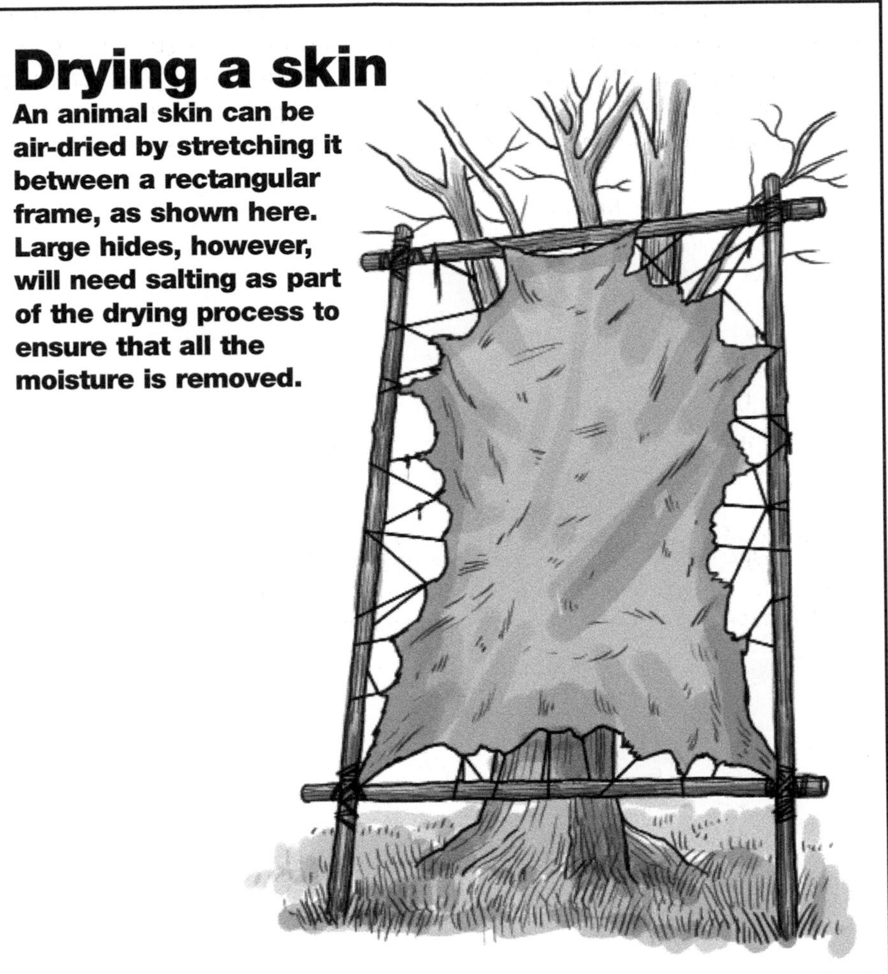

In polar climates, you also have the obvious preservation method of freezing, although don't simply leave the food out in the open – bears can scent food from a considerable distance away. Another preservation method suited to the Arctic is to soak the food in a brine solution and then dry it. You can make the solution by filling a container with sea water and then boiling it. Keep filling the water up as it evaporates to concentrate the salt solution. After a few refills, stop the boiling and let the brine cool. Soak the strips of meat in the solution and then dry them in the air.

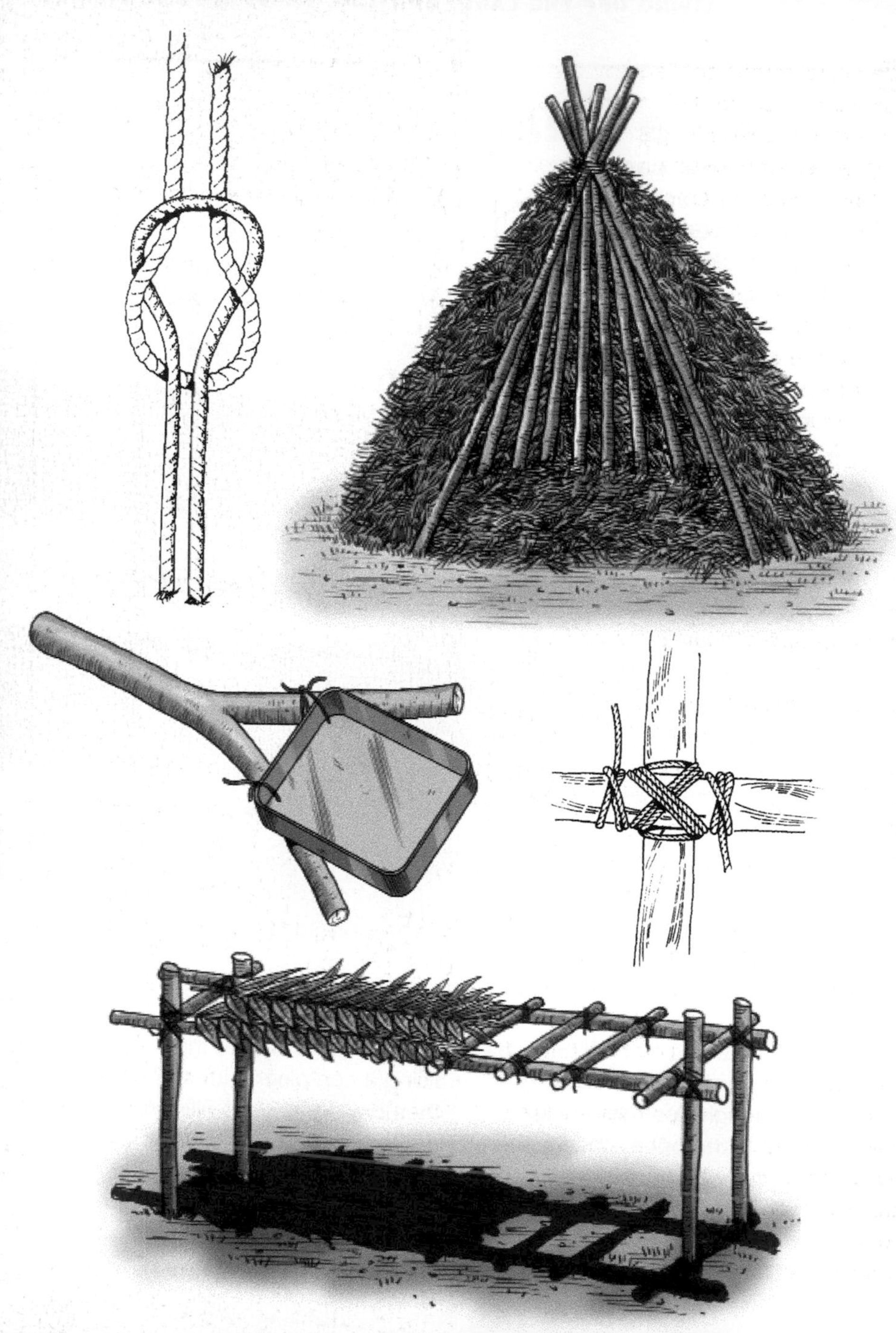

4

Making fire and creating a comfortable camp will help you to prosper in the wild.

Fire, Shelter and Camp Skills

Special forces soldiers, by the very nature of their operations, may have to spend long periods living either amongst native peoples or in hide-outs or camps in the wilderness. Such is a key reason why these personnel receive intensive survival training. Yet not only must they be able to stay alive, they also need to make their experience endurable. This chapter, therefore, looks at some of the practical elite forces techniques for bringing a greater degree of comfort and endurance in the wild, including the ultimate outdoor skill, making fire.

MAKING FIRE

On many levels, making fire has a significance beyond providing heat, light and the ability to cook. A well-made fire also is a morale-booster, something that raises the spirits and provides a sense of wellbeing. Such emotional benefits can have a critical effect on your will to survive.

Any fire requires three elements: tinder, kindling and fuel. The fire always starts with tinder, which consists of any light and small

Special forces survival training includes advanced techniques for making shelters and fire, plus age-old skills of rope-tying. By adding survival skills to your repertoire, your chances of staying healthy are dramatically increased.

Feathering sticks

'Feathering' the sticks that you use for kindling involves creating thin strips of wood with a sharp blade. The feathered stick offers a larger combustible area than a regular stick.

particles of material, usually fibrous in nature. Typical sources of tinder generally include:

- Shredded bark from some trees and bushes (birch and cedar are excellent because of their flammable resin).
- Cotton balls or lint.
- Dried mosses and fungi.
- Crushed leaves and other fibres from dead plants.
- Fine wood shavings or resin-damp wood sawdust.
- Dry straw and grasses.
- Dried-out linings of bird or rodent nests.
- Powdered sap from pine trees.
- Finely-shredded paper.
- Commercially-produced camping tinder – e.g. paraffin-soaked cotton wool, fire sticks (blocks of wood shavings impregnated with flammable chemicals), and paraffin blocks.

The purpose of tinder is to create the very first flames of your fire. It must therefore catch light with little encouragement, so it needs to be bone dry. Dry damp tinder out in the sun or in a warm pocket in your clothing, and keep dry tinder from getting damp by storing it in a waterproof container or bag.

Kindling consists of larger pieces of material, and is added to the burning tinder to raise the temperature of the fire so that more substantial fuel can

TIP: Fire safety

- Don't light a fire at the base of a tree, and keep the fire away from dry foliage.
- In woodland, clear away all debris on the ground to form a circle of bare earth at least 2m (6ft 6in) across, and site the fire in the middle of it.
- Make sure that no tents or camping equipment will be caught by the flames, particularly batteries, gas stoves and flammable liquids.
- In windy conditions, encircle the fire with rocks; this will not only shelter the flames, but also prevent them from spreading.
- Never place wet or porous rocks and stones in or near fires, as they can explode when heated.
- Do not make fires in enclosed spaces without any ventilation, as you run the risk of death through carbon monoxide poisoning.

be added. Typical kindling includes dry twigs about the thickness of a pencil (resinous softwoods are good, but avoid any very green woods), pine cones and needles, and pieces of bark. If using sticks, cut small flaps of wood in the surface of the branch to expand the combustible surface area (the technique is known as 'feathering'). Remember to add the kindling to the fire piece by piece, as a large pile of sticks being dumped on incipient flames will easily smother the burning tinder.

For main fuel, large pieces of dry wood are best. Try to select hardwoods rather than softwoods, as hardwoods provide a more durable flame, meaning that you don't have to spend so much time gathering fuel. (Green woods, however, produce lots of smoke, so are good for signalling fires.) Survival alternatives to wood fuel include grass twisted into bunches, 'logs' of dried peat moss or dried-out animal dung (mix the dung with dried grass and wood chips to make it burn longer).

Starting a fire

In the absence of matches or cigarette lighters (the latter are a useful addition to your survival tin), you have to improvise means of creating fire. Remember, your goal is to create just enough heat or sparks to ignite tinder, not larger kindling or fuel.

The classic outdoor means of firemaking is flint and steel. Natural flint stone is acceptable for making sparks, but man-made flint-and-steel sets are available from outdoor adventure stores. These have a metal (often magnesium alloy) 'flint' and a steel striker, and produce good showers of hot sparks. To use one, hold it just above the tinder and strike the flint with the edge of the steel in a downward glance, directing the resultant sparks at the tinder. As soon as the tinder begins to smoulder, fan or blow it gently to raise a flame. Note that at every stage of firemaking, flames require oxygen to burn. Particularly in the early stages, therefore, keep the fire structure loose and airy, to allow the flames to build up their heat.

When flint and steel aren't available, you may have to fall back on ancient friction ignition methods. The fire plough is a classic technique, as seen performed by Tom Hanks in the film *Cast Away* (2000). To construct the fire plough, take a piece of softwood about 30–46cm (12–18in) long, and carve a groove into the surface of the wood about 2cm (0.7in) wide and about 1cm (0.3in) deep, which runs the entire length of the board. Now put some tinder at one end of the groove. Rubbing a hardwood stick, its tip sharpened to a chisel shape, vigorously up and down the length of the groove will produce both heat and flakes of wood tinder

Fire plough

Fire ploughs work by generating heat from the friction of a stick rubbed repeatedly up and down a wooden groove. The friction produces flakes of smouldering wood, which can then be pushed onto tinder to create a flame.

within the groove, the former eventually igniting the latter. As this happens, use the stick to push the burning embers to the end of the groove and onto the main tinder.

The hand drill involves a more advanced construction. Find a large flat piece of wood and cut a small V-shaped notch into one edge (the mouth of the V at the wood edge), with a small indentation at the point of the V. This will act as the hearth. Now get a strong wood stick about 60cm (2ft) long and 2.5cm (1in)

Bow and drill fire

A bow and drill system works best with woods such as willow, larch, cedar, poplar, sycamore and mulberry. Avoid woods that are very hard or very soft.

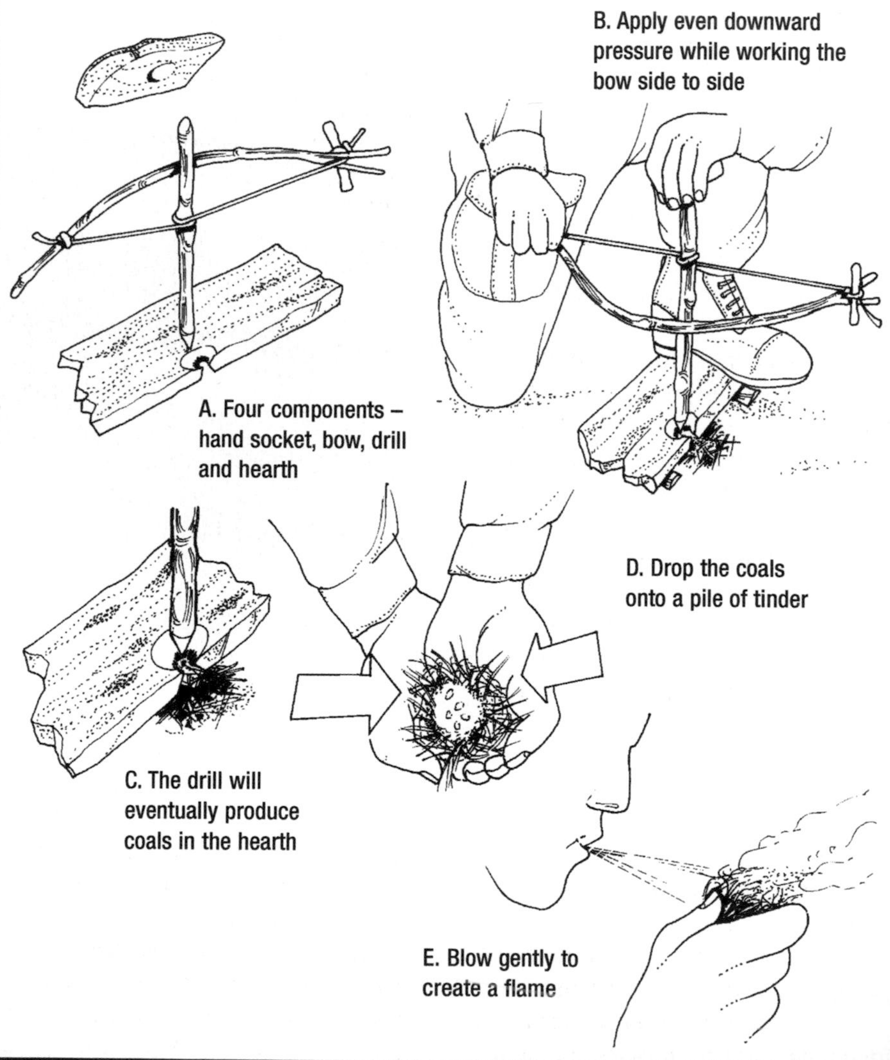

thick. Sharpen one end of this stick to a point.

Place a handful of tinder beneath the V-shaped notch of the hearth, and raise the hearth up slightly using a stick so that it leaves a small air gap around the tinder. Secure the hearth under your knees. Now insert the sharpened point of the stick into the indentation bored into the hearth, and start rotating the stick vigorously between the palms of your hands. Apply downward pressure by working the hands from the top of the stick to the bottom, before going back to the start position and repeating as required. After time, friction generates heat in the indentation and produces smouldering coal and ash. These drop through the V-shaped notch, igniting the tinder underneath. If the embers do not drop through, lift the tinder onto the hearth to make contact. As soon as the tinder ignites, blow gently on it to fan the flames, and then either remove the hearth or add kindling, or move the burning tinder into a pile of kindling.

Making a bow to power the stick rotation can speed up the hand-drill process. Cut a notch around the friction stick about one-third of the length down from the blunt end. Round off the blunt end – this end will fit in a socket made from a palm-sized piece of hardwood with an indentation in the middle. Lubricate the indentation with grease, oil or soap to prevent friction wear. The bow is made from a branch just less than 1m (3ft 3in) long and 2.5cm (1in) in diameter. Tie a piece of cord, line or any other sort of twine to both ends with the stick under tension, so it produces a bow.

To use the bow drill, twist the bowstring once around the spindle notch and place the sharpened end of the spindle into the hollow in the

TIP: Burning glass

Any sort of lens can be used to channel the sun's hot rays onto tinder to achieve ignition. For best results use a magnifying glass, a camera or telescope lens, or the lens of a magnifying flashlight. At worst, a convex piece of bottle glass is also usable.

Simply turn the glass into the sun and channel the rays to a single point of light. On a hot and sunny day – the only day on which this technique will really work – the tinder should quickly smoulder. Blow gently on it to raise a flame.

hearth. Press the hard wood down on the other end the spindle. Holding the bow at a right angle to the spindle, pull it backwards and forwards in a sawing action with long, even strokes. Keep going until smoke is produced and ignition of the tinder occurs.

Fire construction

There are actually numerous different types of fire you can build, each

Types of fire

There are numerous different varieties of campfire. Star fires, for example, give a very controllable heat, while the 'T' fire and keyhole fire are useful for cooking. Long fires and safety night fires are constructed to prevent the fire accidentally spreading.

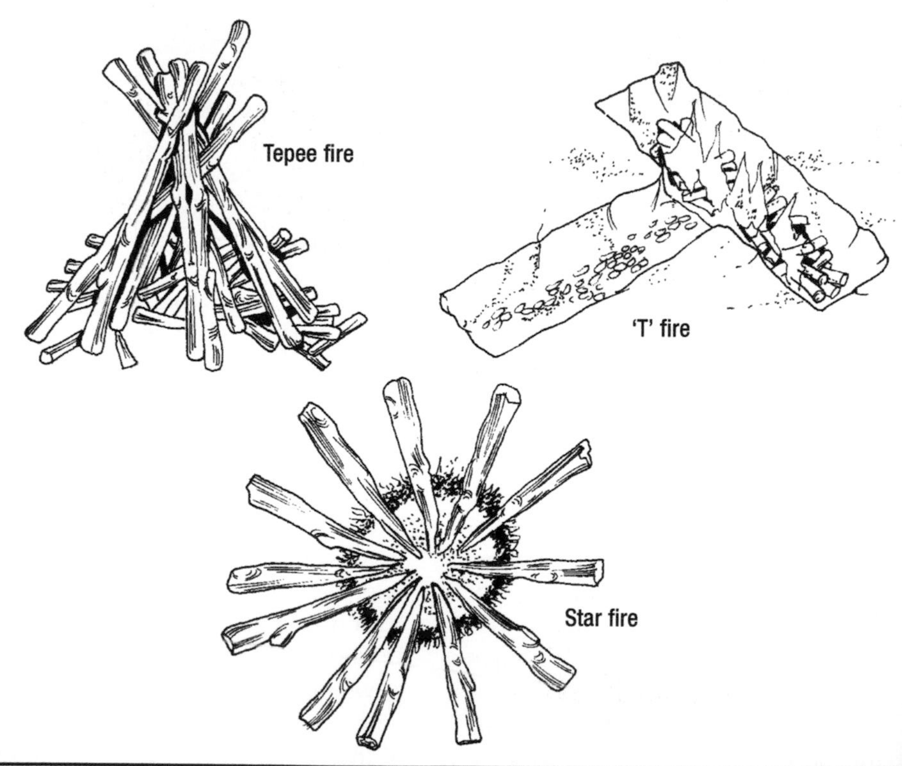

suited to different purposes. A trench fire, for example, is ideal for use in windy conditions. Dig a trench about 30cm (1ft) wide, 90cm (3ft) long and 46cm (18in) deep, and line it from end to end with rocks. Build the fire on the rocks – the rocks will radiate heat out and also protect the fire from the damp earth. The fire can be used for roasting and grilling foods across its mouth. A variation on the straightforward trench fire is

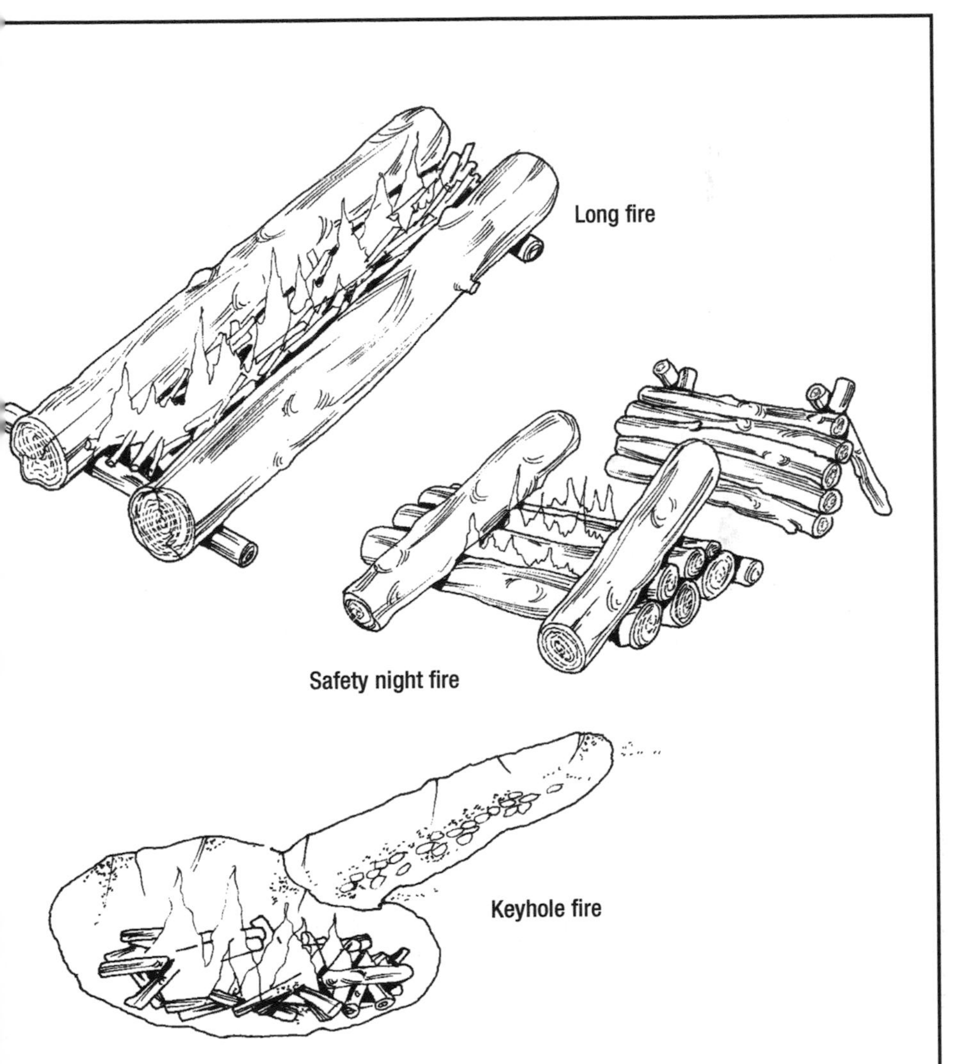

the 'T' fire, in which a T-shaped trench is dug. The fire is kept burning in the top part of the T, while coals are dragged out into the lower part for use in cooking.

One basic fire, the tepee fire, can be used for both cooking and heating. Push a stick into the earth and use it to stabilize a circle of kindling sticks formed into a shape

Rock fire

In areas of dense, dry bush, it may be a good idea to build your fire within a circle of stones, to keep the flames contained and controlled.

like a tepee. Place tinder in the middle of the tepee through an opening left to provide a little wind current. Light the fire with your back to the wind and feed the fire from the downwind side. Once the kindling is well alight, it can be collapsed and larger fuel placed on the fire.

If fires of intense heat and light are needed, build lattice fires. These are

Pit fire

The pit fire is a classic soldier's campfire. Air flow to the fire is provided via a U-shaped vent dug into the soil – restricting or widening this vent will reduce or increase the heat respectively. Wrapped parcels of food can be placed in the pit for roasting, while the opening above can be used for grilling, boiling and drying.

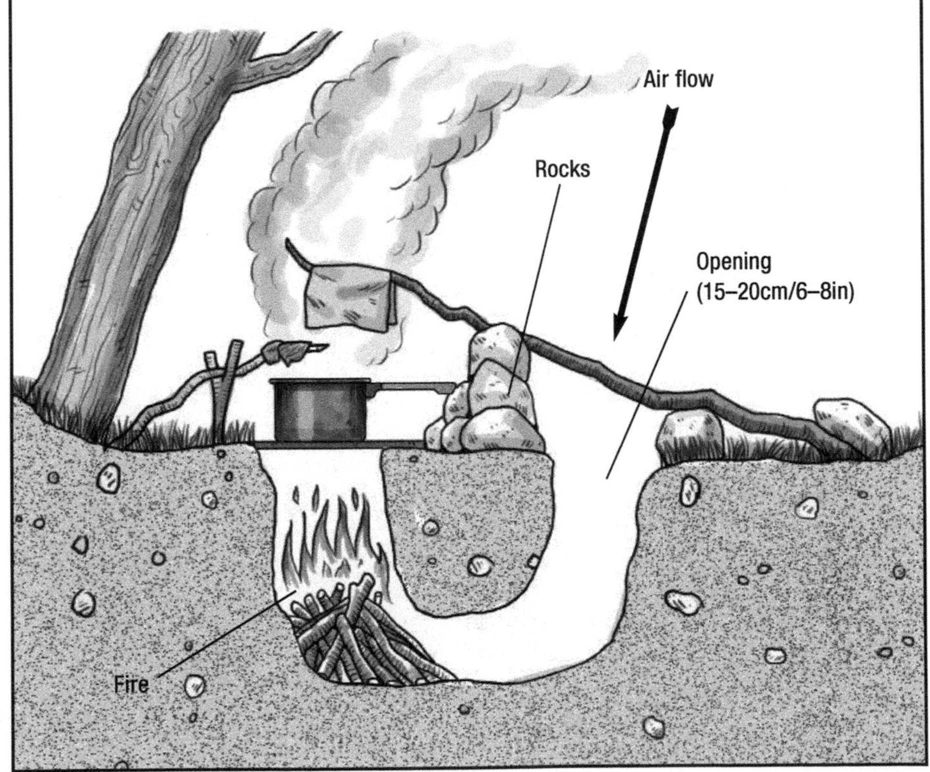

made out of logs stacked on top of one another in open lattice shapes in a pyramid configuration.

The large number of air gaps in the log pile feeds the flames with a strong current of oxygen. The upshot is that this fire consumes fuel quickly, so it is not one to build if firewood is in short supply (reducing the size and number of air gaps will conserve fuel). A less fuel-greedy alternative is the star fire.

This fire is in the centre of a 'wheel', with large pieces of fuel forming the 'spokes' (hardwood logs are best for a star fire). The logs are pushed into the fire according to the level of heat and warmth required.

Windbreak

Strong winds can extinguish a fire, or at least result in too much fuel being consumed. A windbreak, here constructed from a semicircle of stones, not only protects the fire, but also reflects heat back towards you.

Carrying fire

Follow the instructions below to transport smouldering coals from one place to another. Doing this means that you can make instant fire at your new camp.

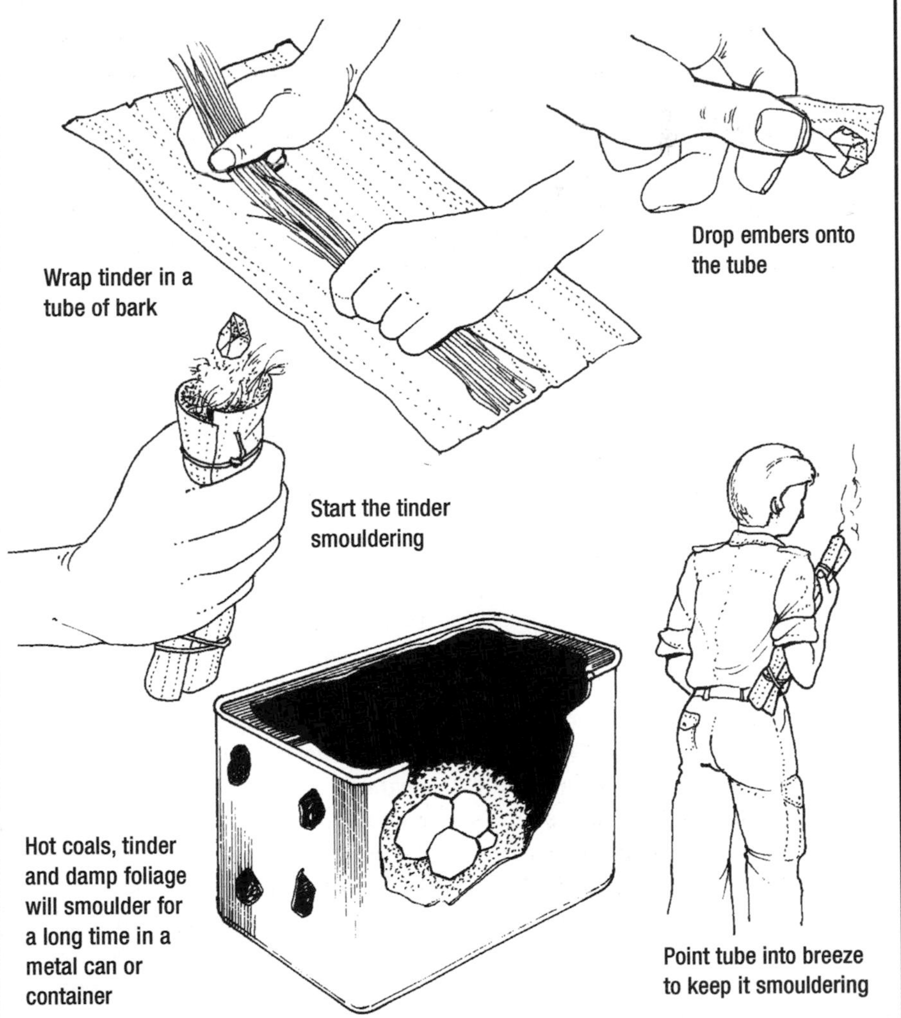

TIP: Special forces fire-building

- If the ground is wet or covered in snow, build a fire platform out of green logs or stones – don't make the fire directly on the ground.
- Choose a sheltered site for your fire, as strong winds make firestarting difficult, or can make an established fire burn too fast.
- If you can't avoid a wind, put your back to it when lighting a fire to shelter the tinder.
- Do not build a fire up against a rock. Instead, build it so that you can sit between the rock and the fire – the rock behind you will reflect heat onto your back. If no 'reflector' is naturally available, build one out of rocks and earth.
- Remember to gather tinder, kindling and fuel in good quantities before attempting to make a flame.
- At night, when you are about to go to sleep, place two large, green logs against the fire to ensure that the fire is kept away from you and your shelter.

SHELTER

Shelters are vital components of outdoor survival. Never think that because a climate is warm, you don't need to construct a shelter. Shelters not only provide you with warmth, they also shield you from sunlight, rain and other precipitation, wind, blown dust and grit, and even insects.

Nature in itself provides several varieties of shelter that need little or no modification. Cliff overhangs, large rocky outcrops, piles of turf, fallen tree-trunks and caves can act as either simple windbreaks or permanent shelters. You can also make shelters by simple modifications to natural features. For example, you can cover a natural hollow in the ground, or a scooped-out hollow on the leeward side of a fallen tree-trunk, with strong branches, sticks, foliage and turf to form a relatively durable and cosy shelter, and one that can be put together fairly rapidly. If you need to

Willow frame shelter

This basic but cosy shelter consists of a frame of willow branches, tied at the top to form a tepee shape, then covered with thick layers of interlocked foliage.

increase the height of the hollow, ring its edge with stones and small rocks, these cemented into place by packing the gaps in the stones with turf and foliage mixed with mud.

Be inventive in your approach to shelters, and use all available materials. For example, if you have a tarpaulin, groundsheet or any piece of waterproof sheeting material with you, you can improvise a tent by tying a line between two trees, then throwing the sheet over the line before stretching it out and securing

TIP: Locating shelters

Do not build shelters:
- On exposed and windy hilltops.
- In deep valleys or hollows, which are prone to frost and damp.
- Too close to rivers or streams, because of the risk from flooding.
- Under rotting trees or crumbling rock faces.
- Under insect nests.
- In drain-off channels from high ground.

Tarpaulin shelter

British Army and Australian Army soldiers regularly build shelters and observation posts from nothing more than a rope and a tarpaulin. Such a shelter is known as a 'basha'.

Fallen-tree shelter

Sometimes natural features provide ready-made shelters. By cutting away some of the inner branches from this fallen young pine tree, and lining the floor with the cuttings, you can make a simple shelter without too much effort.

each corner to the ground using more line and improvised wooden pegs. If no line is available, balance one end of a tree-trunk or long bough in the fork of a tree, and throw the sheeting over it.

More substantial shelters can be constructed from basic combinations of branches and foliage. A popular type is a simple A-frame shelter. Take a long, straight bough, a good couple of feet longer than you are tall, and prop one end in the fork of a tree a few feet off the ground. Then prop numerous other branches vertically against the main support branch, tying them in place with cord or strong saplings. Once you have made the frame, then begin weaving copious amounts of flexible branches and dense foliage into the structure, building the layer up to form a substantial outer wall. You can even 'carpet' the outside of the vegetation-covered frame with grassy sods of earth, to provide further insulation and protection. As with all shelters, make a carpet of

Building a lean-to

Here we see a simple lean-to shelter. The frame is built against a frontal weight-bearing crossbeam, supported between two upright posts (or the fork in a tree, as seen here). Cover the frame with thick layers of leaves and foliage, and build a fire reflector in front to push back the heat from your campfire.

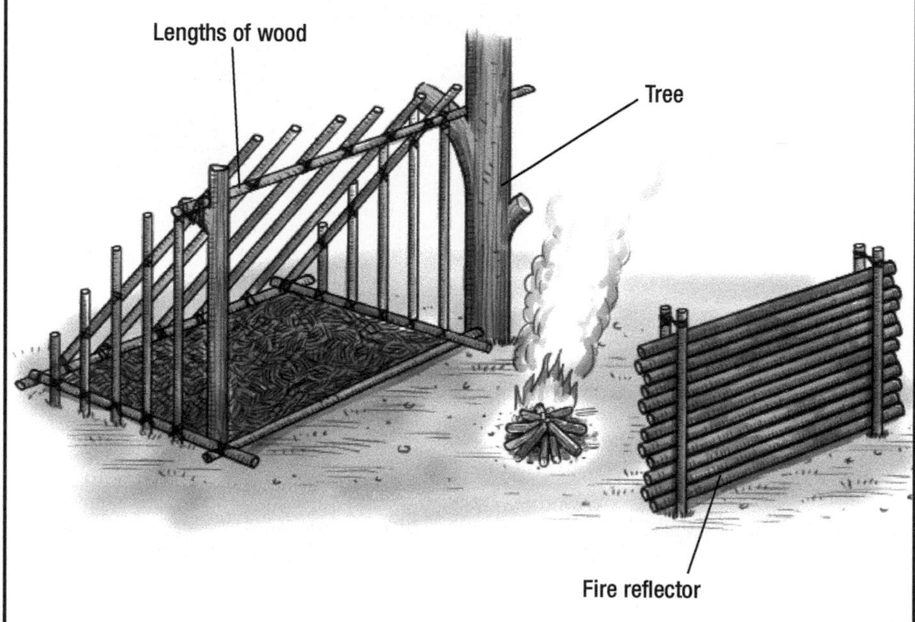

thick, soft foliage on the floor to sleep on (never sleep directly on the floor). The principle of weaving branches and foliage together gives you the opportunity to make all manner of shelters, from simple 'lean-tos' to substantial semi-permanent dwellings.

Extreme-climate shelters

Extreme climates, particularly tropical and polar conditions, present their own unique set of challenges when it comes to making shelters. In polar conditions, a shelter is literally a matter of life and death, a protection from the killing air temperatures and

Earth and log wall

This wall, made from two parallel rows of logs wth the gap packed with earth, is best used for long-term structures such as semi-permanent shelters and animal pens.

A-frame shelter

This soldier sits in a basic A-frame shelter. Note how the large, tropical leaves overlap one another, allowing for the natural drain-off of rainwater.

windchill. In the tropics, shelters are largely to protect you from the wildlife (especially insects), and give you somewhere secure to rest.

In tropical regions, aim to begin constructing your camp and shelter at least an hour before sunset, as darkness arrives quickly. Thankfully, the jungle will provide you with everything you need to build shelters, from plentiful wood to lots of large, glossy leaves that are ideal for outer waterproofing. The key component of any tropical shelter, however, is a

Underground shelter

This desert shelter utilizes two cooling principles. First, by creating the sleeping compartment underground, it takes advantage of the fact that cool air sinks. Second, the double-sheet roof creates a protective space of still air that reflects back the sun's heat.

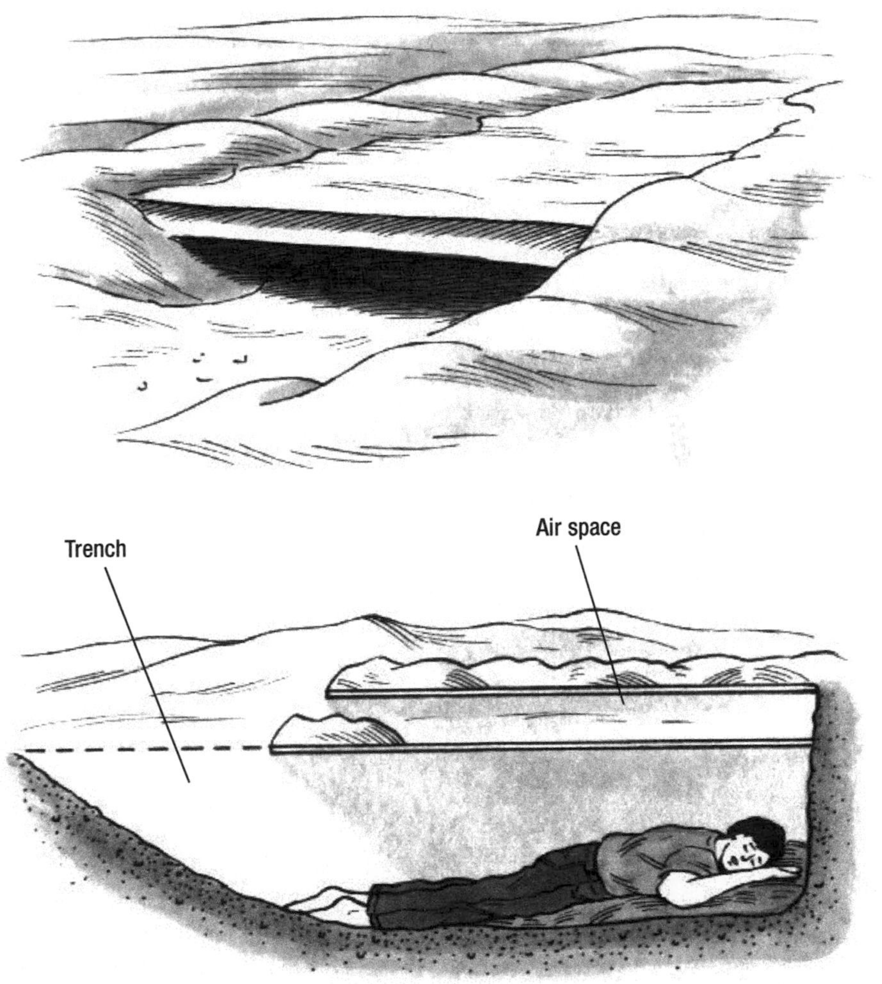

A-frame tropical shelter

Soldiers with tropical training experience know that they should never sleep directly on the ground. The A-frame shelter here elevates the sleeper, while the tarpaulin provides overhead cover.

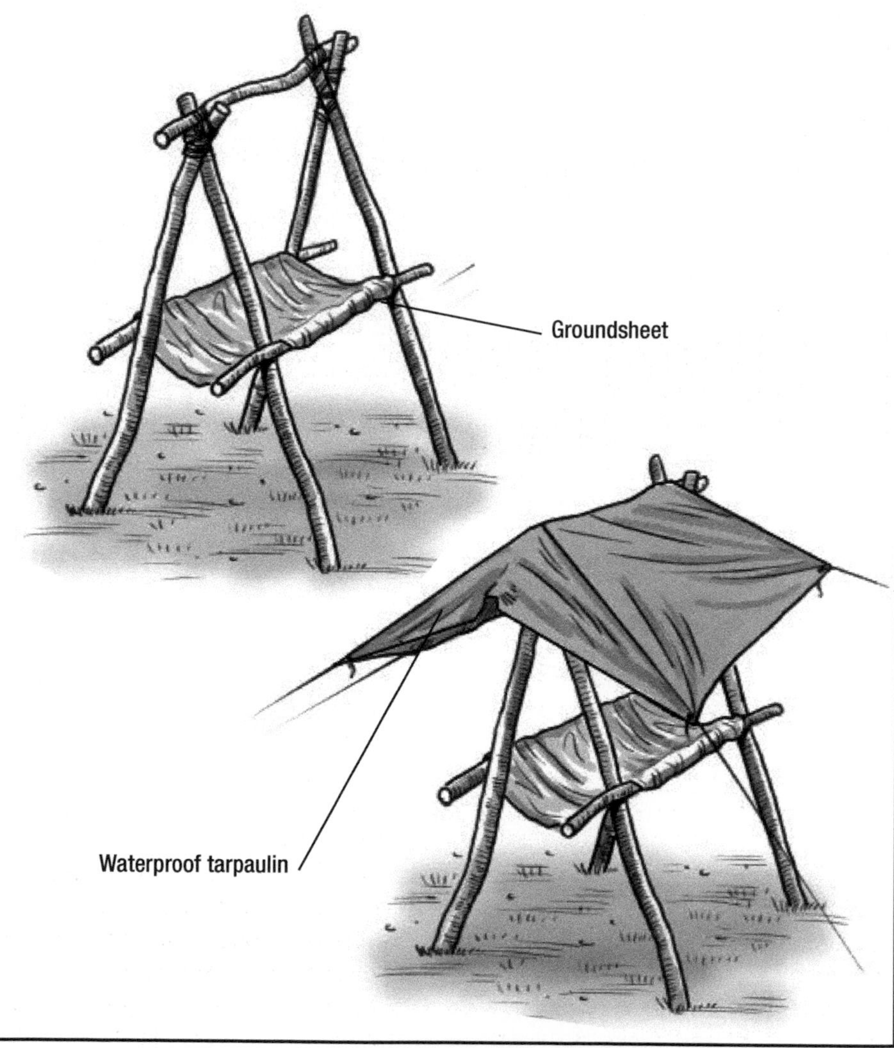

Swamp platform

This platform bed is padded with thick vegetation to create a form of mattress (make sure the foliage is thorn free and contains no irritants). If rope isn't available for construction, vines make decent cordage for binding the poles and cross-members together.

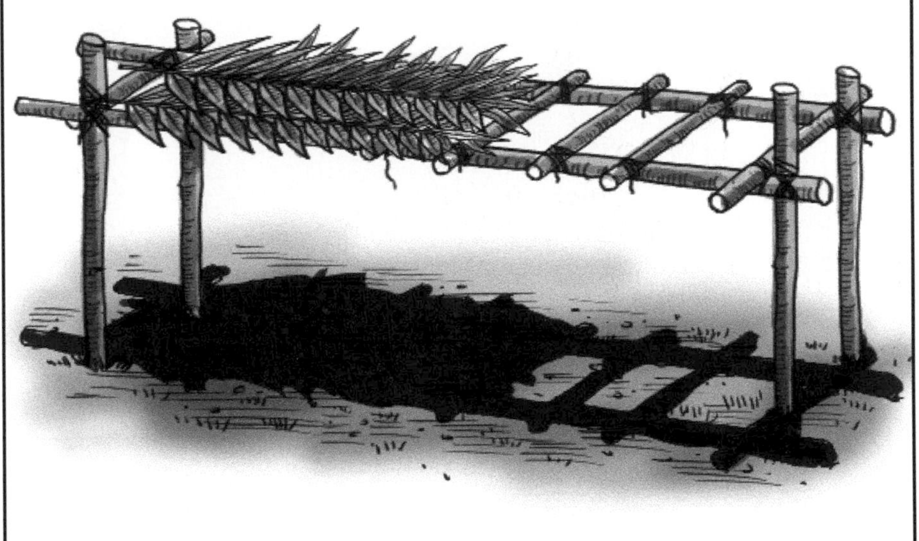

sleeping platform set well above the ground. This means that tropical shelters are slightly more demanding in terms of construction skills when compared to temperate shelters.

To build a basic platform shelter, find four trees set roughly in a rectangular shape, and no more than a few metres apart. Now cut two strong poles or two shafts of bamboo and tie these parallel to each other between the trees above the floor level (if you are in a swamp area, make sure the platform is higher than the visible high-tide mark on surrounding trees). Lay crosspieces between the two poles to make the sleeping platform, covering it with leaves and branches to make a 'mattress', and construct a secondary sloped platform higher up to act as a roof. You can use split bamboo to make roofing – cut the stem in half and lay pieces alternately

Hammock with roof

A hammock with a tarpaulin 'roof' is an ideal shelter for tropical or temperate summer conditions.

to interlock with each other – or simply fix a tarpaulin over the shelter. (Exercise caution when using bamboo; it produces very sharp edges and splinters when cut, and can often spring up at speed when cut under tension.) Obviously, the need to build a platform is obviated if you have a hammock, which in combination with a tarpaulin 'roof' is a far more rapid shelter to erect.

Building a shelter in a desert is a different experience, often because decent materials for construction can be either rare or completely absent. Natural shelters such as shaded cliffs, caves, the lee sides of hills, dunes or rock formations are immediate and useful shelters, although remember that the local wildlife will also think the same way – check out any caves or rocky areas for snakes, scorpions, big cats etc., before you make camp there.

If natural shelter isn't available, or is inadequate, you can adapt sheets of material, ideally light in colour, to create a cool habitation. Find a trench or dip in the ground, then anchor the sheet of material across the trench, using loose rocks, sand, branches or earth to secure the

Brush shelter

A brush shelter's virtue is its simplicity, as one can be put together in minutes. An additional layer of branches on top of the brush material will prevent it from being blown away in strong winds.

edges in place. This structure creates a shaded area underneath. Fabric roofs are greatly improved if you can create two layers of material with an air gap between (using stones to form 'spacers' between the sheets). The gap produces a section of still air, which provides further insulation against the heat of the sun.

If you have to build a desert shelter, do so in the cooler hours of the day, and try to locate the shelter near firewood and water to cut down on your walking time. Also place it away from sloping areas at risk of rock falls, and be aware that in the rainy season low-lying ground may be prone to flash floods. It is a good idea to site your shelter where it will catch breezes to help keep you cool and carry insects away from you.

In striking contrast to tropical and desert shelters, true polar shelters will often feature significant amounts of snow in their construction. The interior of such shelters will never be positively warm, but Inuit igloos, for example, can achieve internal temperatures of roughly 15.5°C (60°F). Note, however, that you should never sit directly on snow or ice, a practice that would quickly

Deep trench latrine

A trench latrine should be dug to a depth of around 1–2m (3ft 3in–6ft 6in). The cover, made from logs lashed together, should be drawn over the hole when the pit is not in use. Note that body wastes in the pit should be covered over with a thick layer of earth after every visit.

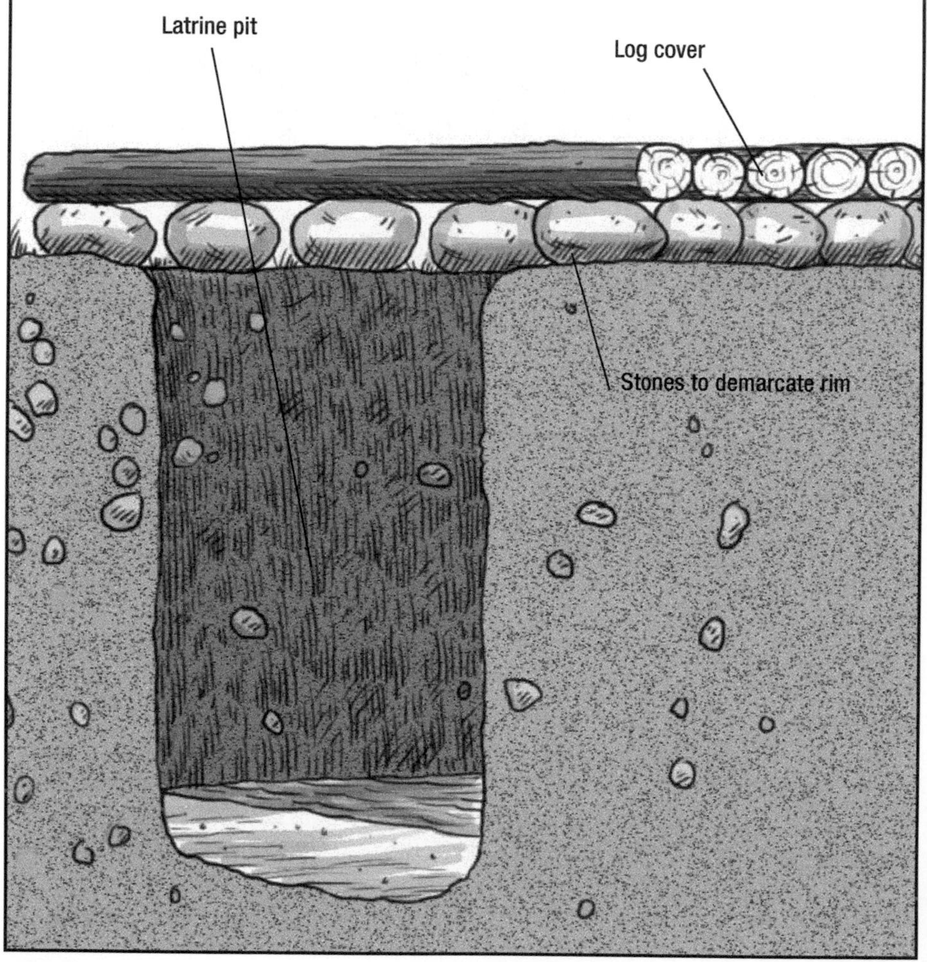

Bough bed

A rectangular log frame, filled with a deep thickness of clean, soft plant material, will form a relatively relaxing bed, although be prepared for various small insects to make an appearance from the foliage at night.

draw out your body heat into the ground. Always cover the floor of snow shelters with insulating material, such as boughs, dry grasses and moss. If these are not available, sit on your backpack or any other suitable piece of kit.

The most elementary polar shelter is the snow cave. As the name suggests, this is literally a dug-out cut straight into a snowdrift. To create the snow cave, first dig a small tunnel into the side of a deep, stable snowdrift to a depth of about 1m (3ft 3in). This is the entrance chamber. At the internal end of this tunnel, dig out chambers to the right and left, set at right angles to the tunnel entrance to be shielded from wind currents. These will act as your living quarters, so make them spacious enough to accommodate you and all your equipment. Give the ceilings a rounded shape for

Desert shelter

This simple desert shelter is made from two waterproof sheets held in place over a trench by banks of earth.

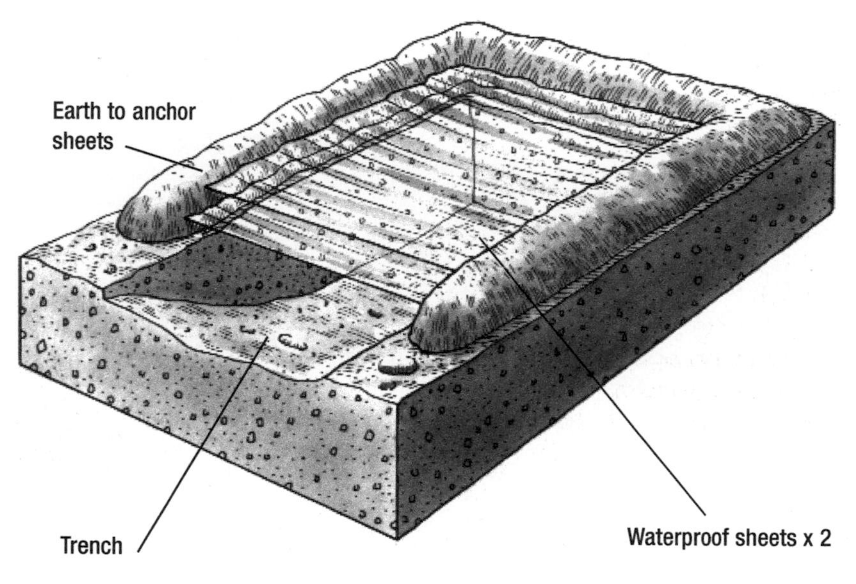

extra strength and to ensure meltwater runs down the sides, rather than drips onto you. Sleep in the higher, warmest sections of the snow cave – all snow shelters should feature raised sleeping platforms – and cook and store equipment in the lowest sections. Block the entrance with a stick bundle, backpack, poncho or snow block to retain the warmth, but remember to allow for some ventilation – bore at least two ventilation holes in the roof at different locations.

If you cannot find a suitable snowdrift in which to make a snow cave, there are other options, such as a moulded dome shelter. For this, build up a large, rounded pile of wooden boughs or foliage, standing nearly as high as you. Cover this pile with a groundsheet or other piece of material, then start piling on snow,

Arctic lean-to

Here the basic lean-to design is adapted by using two trees as the main upright supports, with a thick layer of snow providing some protection against the wind. Such a shelter, however, would not provide adequate protection against serious subzero conditions.

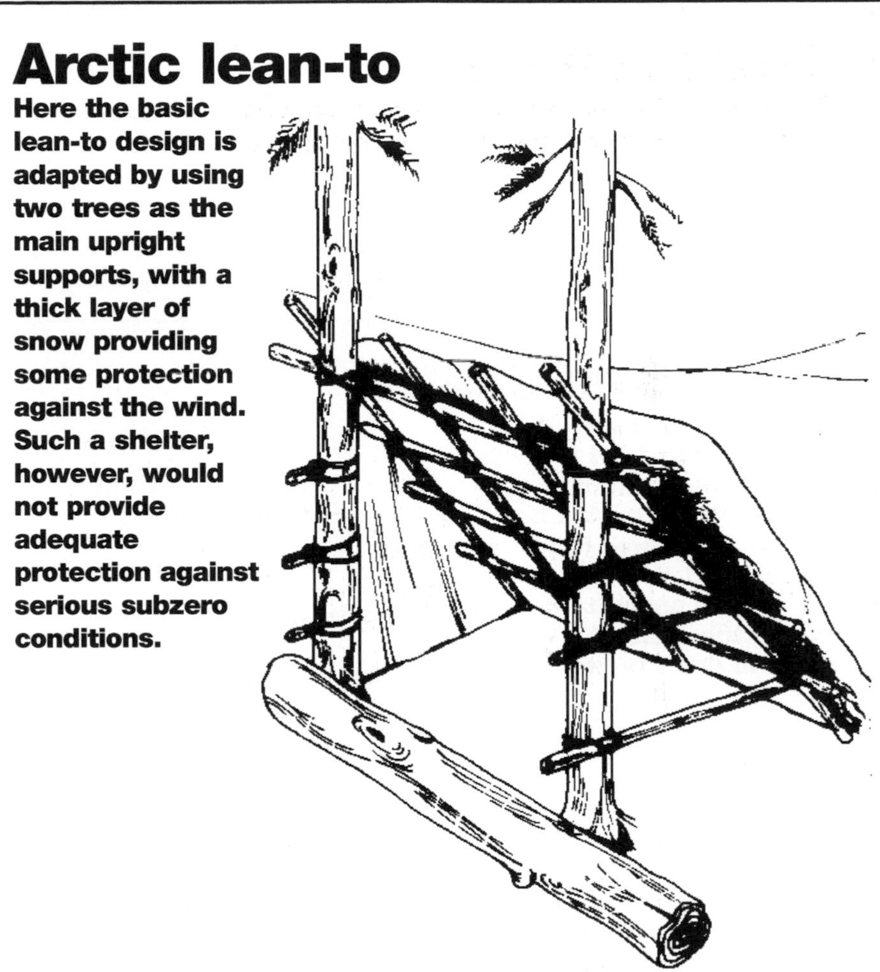

leaving a gap for an entrance. Now allow the snow to harden, then via the entrance remove the wooden boughs from inside the snow cave, and gently pull out the sheet. If the snow has reached sufficient rigidity, you should be left with an igloo-like freestanding snow shelter with an entrance. As with the snow cave, tie up a small bundle of sticks to make an entrance block, or use your backpack.

More advanced polar shelters can be made from snow blocks. For these you need to cut blocks of snow around 50cm (20in) long, 46cm (18in) wide and 10–20cm

(4–8in) thick using a saw, snow knife, shovel or machete, taking the material from deep drifts that have an even, firm structure. Once you have cut the blocks, you can build a variety of shelters. For example, you can arrange them in an oblong pattern to form a sleeping area long enough to accommodate you and your sleeping bag, and rising to about 1m (3ft 3in) high. A top layer of additional blocks will form a roof, although as with the snow cave, scrape the ceiling into a curved configuration and bore ventilation holes in the roof. The trench shelter, as it is known, is only temporary accommodation until you can make

Snow tree shelter

A snow tree shelter takes advantage of the fact that the branches of a pine tree provide a natural and dense form of overhead shelter. Dig out the snow from around the base of the tree and line the floor with thick layers of foliage. With you hunkered down beneath, the low-hanging branches above you will provide some degree of waterproof and windproof protection.

Snow cave

A snow cave is created by digging out a chamber in a deep, stable snow drift. Note how the sleeping platform, which should be covered with vegetation, is positioned much higher than the entrance, taking advantage of the fact that warm air rises.

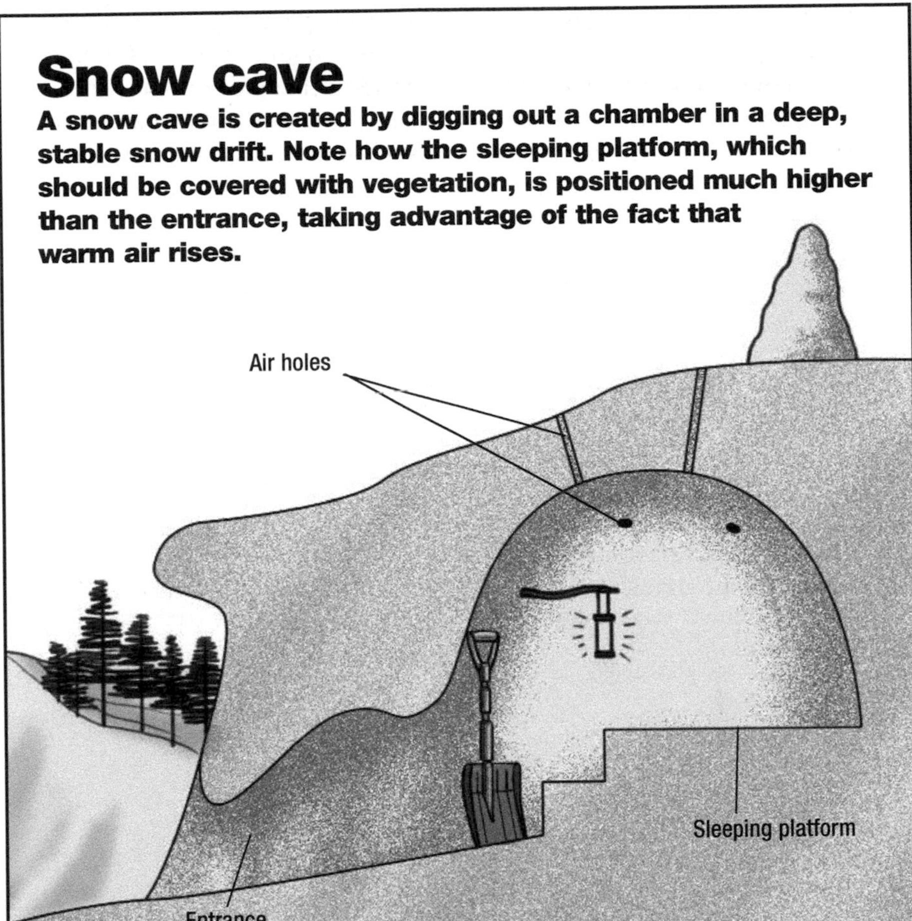

something more substantial.

Of course, the ultimate snow shelter is the igloo. Igloos can be difficult to make in a convincing fashion, so don't attempt to make one if you are unsure of your strength or ability to do so. To start, draw a circle about 2.5–3m (7–10ft) in diameter in the snow, to mark out the inside diameter of the igloo. Cut around 12 snow blocks and begin stacking them around the line. These blocks should lean inwards and the end joints of each snow block need to have faces radial to the middle of the igloo. Now cut more snow blocks and build the igloo wall up higher, bevelling the tops of the

Moulded dome shelter

The moulded dome shelter is a quick and easy method of making a shelter taught to special forces soldiers who operate in Arctic climates. The greatest challenge can be finding enough brush to form the mould frame.

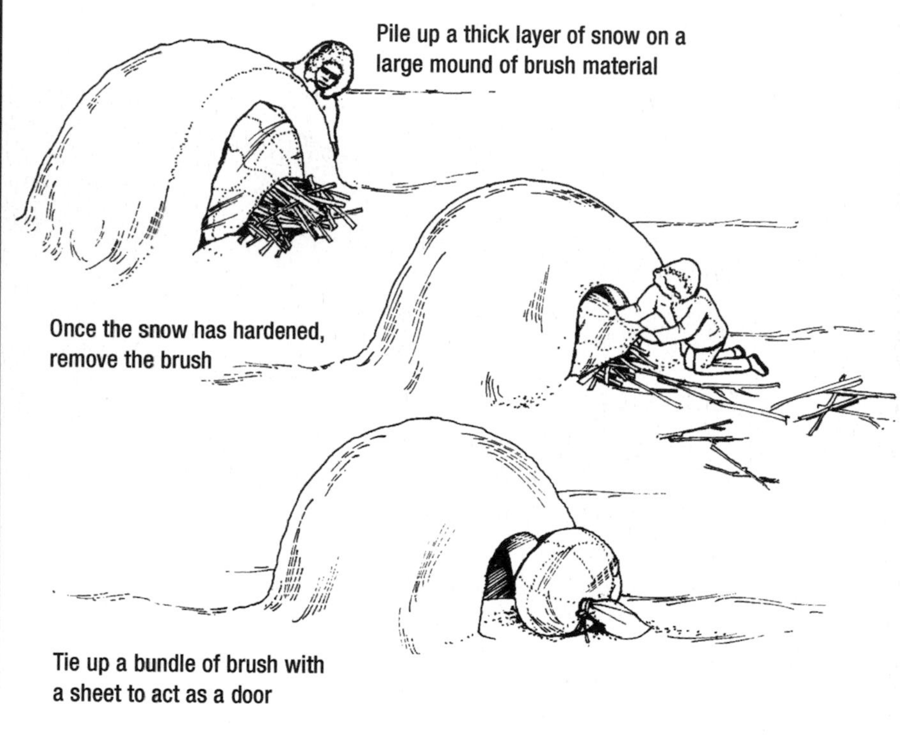

blocks so that the igloo curves in towards the middle. If all has gone to plan, you should be left with a small hole in the middle of what is now a roof. Put a fitted disk of compacted snow – known as a key block – into this hole, moving it into position from the inside. Finally, carve out an entrance tunnel leading into the igloo. Pack any gaps between blocks with powdery snow and leave to harden, and push through one or two ventilation holes. Inside the igloo, make a

TIP: Polar shelters

Soldiers operating in polar conditions obey the following rules when it comes to constructing shelters:

- Build your shelter as near to sources of fire fuel as possible.
- Avoid building shelters on the lee side of cliffs – snow slides might bury your shelter.
- Limit the number of entrances you build; the more you have, the more heat is lost.
- Store firearms outside. Storing them inside encourages condensation to build up on the barrel and in the action, causing either rust or, if it freezes, weapon malfunction. (Always check the end of the barrel before use; a plug of ice could cause the gun to explode on firing.)
- Make a latrine area outside. If the weather is too extreme to venture out, either dig an additional latrine tunnel extending out from your snow cave, or urinate into tin cans and defecate onto snow blocks that are then thrown outside.
- If your sleeping bag gets wet, knock off any frost and then dry it near a fire.
- Check regularly that ventilation holes are not blocked with snow, and chip off any coatings of ice – ice reduces the shelter's insulating properties.
- Do not allow excessive amounts of snow to build up on your shelter. The weight may cause the structure to collapse.

platform of snow for sleeping on (insulated with branches, of course). Place your cooking stove near to the entrance so that the stove is well ventilated, and force sticks into the wall on which to hang utensils and clothes.

CAMP CRAFT

Although survival can be a very stark experience, a bit of ingenuity and practice can make that experience more comfortable. The wilderness surrounding you is replete with natural materials – wood, sinew, bone, leaves,

Building an igloo

An igloo is an advanced polar shelter that takes practice to master. Ideally, experiment with constructing igloos in non-emergency situations before relying on the skills for real.

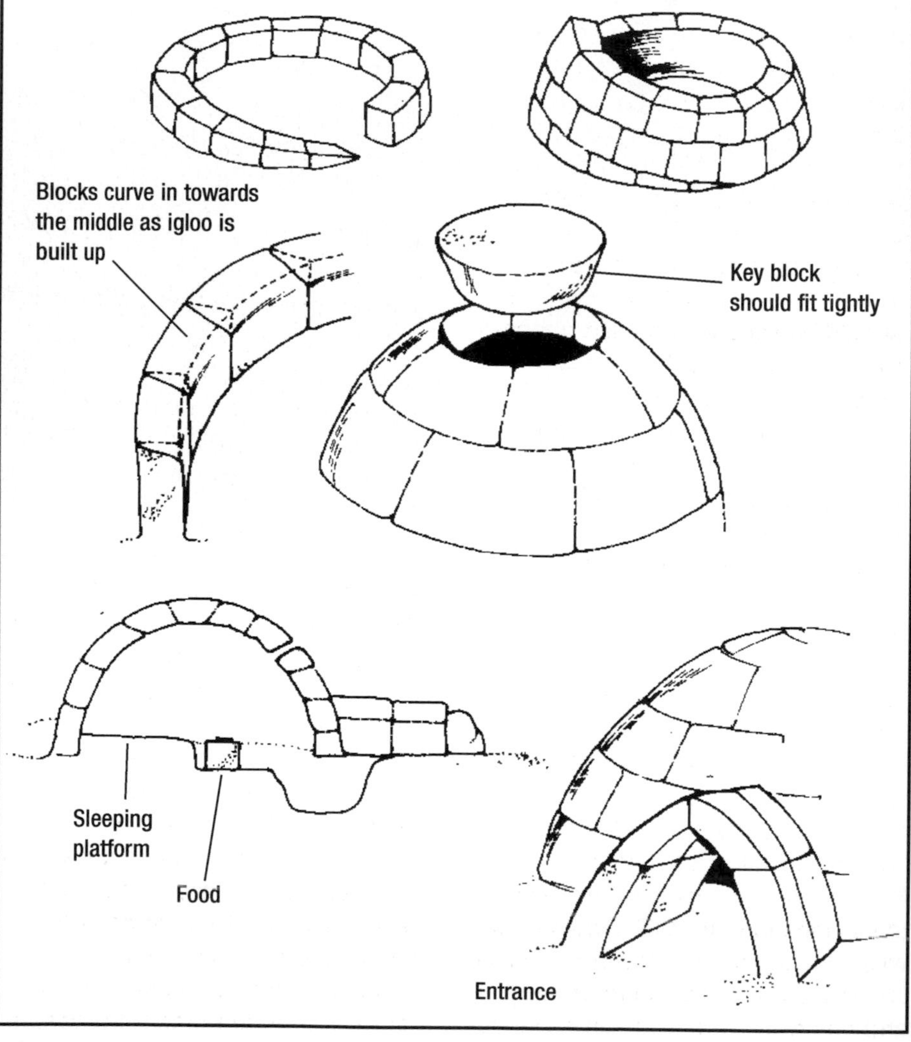

numerous types of rock etc. – and all can be utilized to create additional survival tools or devices to improve the life within and around your shelter.

To be able to create many of these tools you require to have a basic knowledge of rope-tying. The illustrations on the following pages provide you with examples of the most useful types of knots and lashings (lashings are designed to tie two or more objects securely together). Practise them until they become second nature, and learn other useful versions from a good rope-tying instruction manual. Whatever knot or lashing you tie, it should be secure when tied but easy to untie, especially if a knot is connected to your own body.

Regardless of your destination, taking a decent rope with you is always a sound policy. Modern climbing and walking ropes are made from synthetic materials such as nylon, polypropylene, polyethylene and polyester.

All these ropes are strong and light, but take advice from an outdoor expert as to the best type of rope for your journey, explaining exactly the sort of weather conditions you are likely to encounter and the use to which you will put the rope.

Man-made ropes are manufactured to a high standard and should be the first choice, but improvised ropes can be made out of natural materials, and have served traditional communities well enough for centuries. Plant fibres, such as strong grasses plaited or twisted together, or tough vines will make serviceable rope, although the breaking strength will vary considerably with the plant species used. Experiment with various plants until you find one that makes rope suited to your needs, and inspect the rope regularly for signs of wear and tear. (This goes for commercially-manufactured ropes too.)

Some of the strongest natural ropes are those made from animal

TIP: Rope care

- Keep all rope as clean as possible.
- Make regular rope inspections, looking for frayed edges or split points, mildew and rot. Do not use a rope if you find faults.
- Store ropes loosely coiled – do not leave them knotted or under tension.
- Do not let the rope rub against sharp implements or the edges of rock.
- Dry out wet rope by leaving it unravelled near an indirect heat source.

Knots

The overhand knot is the most well-known knot, but the other knots shown have wider utility. Reef knots, for example, are used for tying ropes together, and the figure of eight loop is a good anchoring knot.

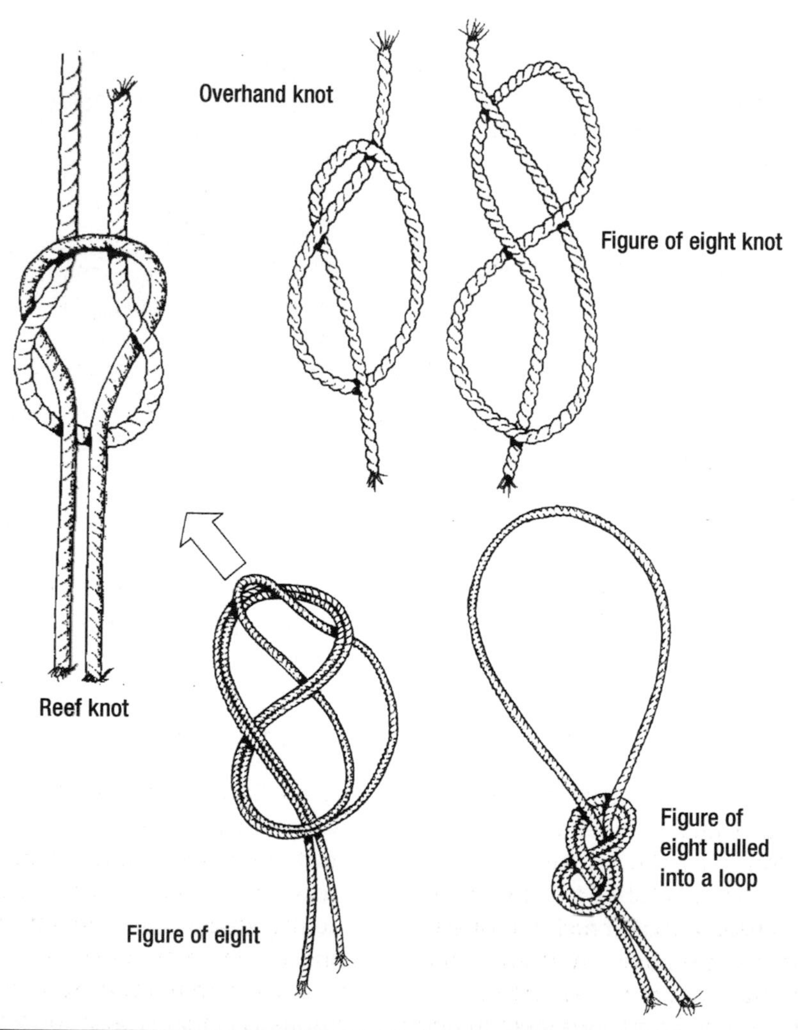

Fixed loop

The fixed loop forms, as its name implies, a stable, strong loop that is useful for tasks such as carrying logs or similar heavy items. Remember, however, that any knot is only as strong as the rope material itself.

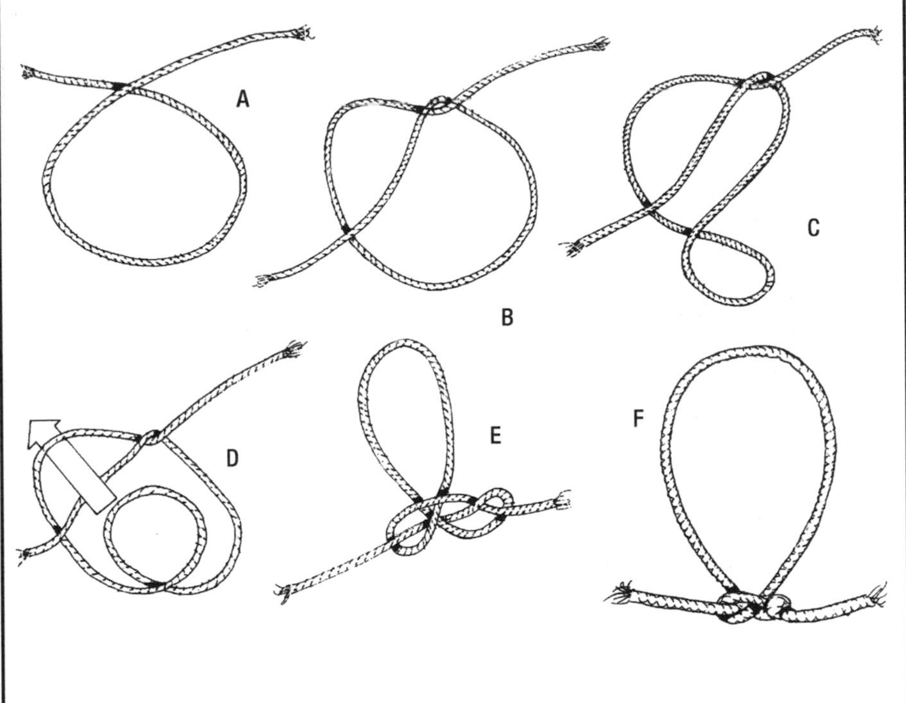

tendons and rawhide. To make tendon ropes, first remove the tendons from the animal on the same day it is killed and dry them out. Using a rock, crush the dried tendons into fibres. Moisten these then twist or braid them into a continuous strand. For rawhide rope, remove the skin of the animal and clean it of all traces of fat. Spread out the skin and cut it into strips. Soak the strips in water for two to four hours until they are soft and pliable, then braid the strips together to form rope. You can also use them singly as individual ties.

Loop-making

The bowline is used to form a loop at the end of a rope, and is also very quick to untie. The more complex triple bowline works as a sling chair or as a carrying harness (with two of the loops worn over the arms).

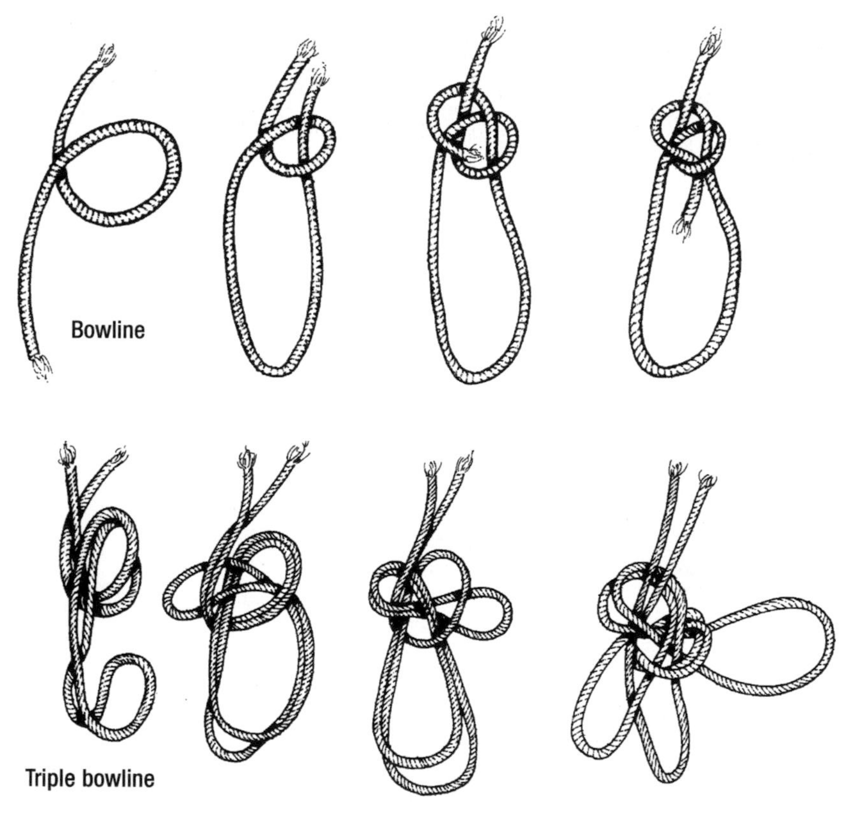

Cutting tools

For thousands of years before the invention of metals, humankind managed to produce a workable range of cutting tools, using materials such as stone, wood and bone. Sometimes cutting tools can present themselves without need for modification. A split rock, for example, may already result in sharp-edged pieces strong enough to cut wood or bone, and small slivers of naturally-occurring flint can be tied to handles or poles to make cooking knives or spears.

For more advanced stone-cutting tools, flint, quartz, obsidian, chert or other stones with similar glassy qualities are ideal, as they can be shaped to take a surprisingly sharp edge. Strike the stone that you intend to be the blade with another

Hitches

Hitches are used for attaching ropes to poles, posts and bars. The rolling hitch seen below is especially good for its non-slip properties once tied.

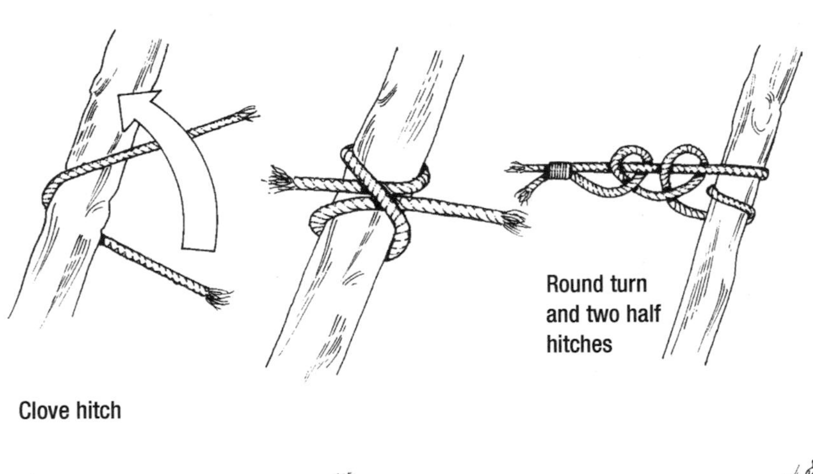

Clove hitch

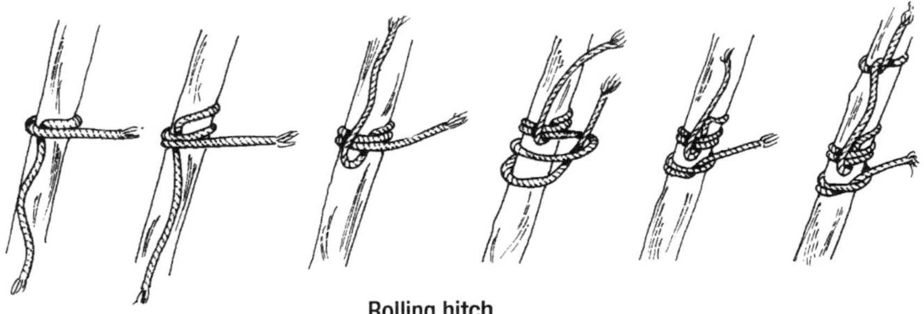

Rolling hitch

Lashings

Lashings are useful in the construction of shelters, equipment, racks, rafts and other structures. The most commonly used is the square lash, but the shear lash is a particularly strong variation.

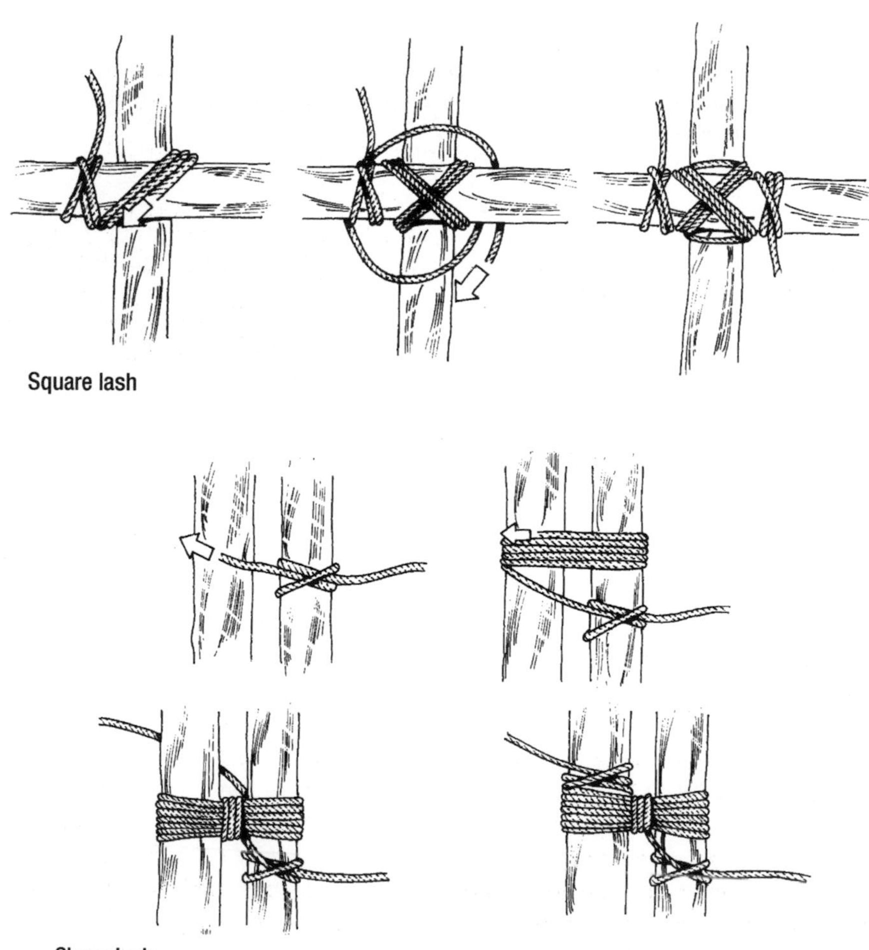

Square lash

Shear lash

Improvised axe

This improvised axe is made by binding a chipped stone axe head into a partially split wooden shaft. Once the head is in place, make the structure more solid by wrapping it with a shear lash.

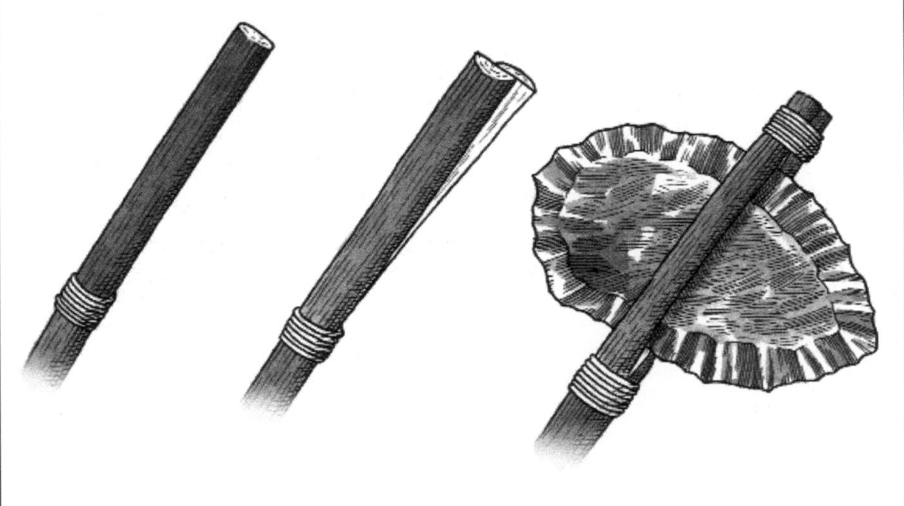

stone at about a 45-degree angle, chipping the surface until the sharp edge is achieved. Antler can also be used to push away flakes of stone to form the blade.

Bone is also receptive to being fashioned into cutting tools. A bone saw, for example, can be made from a large shoulder blade or a jawbone by splitting the bone in half, producing a lively edge on the split. Use your knife (bought or made) to cut teeth into the edge of the split, thus creating an improvised saw with resilience enough for cutting softwoods or for butchering large animals.

Knives and other cutting tools can be made out of bits of junk and refuse, of which there is unfortunately much lying around in today's natural woodland.

A piece of glass or the lids from tin cans (especially those lids made by can openers that cut inside the rim rather than beneath), for example, can be inserted into a split stick and tied securely in place to make a sharp knife.

For more substantial cutting work, it is possible to manufacture a basic axe. Be careful here – a stone axe head is a lethal missile if it comes lose and flies through the air, so test the axe gradually and inspect it frequently for any signs of the shaft/lashings breaking or splitting around the head. To make the axe head, take a hand-sized flat stone and scrape and chip a cutting edge, working in from both sides of the stone. Now find a thick piece of hardwood about 46cm (18in) long and tie cord very tightly around it about a third of the stick's length from one end. Split the wood from the tip down to the tied point, then set the axe head into the split. Bind the wood very firmly with twine just above the stone to hold the axe head in place, then use lashings in a

Cutting a tree

Tree-cutting is dangerous if not performed correctly. Note the correct pattern of cut to control the direction of fall.

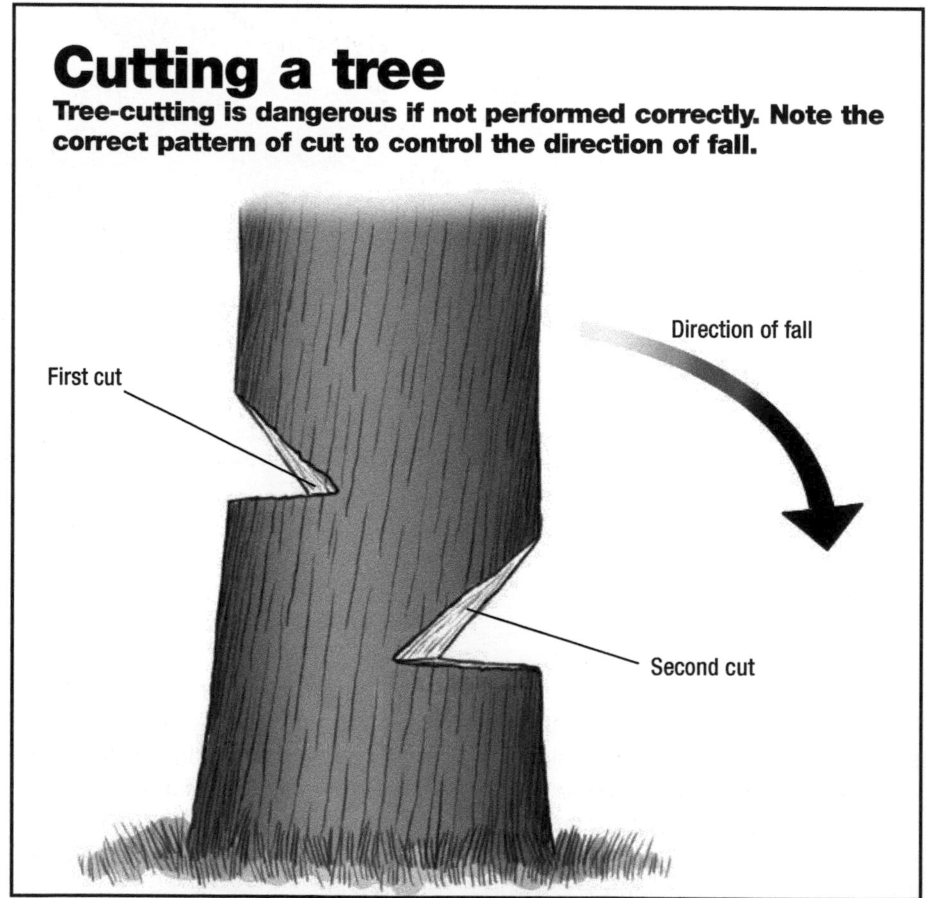

Survival 'pan'

Here a simple military mess tin is tied to a forked twig to create an elementary form of frying pan. Such utensils may seem crude, but they can reduce the risk of campfire burns.

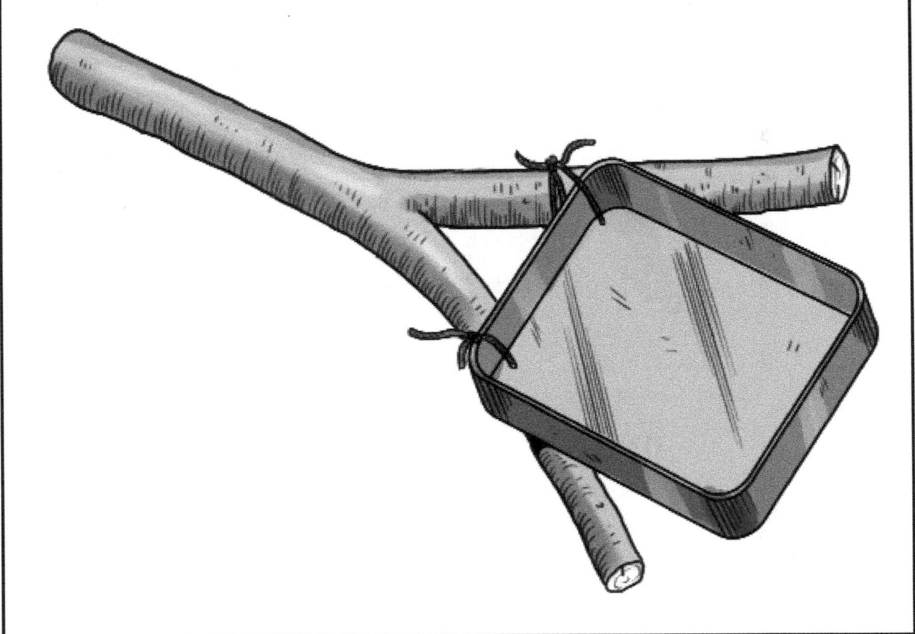

criss-cross pattern to secure the entire axe head firmly in position. You will now have a usable axe sufficient to cut small trees and thick branches, and a hunting weapon if necessary.

Camp utensils

The secret to survival tools is to find a use for everything. Small bones and ribs, for example, can be sharpened into needles, pins and even stabbing weapons. Antlers and horns can be used for digging, gouging and hammering. A forked stick is ideal for holding cooking pots or for drying clothes – push the forks into the ground at an angle of 45 degrees, secure them with rocks, and prop the stick up at the midway point with another Y-shaped stick or a large rock. The end of the forked stick can now be used to suspend items over or near a fire. Basic

Making a clay pot

If you find clay of a smooth, non-crumbly consistency, you can use it to make a basic drinking cup or storage pot. Let the pot dry out after construction, then stand it close to a hot fire to harden it.

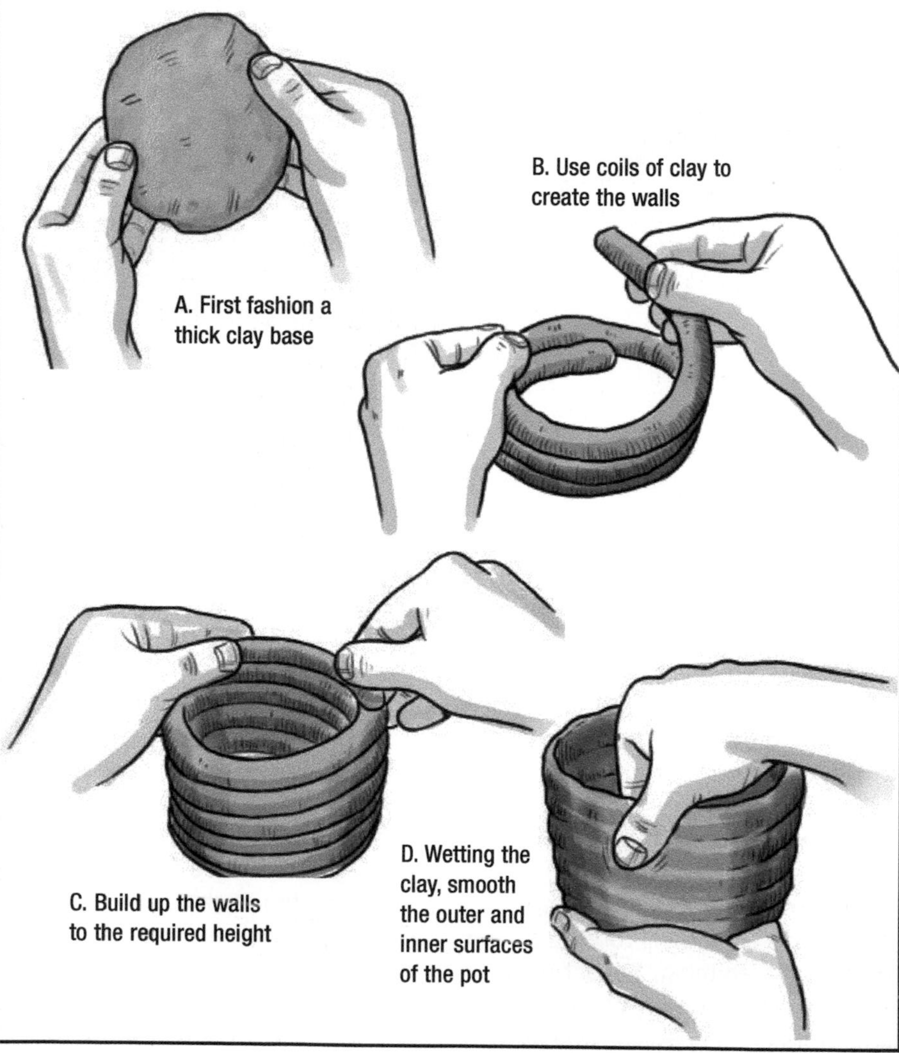

Making a wooden bowl

This wooden bowl is made by burning the centre of a block of wood with embers from a fire, then carving out the burnt material to form an receptacle.

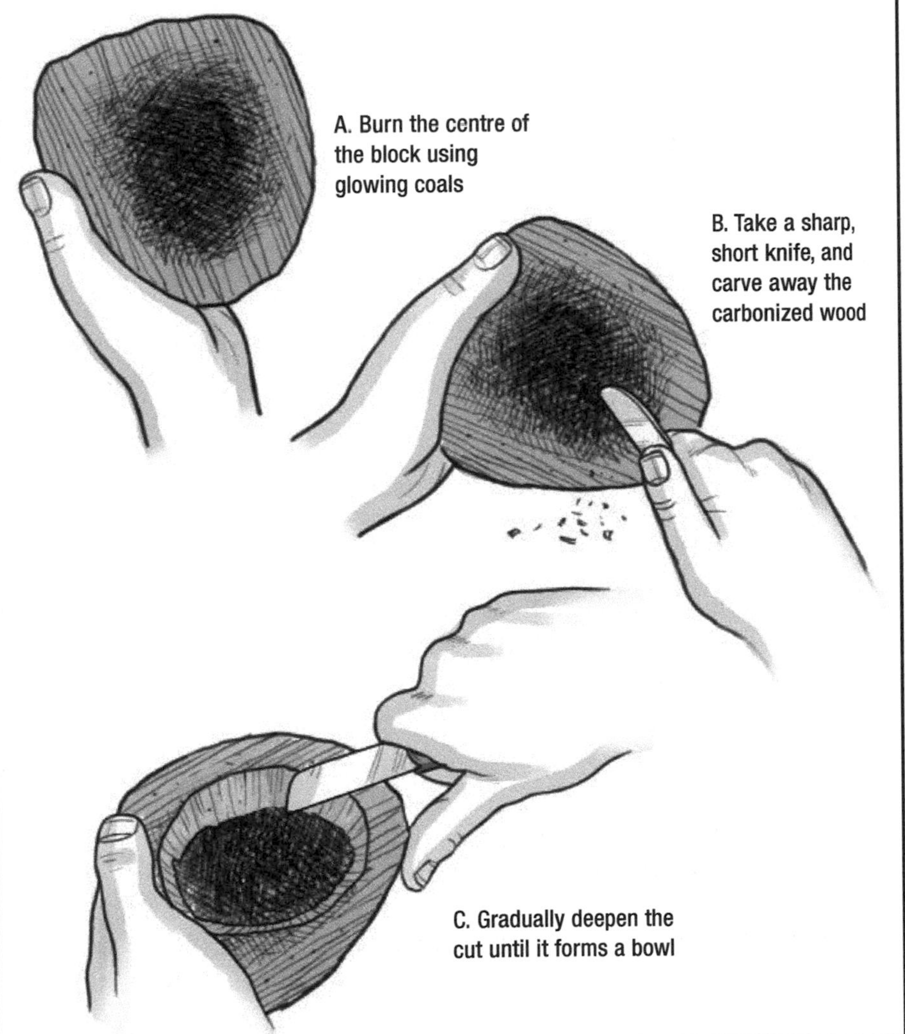

Bark container

Birch bark has long been used by traditional communities to manufacture containers, the bark being both flexible and, when properly treated with resin, waterproof.

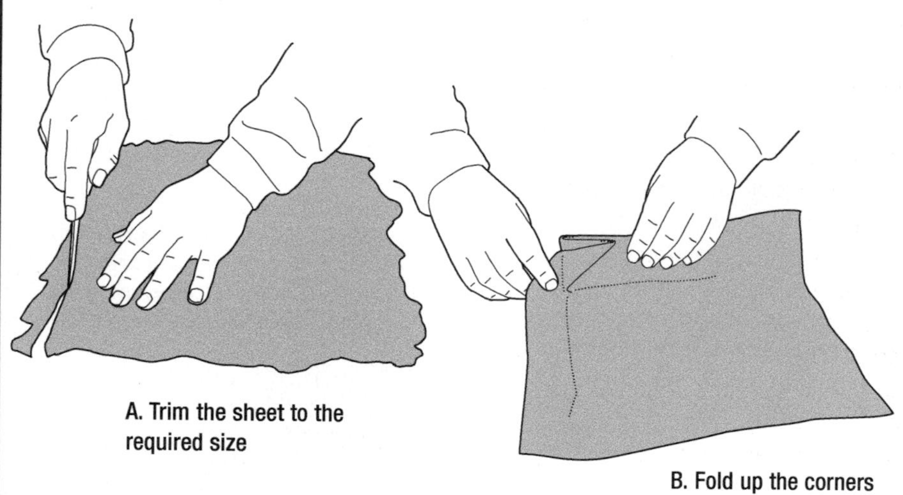

A. Trim the sheet to the required size

B. Fold up the corners

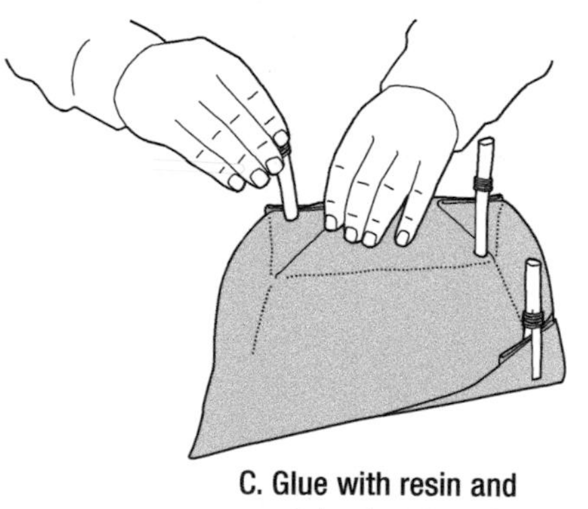

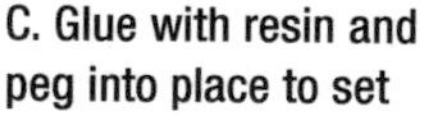

C. Glue with resin and peg into place to set

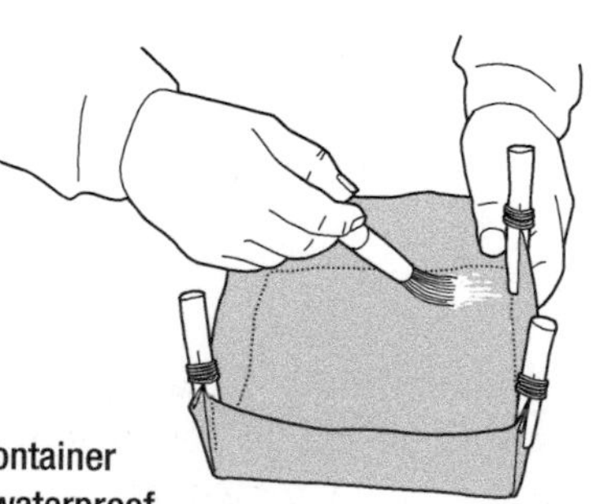

D. Paint the container with resin to waterproof

cutlery, such as ladles, spoons and forks, can also be made with tree branches, sticks, and a bit of imagination. Note that if the outline of the carved tool follows the grain, it is more water-resistant.

Tree bark is another useful material – it can be shaped into objects such as guttering and containers, even temporary cooking vessels. The best type of bark for these uses is green bark from young, healthy trees, as it is usually flexible and easily bent into shape (birch bark is ideal).

To make a simple rectangular container out of bark, cut a large square of the material from a tree and soak it in water so it will be less liable to split when bent. Now fold up the sides of the bark to make a lip around the edge about 5–8cm (2–3in) high, with the exterior face of the bark on the outside. Glue the joints of the container together using tree resin (from birch and pine trees especially) and hold them together while drying by using partly-split sticks as pegs. Finally, rub some pine resin on the inside of the container and allow it to dry, thereby providing it with additional waterproofing.

Survival is as much about improvisation as it is about knowledge, so the important point is that you utilize everything around you to your advantage. Think of survival as a practical problem, therefore, and you will tend to find practical solutions.

TIP: Wood for carving

Frontline soldiers have often carved wood both as a useful survival skill and a way of combating boredom. Each wood has its own distinct carving properties:

Sycamore – Soft, easily carved.

Ash – A tough wood to carve into intricate patterns, but excellent for tool handles, bows and weapons.

Beech – A hardwood, it is unsuitable for beginners or those equipped with blunt carving tools.

Birch – Good carving wood, but decays easily.

Hazel – Easy to carve, but also splits easily.

Yew – Very hard, flexible wood good for cutlery and bowls and also for hunting bows.

5

Dangers in the Wild

The wilderness can be an unforgiving place, with dangers ranging from avalanches to venomous snakes.

Soldiers on operations are, of course, faced with the obvious danger posed by the enemy. Yet the wilderness around them is a further hazard that takes its toll in every campaign. The list of dangers not only includes lack of food and water, and extreme weather conditions, but also disease, dangerous terrain, venomous or predatory animals, lethal plants and fungi, and hostile atmospheric conditions. While for us there is a danger of over-magnifying such threats, we must acknowledge their true extent in any particular environment, and prepare for them in advance. Never assume that everything will work out fine – as with elite soldiers, being ready for an emergency both practically and mentally means that you will be able to make judicious decisions should the worst happen. This chapter, therefore, looks at some of the dangers inherent to a variety of wilderness environments, from subzero polar regions through to scorched desert.

Each environment presents a unique set of dangers, including indigenous animal species, endemic diseases, terrain and regional climate. Prior research is the key to preparing for these dangers, so make sure you put in the time with books and good Internet sources before you travel.

SUBZERO DANGERS

As all mountain and Arctic-trained soldiers know, few climates are quite as aggressive to health as subzero winter conditions. The biggest danger of all is, naturally, the sheer cold, exacerbated by precipitation and windchill. Windchill is the lethal ingredient. A wind of 32km/h (20mph) will push a temperature of -14°C (5°F) down to a felt temperature of -34°C (-30°F), and can freeze exposed human flesh in about 60 seconds. If you get wet in such conditions, the windchill effect is increased, your body heat being wicked away rapidly as the freezing wind attempts to dry out your clothing. Once you have hypothermia or frostbite, your options for self-treatment become very limited, so as always preventative measures are your first line of defence.

Frostbite consists of localized tissue damage from exposure to severe cold. It is graded according to several degrees of severity, from red, tingling and inflamed skin through to the literal freezing of muscles, tendons and blood vessels. A similar condition, albeit one that affects only the feet and which doesn't require subzero temperatures, is trench foot. This is the result of feet being kept in damp, dirty conditions for prolonged periods without drying out, resulting in tissue damage and problems with blood supply, which in turn can lead to gangrene.

To prevent frostbite and/or trench foot, you need to keep your skin as dry as possible. In particular, look out for patches of white, waxy skin forming (don't forget your ears, which are particularly vulnerable to frostbite), and quickly cover them and keep them dry and warm. Limit your exposure of bare skin to the elements – keep gloves and hats on at all times if you are outside, and if your shelter is freezing, dress and undress in your sleeping bag. Try to maintain your natural circulation – make sure you bend and flex your toes and fingers regularly, and wrinkle your facial muscles to stop stiff patches forming there. Also ensure that your clothing isn't so tight that it restricts circulation. Do not touch metal with your bare hands, as the freezing steel can burn your skin and pull it off.

To protect yourself against the broader, and more serious, threat of hypothermia (a drop in core body temperature to below that required to sustain normal body functions), you should naturally be wearing the appropriate clothing, working on the layering principle outlined in Chapter 1. Avoid overheating as much as getting cold; getting seriously sweaty inside your clothing increases the risk of the sweat wicking away your body heat when you stop exerting yourself. Loosen or remove some clothing to avoid the sweat building up, although beware – feeling unusually warm can be a

TIP: Winter sun

Sunburn is a surprising threat to soldiers in subzero environments, because the ultraviolet rays of the sun are intensified when reflected off the snow and ice. The same effect can also lead to snow blindness – red, watering and sore eyes accompanied by intense headaches. To prevent these conditions, troops take the following precautions:

- Apply high-factor sun cream to all exposed areas of the face, especially the nose, lips and eyelids.
- Wear sunglasses or at worst improvise a pair of goggles out of cardboard or tree bark.
- Smear streaks of charcoal underneath the eyes – the dark smudges help reduce the amount of reflected light going into the eyes.
- If affected by snow blindness, rest eyes until they recover, ideally (and obviously) in a dark place.

symptom of hypothermia, usually in tandem with disorientation.

One important note is to be aware of the risks of dehydration. Freezing climates are often very dry climates – there is little airborne moisture. Especially when you are working your body hard, you can easily become dehydrated and leave yourself more exposed to hypothermia. If your urine is dark yellow and you feel drowsy or have headaches, rest and drink plenty of fluids (but not alcohol).

Hygiene is also important in subzero climates. Try to have a regular wash, particularly of the groin, armpits, feet or other sweaty areas. Change socks and underwear at least every two or three days (more frequently if the socks become wet), or at least massage and dry your feet. If you haven't a change of underwear, then air the items for a couple of hours. Keep your teeth clean, and if

Basic snowshoes

Snowshoes are essential if you have to move through very deep, soft snow. Take care that none of the bindings cut into the flesh of your ankle or lower leg.

TIP: Bear attacks

Canadian special forces are trained for encounters with polar bears, brown bears and grizzly bears. All these species can be extremely dangerous if accidentally confronted, so observe the soldiers' following rules:

- If walking through an area in which you know there are bears, make noise as you move through the landscape to alert the bear to your presence (bears are far more likely to attack if suddenly surprised). An old trick is to tie a tin can with a spoon in it to your backpack – its rattling noise will warn the bear of your presence in advance.
- Try not to keep food in your shelter, as bears are particularly attracted to the smells of food and cooking. Keep your sleeping area about 30m (100ft) away from your cooking area and hang your food in a sack from a branch about 3m (10ft) up in the air.
- If confronted by a bear, talk softly, stand upright and back away slowly, giving the bear plenty of room to escape. Do not run – the bear will be more likely to give chase if you do, and can run much faster than you.
- If the bear attacks you, at first roll up into a ball and play dead, covering the back of your neck and head with your hands. If the bear doesn't lose interest and continues to attack, fight back, using sticks, rocks and any other weapons you have.

you have no toothbrush use a clean piece of cloth wrapped around a finger or the end of a twig chewed into a pulp. Don't allow your clothes to become too dirty – filthy clothes have poor insulating properties.

Winter terrain and weather presents a series of other dangers. In blizzards, for example, 'whiteouts' can occur when land and sky merge into one uniform sheet with no visible landmarks. Do not travel in these conditions, as you will lose all sense of direction (people have been lost and died only metres from their shelters in such storms). The snowfall will also obliterate your tracks, making it harder to retrace your steps.

Falling through ice

If you fall through ice, push as much of your upper body back onto the ice while pulling with your hands. Simultaneously kick with your legs to 'swim' back onto the ice.

Ice rescue

This ice rescue involves one person lying flat across the ice sheet, this posture spreading his body weight over a wider area and thereby reducing the risk of the already fragile ice cracking further.

Take care when walking across ice sheets, which can give way suddenly and plunge you into freezing water. When walking across frozen lakes or rivers, therefore, use a pole to probe the strength of the ice ahead of you. If you do fall in, get onto land with great speed and roll in the snow to absorb excess water. Then move quickly inside a shelter, make a fire if possible and get into dry clothes before you start to freeze. In coastal regions, also watch out for plates of ice shifting and crushing together, suddenly pushing up ridges of ice at steep angles while opening up gaps into the freezing sea water in other places. Don't attempt to negotiate such terrain.

MOUNTAIN DANGERS

The dangers of mountainous environments are in many ways similar to those of polar regions. At high altitude especially, air temperatures are frequently low and wind speeds high, making a potentially lethal combination. The weather conditions are also prone to rapid changes. Even in the course of a single hour, the mountain climate can shift from pleasant sunshine to driving rain or snowstorms.

Mountains have the obvious added danger of precipitous drops and slopes, which not only threaten the traveller with a fall, but also with rockfalls and avalanches. Just

Roping together

In freezing, mountainous landscapes, being roped together is an essential procedure. Here we see how one person has fallen into a crevasse, but is saved by the two others on the rope. Note how they use their ice axes correctly, pushing their shoulders up against the adze of the axe while driving the pick deep into the ice for grip.

movement alone can be treacherous. Wet or smooth stones, or those covered in grass or moss, are slippery, and mountain soil can also be extremely loose and prone to giving way underfoot without warning. Snow can harden under freezing temperatures to become a lethal sheet of ice, or deep crevasses can be hidden under seamless snowfall.

Landslides and slumps

In geological terms, a slump occurs when the natural material moves in a block, whereas a straightforward landslide consists of fragmented blocks.

Mudslides and rockfalls

Mudslides and rockfalls are dangers of any precipitous slope, so give such terrain a wide berth if it looks sagging, unstable or crumbly.

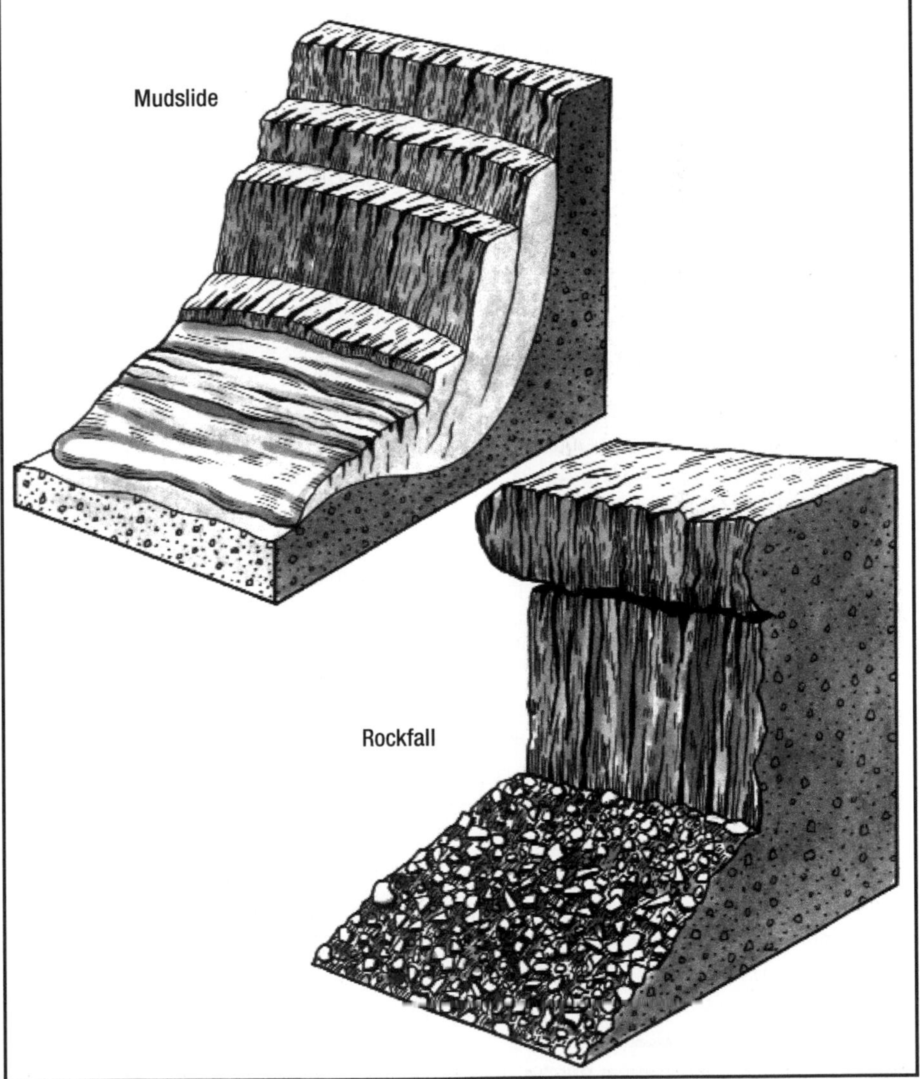

For all these reasons, always stay roped to other members of your team when crossing mountainous terrain, and carry an ice axe to help arrest your descent should you fall. To do so, drive the shaft vertically into the slope and keep hold of it with one hand near the base. Drive your toes into the snow to get a foothold. On harder snow, brake yourself by forcing the pick of the ice axe into the snow. One hand should be on the head of the axe and the other on the shaft. Force the pick into the slope by pushing down with your arm and shoulder.

Avalanches

Avalanches are a danger peculiar to mountainous environments, and kill dozens of people around the world every year. Although an avalanche is made from just snow, its huge weight and velocity – speeds in excess of 120km/h (75mph) are possible – means that if a person caught in one isn't killed by impact injuries, then they are typically buried beneath metres of snow. In such circumstances, survival is a race against time. People buried in avalanches have an 85 per cent chance of survival if found and extracted within 15 minutes, but that figure drops to around 30 per cent after half an hour, the killing mechanism usually being suffocation underneath layers of snow.

Avalanches are caused when surface snow slides over a harder base layer of snow or ice, or smooth ground. Wet snow is the more dangerous type, as water acts as a lubricant while making the snow denser and heavier, and thus more likely to slide. The following are typical factors in the origins of an avalanche:

- Smooth slopes of between 20 and 50 degrees – the steeper the gradient the more the danger.
- Wind speeds of more than 25km/h (15mph).
- Convex slopes are more likely to produce avalanches than are concave slopes.
- In winter, north-facing slopes are more prone to snow slides, whereas in summer south-facing slopes are vulnerable.
- Heavily snow-laden cornices breaking off.
- Loose snow beneath compacted snow, as the loose snow forms a fluid base over which the hard snow can run. If you prod the snow with the shaft of your ice axe and notice softening in resistance beneath the surface, there is an avalanche danger.
- Sudden heavy snowfall that doesn't have time to settle and become stable.
- Rapid changes of temperature.

The best protection against avalanches is to avoid danger areas altogether. In areas popular with

Avalanche path

Victims of avalanches are likely to be found below the fracture zone (where the avalanche initially starts), particularly in the deposition zone at the bottom.

walkers and skiers, avalanche notice-boards are often posted up to warn of zones particularly at risk. Should you have to walk across a potential avalanche area, stay roped together with other team members, and try to limit the extent to which you disturb the snow as you cross. Take advantage of natural protective features, such as dense areas of trees or rocky outcrops, as these can break up the force of an avalanche.

Should an avalanche begin to run, and you are in its path, try to reach the peripheries of the avalanche zone as fast as possible, but remove your backpack and skis immediately – the weight of the backpack could drag you down, while keeping your skis on could result in leg injuries. When the snow strikes, you will be tumbled or pushed violently down the mountainside. If possible, keep your head above the surface of the

Avalanche survival

If caught in an avalanche, try to keep yourself on the surface by using a strong swimming action with the arms, pushing towards the outer edges of the avalanche's run.

Breaking a fall

Should you fall down a rocky mountainside, you need to arrest the descent and avoid tumbling. The positions here can help slow you down, digging in with the heels or toes to act as brakes. On icy surfaces, however, you need to use an ice axe to stop your descent.

Rescue search

When searching for someone buried in an avalanche, work downhill methodically from the last place at which they were seen.

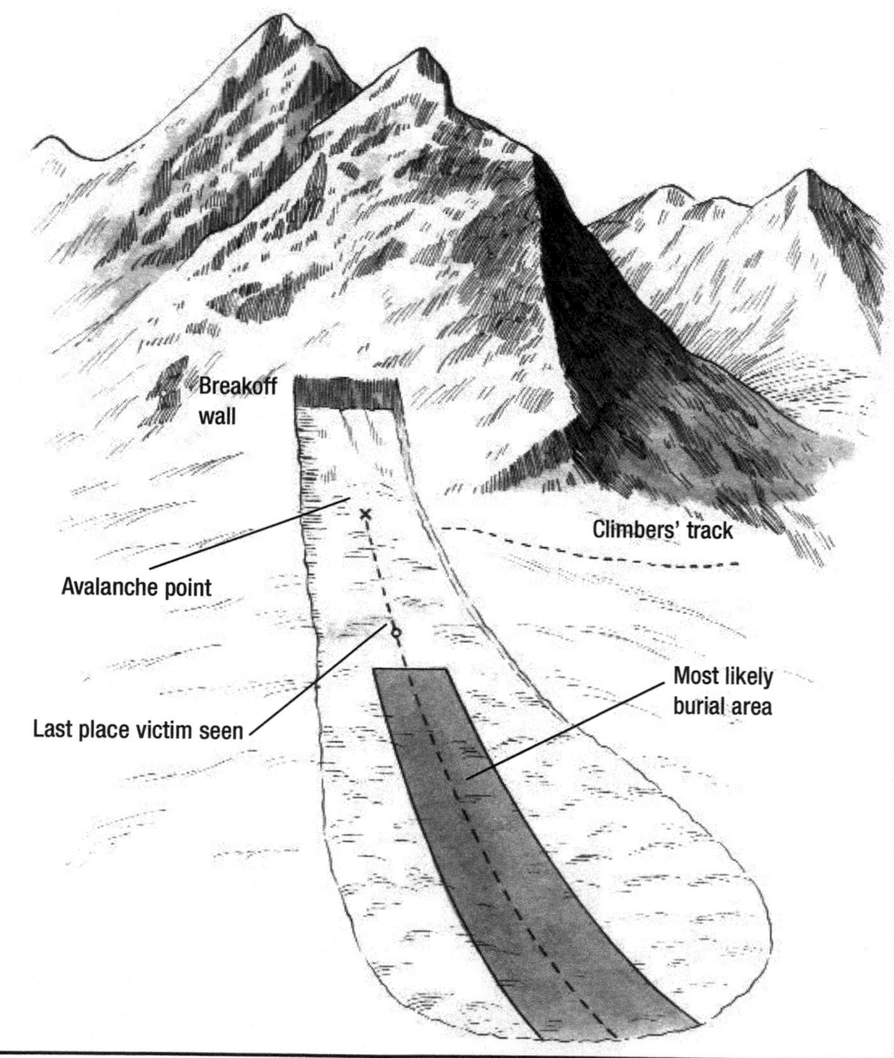

avalanche by using a strong swimming action with your arms, clawing your way to the surface. Keep your mouth tightly closed, and cover your nose with clothing if it is filling with snow.

The worst-case scenario is if you are buried, as you will be in pitch darkness, disorientated and with a limited air supply. Note that there are several devices you can wear to increase your chances of being found. Avalanche cords, for example, are brightly-coloured cords about 15m (49ft) long, which are attached to your belt, trailing harmlessly behind you when you go out walking or skiing. If you are buried by an avalanche, the end portion of the cord remains visible on the surface, giving rescuers a clear lead to your location. More sophisticatedly, avalanche beacons or transceivers are electronic devices that emit a locating signal which is picked up by rescue parties' monitoring equipment. GPS locating beacons can also provide a similar service.

If you are buried and you are able to move, first clear a breathing space in front of your face. Reduce your rate of breathing as much as you can, and avoid shouting unnecessarily. If you are disorientated, and don't know the direction to the surface, allow some spittle to drip from your mouth – the direction in which the spittle drips is the opposite direction to the surface. Now start digging slowly and methodically towards the surface, until you break free.

If you have to rescue someone else buried by an avalanche, your most essential pieces of equipment will be a probe and a shovel. You should be carrying professional versions of both, but if you haven't a probe, at the very least a long branch will provide some utility, or you can (gently) use the shaft of your ice axe. Note that where you last saw a person may not be where he or she is actually buried.

First, try to mark the person's position at the point at which the avalanche hit (use a backpack, stone or similar marker). Work downwards from this point to try to find the place of burial, looking out for any personal belongings that might suggest the direction of travel. (If there are several of you in the search party, space yourselves out to cover as much ground as possible.) Using your probe, explore the snow in front and to the sides of you, feeling for any sudden resistance from a human body. Should you find the victim, dig them free and immediately clear their mouth and airways of snow. Give artificial respiration if they are not breathing.

Altitude sickness

Any discussion of mountain dangers would be incomplete without mentioning the threat of altitude sickness. Altitude sickness is caused by the way atmospheric pressure decreases with height. The physiological effects of altitude begin to be felt above 2400m (8000ft) and at around 5500m (18,000ft) air pressure is about half of what it is at sea level. This means a dramatically-reduced oxygen intake on inhalation. The following symptoms can occur with sudden exposure to high altitudes:

- Stage 1 (mild) – shortness of breath, mild headache, nausea, fatigue, slight dizziness.
- Stage 2 (moderate) – fatigue, severe headache, persistent nausea, vomiting.
- Stage 3 (severe) – chronic fatigue, severe breathing difficulties, fluid in the lungs, cyanosis, cerebral and pulmonary oedema, staggering, confusion, unconsciousness, even death.

The way to avoid altitude sickness is through acclimatization, allowing the body to adjust to the reduced oxygen levels before putting it under the strain of exercise. If taken by helicopter or light aircraft to a high-altitude position (not advisable for the inexperienced, as the transition from low to high altitudes is abrupt), spend two or three days becoming acclimatized and allowing the body to adjust its operation to the reduced air pressure. The best method is to hike to a high mountain area over a period of several days to provide a slow transition. An acclimatization period of two to three days should cure someone with mild altitude sickness, but if moderate symptoms develop, the

Tropical rainforest

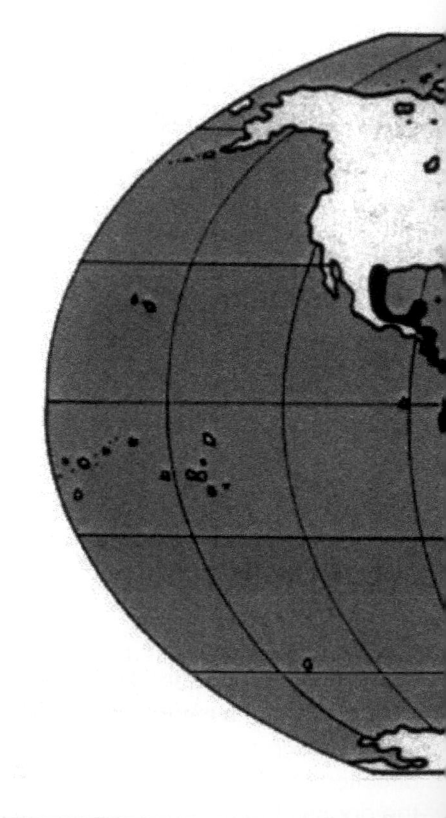

casualty should descend by 300–600m (1000–2000ft) and rest until the symptoms disappear. Severe altitude sickness is life-threatening and requires an immediate, emergency descent of at least 600–1200m (2000–4000ft), preferably by helicopter or some other high-speed vehicle.

TROPICAL DANGERS

Tropical regions are replete with dangers. As Allied soldiers discovered in World War II, probably

Tropical rainforest covers very little of the planet's surface, but it constitutes some of the most environmentally dangerous territory on Earth. Disease, heat exhaustion and venomous/poisonous creatures are the greatest threats here.

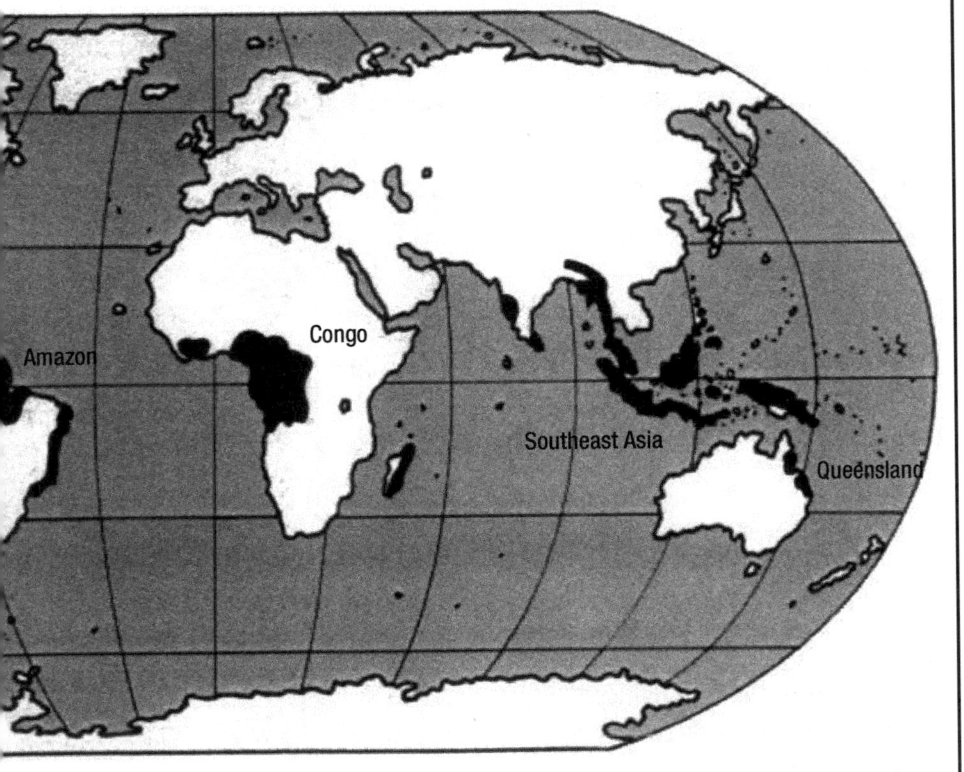

the most serious hazards come from disease, infections and parasites. Tropical diseases, for example, include bilharzia, amoebic dysentery, malaria, dengue fever, yellow fever and typhus. Also remember that many tropical countries may have far higher instances of sexually-transmitted diseases, such as HIV/AIDS and hepatitis, compared to your home country – the wilderness is not the only threat if you don't take care. With exotic travel becoming far more common, it is not unusual for travellers to become ill days or even weeks after they return from a foreign trip, finding that they have picked up something nasty on the way. Always ensure that you have received all relevant vaccinations before taking a trip to the tropics. Visit your doctor at least six months in advance of travel, as some courses of vaccination may have to be ordered in or administered over a period of several weeks.

Once you are in the tropics, you need to put in place strict regimes of hygiene and disease prevention. Cleanliness takes on special importance, as the sweaty parts of your body are vulnerable to 'jungle rot' in very hot and humid conditions. Here bacteria breed on the damp flesh, which actually starts to soften and decay. Wash regularly in purified water, and allow your body to air itself as often as possible. Be careful about bathing in tropical waters – keep your shoes and underwear on, and avoid taking mouthfuls of the water (you should filter and purify any water before drinking it). Also put waterproof bandages over any wounds, no matter how small – many parasites are almost microscopic, and will find wounds easy entry points into your body. Build an earthen latrine a good distance from your shelter and cooking area, and cover over excrement with a thick layer of earth to prevent the spread of disease or the proliferation of insects. Be wary about eating local produce that hasn't been thoroughly cooked, or drinks where you have not had the opportunity to identify the water source.

If you are injured in the tropics, the wound will become infected very quickly if you don't take extra-special care. Keep it as clean as possible, regularly changing the dressing and applying (unless the injury is a burn) antibiotic ointment. Try to have some antibiotics in your medical bag (as long as you know how to use them) in case you or another member of your group gets an infected wound or systemic infection.

Animal threats

Tropical regions have an unusually wide range of dangerous wildlife. Actually, the most dangerous creatures in terms of death toll are insects, on account of their role in disease transmission. Malaria, for example, is distributed by the

Protective clothing

Soldiers are often provided with protective clothing for tropical environments. Mosquito netting, however, can be used to make an improvised insect shield for the head and neck.

TIP: Removing a tick

If you find a tick has attached itself to your skin with its powerful jaws, do not simply attempt to pull it off – it will leave its head parts inside your skin, which can then cause infection. Instead, grip the tick with a pair of fine tweezers near to its mouth parts – don't grip the body or this will squeeze the tick's bacteria-filled fluids into you. Don't twist or yank the tick, but instead maintain a firm upward lift – strong enough to raise your skin – for several minutes until the tick finally relents and releases its grip.

anopheles mosquito and kills around 1.2 million people globally each year.

Although it will be almost impossible to avoid all insect bites in the tropics, there are things you can do to limit your exposure. First, apply insect repellent regularly to all exposed skin, and make your camp well away from swampy areas, which are breeding-grounds for insects. Sleep under a mosquito net at night, and a smoky fire burning through the night will also help keep away small biting creatures. Always wear your boots, as these will protect you from ticks, chiggers and ants, and do a thorough inspection of your body each day to check you are not carrying any ticks, leeches or other parasites. Don't sit or sleep on the bare ground, or amongst tall grasses, and obviously avoid making your shelter near an ant nest, wasp/hornet nest, or other evident danger.

Leeches are another regular nuisance of the tropical world. These aquatic creatures can drop onto your skin, latch on to you with a painless

Hornet

Hornets deliver the most excruciating sting, likened to the feeling of a red-hot rivet being driven into the skin. Don't kill a hornet, as its distress signals can encourage the others in its nest to attack you.

bite, and feed on your blood, dropping off when they are finished. Check your body for leeches after passing through water or after moving through wet foliage by the side of a watercourse. As with ticks, do not attempt to pull a leech off because it will leave its head parts under your skin and cause infection. Instead, using your fingernail, first prise off the sucker from the small end of the leech, then quickly flick or scrape off the fat posterior sucker to remove the leech. (Do this quickly, as the leech will be trying to reattach itself.)

Beyond insects, the tropics present many other animal dangers. Venomous spiders and scorpions, for example, bite thousands of people every year, although fatalities only

Scorpion

Scorpion stings range from merely painful through to lethal. US Army tropical survival courses actually include eating scorpions for food, as only 25 of about 1000 scorpion species are dangerous to humans.

Snakes

The three snakes here are all highly venomous, and should be avoided at all costs. If confronted by a snake, move slowly away from it, giving it plenty of room to escape. If you have to kill one, chop at its head with a club or machete, or drop a large rock on it.

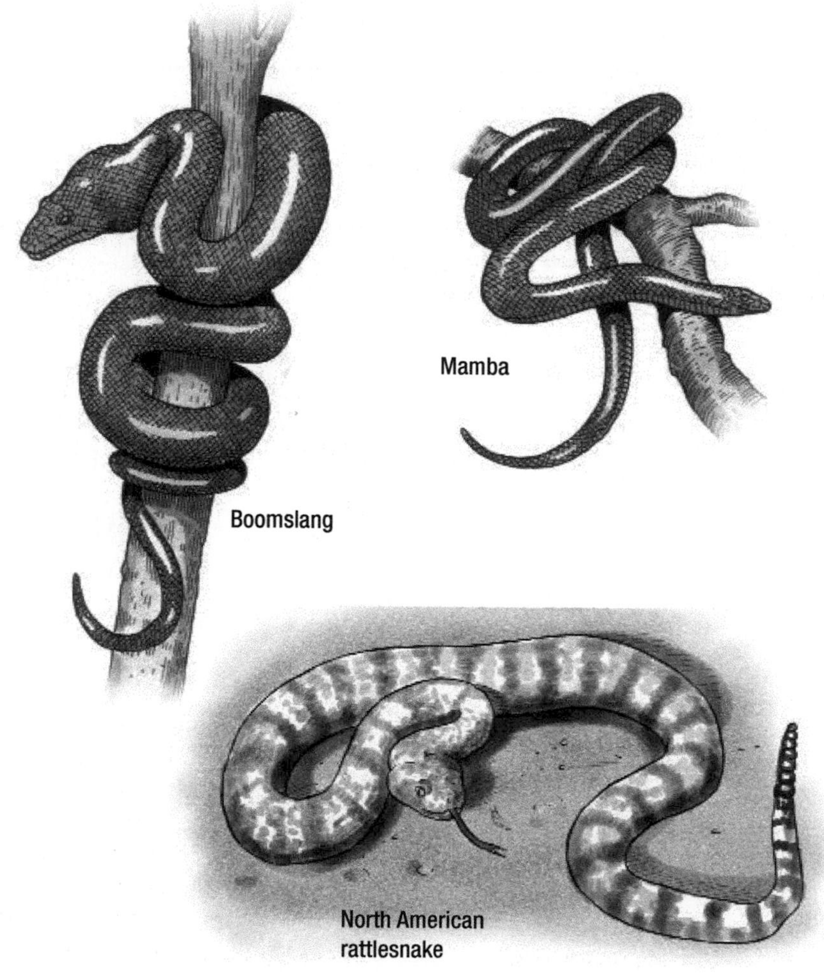

Coral snake

Coral snakes are amongst the most lethal snakes in the world. Just 3–5mg (0.0002 ounces) of their venom can be fatal to an adult human. Thankfully, they prefer to flee rather than attack people when confronted.

tend to occur in the young and the old, or amongst sick people. Scorpions like to sleep in dark, protected spaces, so to avoid getting bitten or stung, knock out your boots, clothing and pack every morning before getting dressed. Do not touch spider webs. If looking under rocks or logs or in rodent holes, use a long stick to probe – never use your hand.

Snakes can be a far more serious problem, as there are some truly lethal varieties, such as vipers, cobras, tropical rattlesnakes, mambas and kraits. Keep your boots on at all times when walking through a tropical landscape, as they will protect your ankles should you tread on a snake – the reason most snake bites occur. Be careful where you

Wild pig

Wild pigs provide a good meal, but they are highly dangerous – they can charge at high speeds, and inflict terrible lacerations with their mouth tusks. Only tackle such creatures with weapons such as rifle-calibre firearms, bows or spear traps, and have a back-up weapon at the ready.

step, therefore, particularly when stepping over logs and stones, and watch that a snake is not coiled around a branch when you go through foliage. Always check bedding, clothes and backpacks for snakes in the morning.

If a snake bites you, try not to panic – your increased heart rate will pump the venom more efficiently around your body. Before the snake escapes, check what type it is, or if you do not know remember features such as markings, size and colour so you can give this information to medics. Immediately wash the bite area with soap and water. If the snake is venomous, the symptoms will depend on the snake type, but can range from a small bleeding wound to respiratory, cardiac or nervous system failure. Do not attempt to suck out the poison, and unless you have specific antivenoms and the knowledge to use them, focus all your efforts on getting into the hands of medical professionals.

The tropics are also home to a range of dangerous creatures far larger than insects and snakes. In Africa, for example, the hippopotamus ranks as one of the most dangerous animals, killing more people than spiders, snakes and big cats combined. Hippos are extremely territorial creatures, and most attacks result when people either walk into a hippo's territory, or attempt to pilot a small boat through the same waters. For this reason, avoid fishing in or walking through areas where hippos gather, especially if there are calves in the water – female hippos can be very aggressive in the protection of their young.

Another semi-aquatic threat comes in the form of crocodiles and alligators. These creatures attack prey at the water's edge, approaching silently just beneath the surface (little more than the eyes will be visible as the creature glides in to attack) before leaping out and dragging the animal, or human, into the water. Avoid splashing about at the water's edge or swimming in an area where crocodiles or alligators are suspected – check out the riverbank for these animals' distinctive footprints. If you have to be at the water's edge, have another person on dedicated lookout. Should you spot groups of alligators or crocodiles, give them a wide berth, as they can actually run faster than you over short distances. If chased by a crocodile, however, ignore the advice to zig-zag. Sprint with all the speed you can and attempt to climb quickly up a tree.

Big cats such as tigers, jaguars, lions and leopards are rarely a problem, as they rightly fear humans more than we fear them. Normally

TIP: Rabies prevention

- Do not fuss over or attempt to feed local dogs or cats in tropical or desert areas.
- Steer clear of violent, staggering animals that are foaming at the mouth – these symptoms can indicate a rabies infection.
- Should someone else have advanced rabies, tie them down and do not go near them.
- If the rabies victim dies – which they almost certainly will do – do not handle the body or attempt to bury it.

Head protection

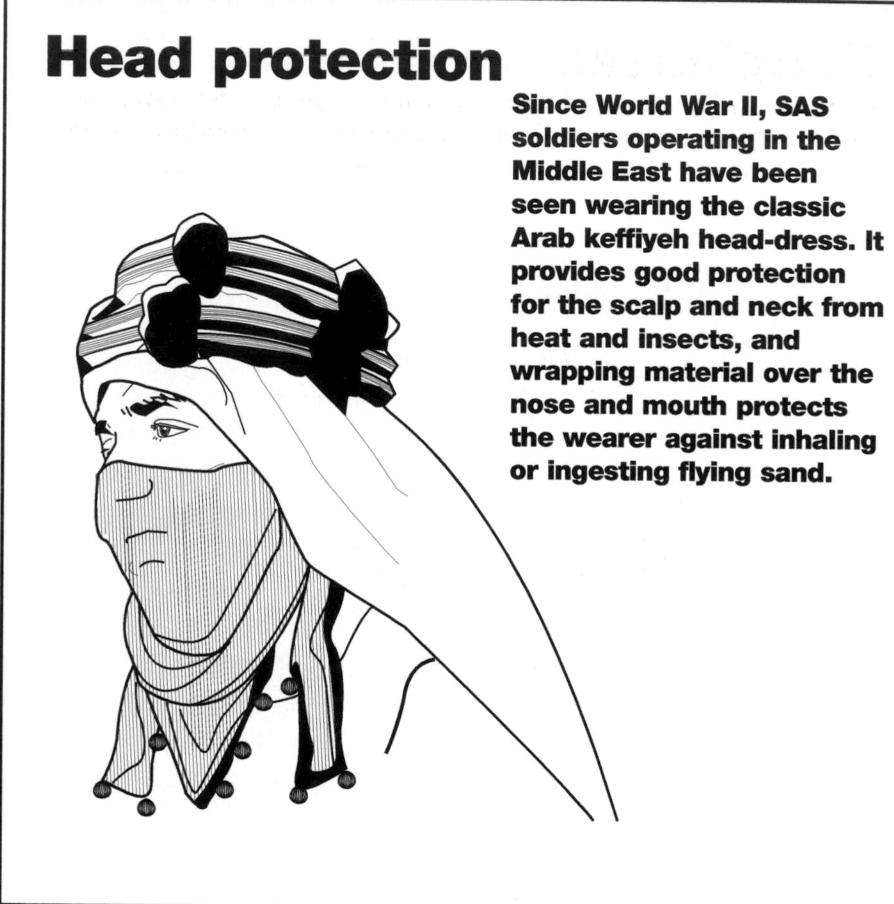

Since World War II, SAS soldiers operating in the Middle East have been seen wearing the classic Arab keffiyeh head-dress. It provides good protection for the scalp and neck from heat and insects, and wrapping material over the nose and mouth protects the wearer against inhaling or ingesting flying sand.

only sick, old or wounded creatures will attempt attacks on people. If there are any reports of such attacks in an area, stay away from long grass, from where big cats will usually spring an ambush. If you inadvertently corner a big cat, simply back away slowly without making any threatening movements and allow the cat to escape.

DESERT DANGERS

The desert actually presents many similar threats to those of jungle regions, particularly in terms of dangerous creatures and insects, and disease. Follow all the precautions outlined above to protect yourself again such threats. The two environments also share the danger of rabies-infected animals. Rabies is a

Sunglasses

Crude sunglasses can be made from strips of cardboard or bark, with slits cut into them for the eyes. Of course, proper sunglasses with full ultraviolet protection are far better.

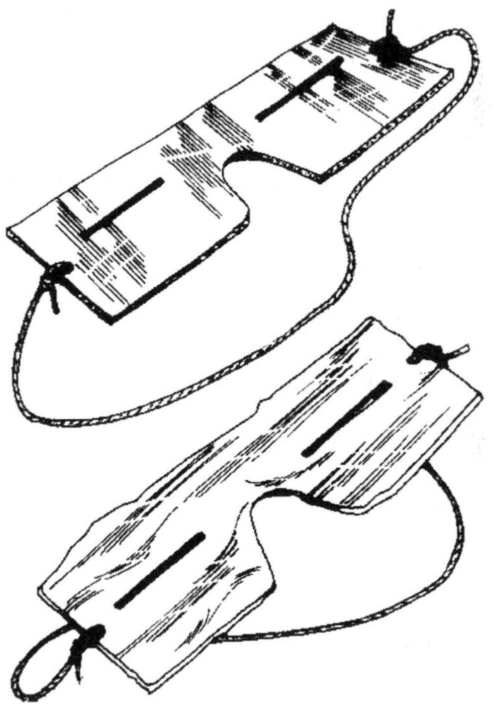

lethal viral disease transmitted by the bite of an infected animal, often a dog or fox. The early symptoms are flu-like, but it may take anywhere from two weeks to two years for the final, devastating symptoms of paralysis, hydrophobia and severe brain damage to develop, which are invariably fatal. There is a treatment for rabies, but it must be applied within 24–48 hours of the bite to work, so as soon as you are bitten by any animal, clean the wound vigorously with soap and water, and a

Protection in a sandstorm

In a sandstorm, cover your face and as much of your body as possible, and put a solid object – such as the rock outcrop here – between you and the wind. US and British soldiers in the Middle East also carry eyewash and nasal spray to treat the physical after-effects of the storm.

disinfectant if you have it, and get to hospital immediately.

Of course, the far greater dangers in the desert are dehydration and heat-stroke. Chapter 2 explains the principles of finding water in even arid conditions, and the hunt for adequate water supplies should be your number one priority. Do this, however, in the cooler dawn and dusk hours, before the sun, and temperature, rises. If you have water with you, ration it sensibly between yourself and other members of the party, although don't make the ration so small that it is effectively useless at preventing dehydration.

To protect yourself against the desert sun, keep your skin covered with clothing and wear a good

Escaping quicksand

To escape from quicksand, try to 'swim' yourself to safety, pushing across the surface with your hands while wriggling your legs free from the sand's sucking effects. Reach for any nearby branch or handhold to help.

Sources of heat gain

This diagram illustrates why daytime travel in the desert is dangerous, as you are being struck by various sources of heat, not just direct sunlight. If you can, travel at night or in the cooler dawn or dusk hours.

protective hat (see Chapter 1) that also shields the back of the neck. Travel at night or at dawn or dusk if possible, and shelter up during the day.

Don't be tempted to drink your own urine, although advice on this matter varies. A fully hydrated person could probably drink a small quantity of urine with few ill effects, but the salt and mineral content of urine would hasten the dehydration of an already fluid-starved person.

TORNADOES, HURRICANES AND STORMS

Hurricanes and tornadoes afflict specific parts of the world, but millions of people live within affected corridors, particularly in the middle and southern states of the US and across the Far East. Tornadoes have wind speeds of up to 560km/h (350mph), and can be up to 1km (0.6 miles) wide. They are quite capable of tearing a house to pieces, and throw out debris at lethal speeds and to extreme distances. Hurricane winds tend to reach a maximum speed of up to 350km/h (200mph), but they cause damage over a much greater area and often bring massive flooding. General storms, by contrast,

Rain-shadow effect

When reading the weather, note that mountains often receive most of their rain on the side facing the prevailing winds, while the opposite side can live under the drier conditions of a 'rain-shadow'.

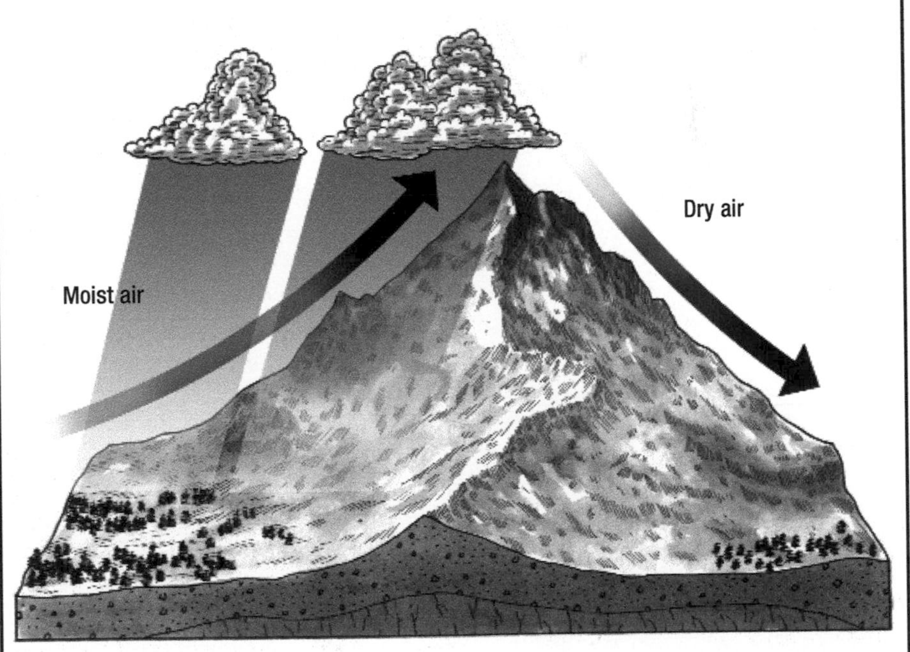

can strike anywhere in the world, but can have almost equally ferocious effects for their duratlon.

These extreme weather conditions present a variety of dangers – flash flooding, lightning strikes, injury from flying debris, accelerated exposure – so preparation for such events is essential if you are to avoid being caught out in the open. Most important, keep a judicious eye on the weather. Look out for the signs of an impending storm, such as:

- Towering, dark clouds gathering in the sky.
- An increased windspeed, particularly if it is accompanied by low, overcast skies and rain.
- Hailstones falling.
- Lightning in the distance.

Developing tornadoes offer an additional set of indicators. Watch out for a rotating cloud base, with dust or debris being whipped up below, and listen for a loud, continuous rumble or

TIP: Lightning avoidance

Lightning strikes are a threat in storms, particularly in mountain environments. Here are some US 10th Mountain Division precautions to take to lessen the risk:

- If caught in a thunderstorm, avoid summits, vertical cliffs (remember that even standing under an overhang will not protect you from a strike), exposed ridges, lone trees, pinnacles and gullies with running water.
- Leave wet ropes and metal equipment at least 15m (50ft) from your shelter.
- Remove anything metal from your clothing.
- Sit in a squatting position with your arms wrapped around your body. This is the best position for surviving earth currents, as it protects the brain and major organs from being struck by the lightning bolt.
- Wear rubber-soled shoes if possible, or place rubber or plastic material beneath you, such as a sleeping mat or plastic coat.

roar that does not fade away. This noise may be your only indication of a tornado during night hours, although you can also look for blue-green to white flashes of light at ground level – this is not lightning, but the flashes from power lines being destroyed. Occasionally, the air may become very still before a tornado strikes.

When a tornado does emerge, it will form into the distinctive funnel shape (made by the dust sucked up by the winds and by condensed water droplets). Look out for other funnel shapes dropping down from the clouds around you – tornadoes can form into groups under the right conditions.

Obviously, one of the best preparations for storm conditions is meteorological forecasts, so you should stay tuned in to the radio or check conditions on your mobile phone. If you become aware of an approaching storm, find a cave, ditch or rocky outcrop to shelter in or under. (Avoid sheltering under trees if

Storm cloud anvil

A towering, anvil-shaped cumulonimbus cloud is a clear warning of severe weather. Such clouds not only produce strong winds, hail, lightning and heavy rain, but in certain regions (particularly North America) they can also be a prelude to tornadoes.

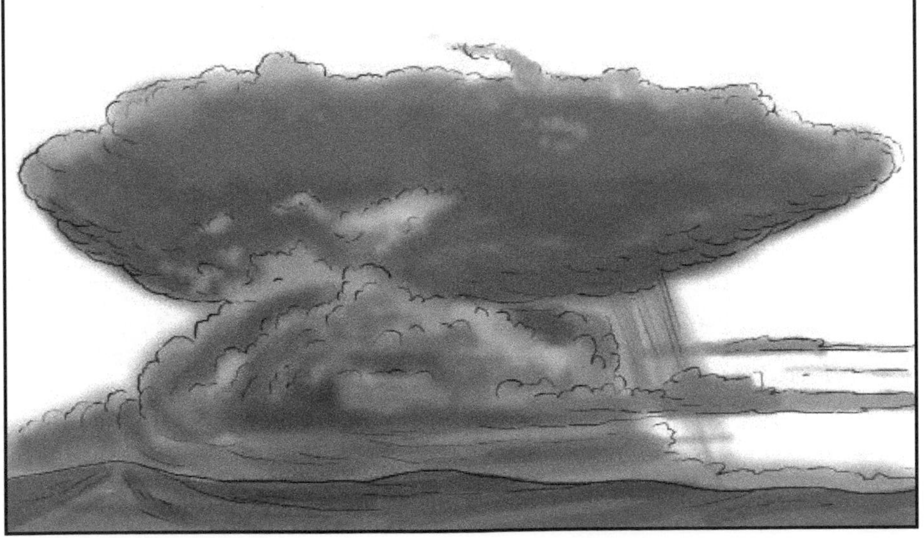

Tornado

Tornado funnels vary tremendously in size, from about 80m (260ft) to several kilometres. Note that their direction of travel can be unpredictable, and given to sudden change.

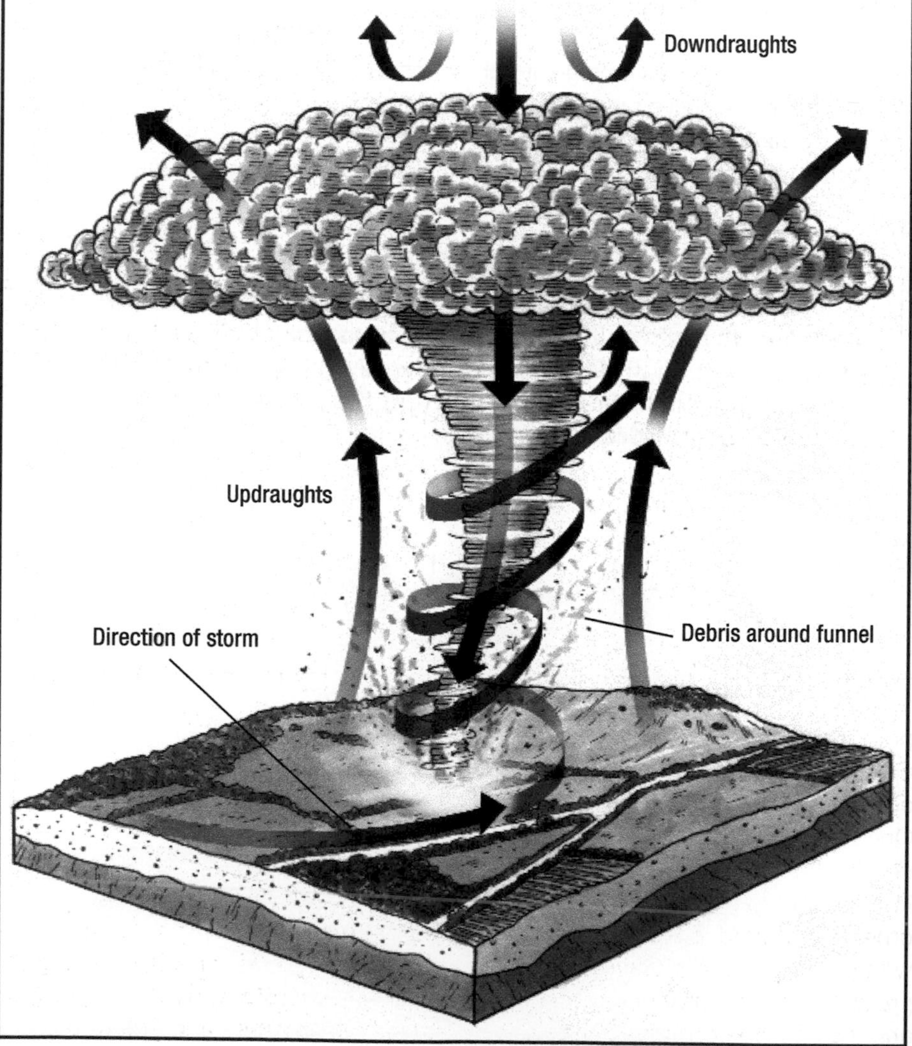

Sheltering from a tornado

If you are caught out in the open in a tornado, lie down in a ditch or area of low ground to protect yourself from the flying debris above. Don't try to outrun a tornado if it is heading towards you – the average forward speed of a tornado is about 48km/h (30mph).

possible, as they might be brought down by the storm or on high ground could act as lightning conductors.) Once in shelter, wait for the storm conditions to pass. If you are caught in the open, get down in a ditch or other low ground, cover your head with your arms and clothing (to protect your head from flying debris) and wait for the tornado to pass.

FOREST FIRES

Forest fires are a perennial danger in wooded or grassy areas, particularly in the summer months when foliage is dried out and can easily ignite. Improperly-sited campfires are a common cause of localized fires. When constructing your fire, therefore, clear the ground of leaves, grasses and twigs to make a patch of bare earth at least 2m (6ft 6in) in diameter, and build the fire in the middle of the circle. You can also prevent a fire from spreading by building it in a trench or surrounding it with a circle of substantial stones.

Be particularly careful if you have to light a fire on a hot and windy day – sparks and ash can be blown into the dry brush, where the wind quickly fans them into flame. On such days, try to locate your fire so that any sparks are carried towards areas of

Clothing on fire

If your clothing catches fire, you need to follow the STOP, DROP and ROLL procedure. Immediately STOP where you are, DROP to the floor, and then ROLL around, pressing the flames down into the earth. The rolling action will hopefully smother the flames by depriving them of oxygen. If someone else's clothes catch fire, you can achieve the same result by throwing a thick rug over the flames.

TIP:
The AVPU scale

A casualty's degree of consciousness can be assessed fairly accurately using the AVPU scale, which is used on US military training courses:

- A = Alert. The casualty is fully conscious, aware of their position, and is able to interact fully with the outside world. The diagnostic process for this is simply that you can interact with the person as usual.
- V = Voice. At this level of consciousness, the casualty is still responding to your voice, though they may be sluggish or incoherent. Give the person simple commands to follow, such as getting them to blink their eyes or squeeze your hand if they can hear you.
- P = Pain. Here the casualty will only respond to physical stimuli. Try inducing particularly sensitive pains or sensations (non-damaging, of course), such as squeezing the ear lobe or scratching the soles of the feet. If the person tries to pull away or moves, then there is still activity being processed between the nerves, spinal cord and brain.
- U = Unresponsive. This is a very serious state in which the casualty is totally unconscious, and does not react to any form of stimuli.

The AVPU scale helps you to judge the condition of the nervous system and spot any wider injuries or illness.

vocalizations at least prove that they are conscious and breathing, suggesting some degree of stability, whereas a completely silent and inert casualty could be at death's door. When performing triage, however, always take into account continuing threats to wellbeing. If, for example, an injured person is lying in an area at threat from rockfalls, it makes sense to move them first before treating other casualties.

When assessing any casualty, your highest priority is to identify conditions that might be impairing breathing or circulation. Remember that these two bodily functions are critically interlinked – breathing oxygenates the blood, and the circulatory system takes that blood around the body to vital organs and tissue (without the oxygenated blood, the organs and tissue will start to die). The brain is particularly sensitive to oxygen deprivation, with brain damage occurring in five minutes if action is not taken to restore circulation and breathing.

For this reason, many doctors and paramedics are taught that the top priorities for first aid are remembered by the abbreviation ABC:

- A = **Airway**: Open the casualty's mouth and check that there is nothing obstructing the throat or

Airways

Tipping the head backwards opens up the windpipe for delivering artificial respiration, although do not carry out this procedure if you suspect a spinal injury.

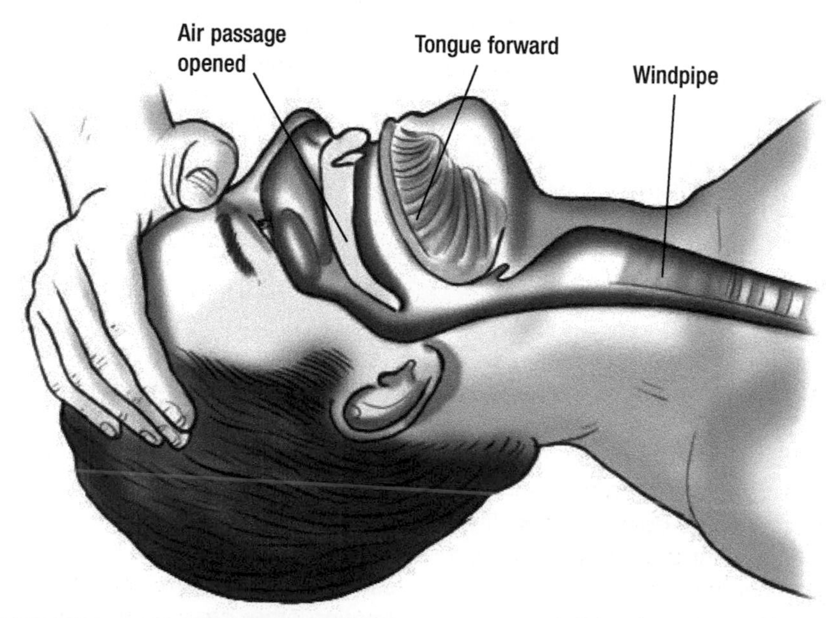

interfering with breathing, such as blood, vomit, loose teeth, the casualty's tongue or food. Clear out any loose obstructions with your fingers, or pull the tongue free from the airway.

- **B = Breathing**: Put your cheek next to the victim's nose and mouth – listen and feel for breathing. Look at the chest to see if it is rising and falling. Place your hand on it to make sure.
- **C = Circulation**: Check for a pulse. Place your fingers (not your thumb, which has its own pulse) against the inside of the wrist about 1cm (0.3in) in from the thumb side, on the outer side of the wrist tendon. Alternatively, another pulse is found in the groove either side of the windpipe just beneath the angle of the jaw. The pulse should ideally be strong and regular – if it is not present, or is weak, unusually slow or fast, and erratic, then there are problems.

Having run through the ABC assessment, and delivered treatment accordingly (see below), you should make a more complete assessment. In some cases, the casualty's own narrative of their symptoms or injury will guide you to the right place – such as a broken leg or abdominal pain – but a thorough check-over can reveal injuries that even the casualty may be missing. The following checklist is not exhaustive, but gives you a good idea of what to look for in a casualty.

- **Head** – Check for any bleeding hidden under the hair, or blood or fluid leaking from the nose or ears (which in certain situations indicate an injury to the skull or brain). Look closely at the eyes – pupils that are significantly different in size, or eyes that cannot follow a slowly moving object, could indicate brain injury or stroke, as can facial asymmetry. Look for mouth injuries such as a broken jaw, lost teeth or heavy gum bleeding.
- **Skin** – Examine the skin for any unusual coloration. A blue or blue/grey colour, for example, especially if prominent in the lips and fingernails, can indicate problems with circulation or breathing, whereas pale skin combined with a cool, moist texture suggests circulatory shock (see below). Also look out for any rashes, which could indicate poisoning or a virus, and for swollen lymph nodes in the neck, armpit or groin (see illustration on page 225 for locations), which suggest the casualty is fighting a virus or infection.
- **Neck and spine** – If the casualty has suffered from an impact injury, such as a fall, check the neck and spine for any bruisings,

swellings, marks, and so on. Don't, however, move the casualty, especially if they are lying awkwardly and complain that they cannot move – they may be suffering from damage to their spinal cord (the major component of the central nervous system), and moving them could result in further damage and even death.

- **Chest** – Make sure that both sides of the chest move equally when breathing. Listen to the chest for any wheezings, cracklings or whistlings, which may indicate the presence of fluid.
- **Arms and hands** – Check for any breakages or swellings, and look at the fingernails for the blueness associated with circulatory/respiratory problems. Ask the casualty about any unusual sensations (numbness, pins and needles), which may be related to nerve or spinal damage. Have the casualty squeeze your two forefingers, and note any dissimilarity in grip strength between the two hands (which could indicate a brain impairment such as stroke or physical damage to the limb).
- **Abdomen** – Check for unusual swellings or marks, or if the abdomen is very hard or rigid (could indicate such illnesses as peritonitis or blocked gut). If there is pain, have the patient identify the location, and pass this information over to a doctor.
- **Pelvic/genital area** – Note any bleeding or significant fluid loss from the orifices, which could indicate internal injuries or infections. Are any scabs, rashes or marks present that may indicate a sexually-transmitted disease?
- **Legs and feet** – If the casualty is walking, get them to walk in a straight line to check their balance. If they are conscious and lying down, get them to pull and push their feet backwards and forwards against the resistance of your hands – note any differences between the strength levels of the two limbs which may indicate nerve/spinal damage. Check nerve responses by scratching the soles of the feet to see the tickle response.

Based on what you find from your assessment, you will then have to deliver first aid treatments. Remember, the goal is to stabilize the patient – it is unlikely that you will be able to heal them if an injury or illness is serious – until you reach medical help.

BREATHING AND CIRCULATION

If an ABC assessment reveals that the casualty's heart has stopped, and/or that they are not breathing,

Finding a pulse

The two best locations for finding a pulse are on the outer edge of the wrist and next to the windpipe just beneath the angle of the jawline. Count the pulse beats for 10 seconds, then multiply by 7 to get beats per minute.

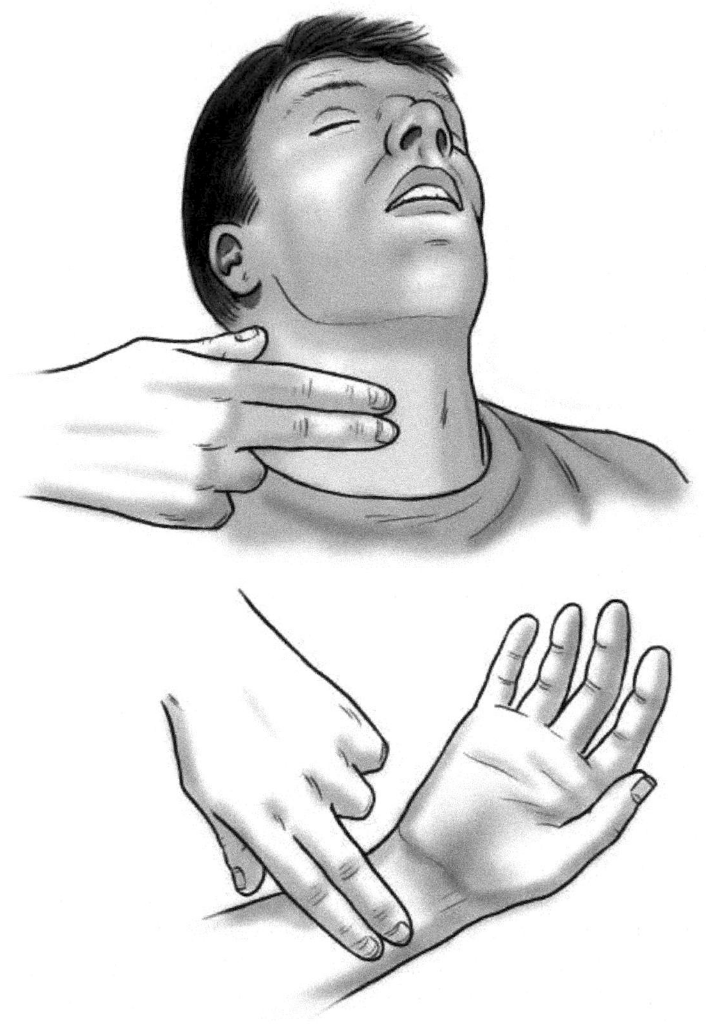

then you will have to perform one or both of the techniques of cardio-pulmonary resuscitation (CPR). CPR's objective is to artificially sustain, and hopefully restore, a casualty's circulatory and respiratory systems in the event of their failure. It consists of two elements – artificial respiration and cardiac massage.

Artificial respiration essentially involves you breathing for the patient, using your own breath to push air into the lungs. To perform this technique, first lay the casualty on their back and open the mouth. (Your ABC assessment should have already cleared out any obstruction from the mouth or throat.) Next, tilt the casualty's head gently backwards by placing the palm and fingers of your hand on their forehead and applying firm, gentle backward pressure. At the same time, put two fingers of the other hand under the chin and lift gently upwards. This action opens up the airway. Pinch the casualty's nose shut and make a tight seal with your mouth around theirs. Then blow into

TIP:
Treating shock

Circulatory shock is a common battlefield injury, and sets in when blood pressure (the pressure required to keep blood circulating around the body properly) drops to dangerous levels. It is caused by internal or external bleeding or through severe dehydration. Indicators can include pale, cold and clammy skin, a rapid but weak pulse, fast, shallow breathing and dilated pupils. Your first-aid priority is to keep as much remaining blood as possible circulating around the vital organs in the core of the body. With the casualty lying down, raise and support their legs about 15–20cm (6–8in) from the ground, to reduce the amount of blood going to the lower limbs, and keep them warm and dry. Naturally, try to control any obvious bleeding as quickly as possible. Only give sparing sips of water to drink if the casualty is conscious and is not suffering from abdominal wounds, and do not give them anything to eat. Get the casualty to a hospital or doctor (or bring emergency services to you) as an immediate priority.

their mouth, pulling away when you reach the end of your breath. The chest should rise when you blow in and fall when you pull away. (If the chest doesn't rise, check that you seal your mouth tightly around the casualty's and that there is no obstruction in the casualty's airway. If there is an obstruction, follow the guidelines for choking, below.)

After these first quick breaths, establish a rate of around 12 breaths per minute. Check every minute to see whether breathing has resumed. As soon as it does, stop the artificial respiration.

The aim behind cardiac massage is essentially to squeeze blood through the casualty's circulatory system by manually compressing the chest. By doing so, the first aider can maintain some flow of oxygenated blood to the major organs and potentially restart the casualty's heart. To perform the basic compression technique, lie the patient down on their back, with you kneeling to one side by the chest. Using two fingers,

Chest compression

The diagram here shows the correct location for delivering chest compressions, the heel of the compressing hand sitting directly over the lower sternum.

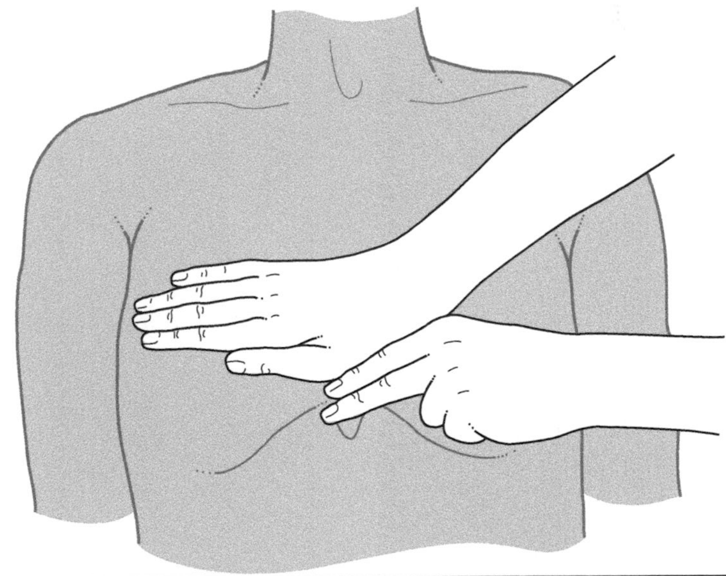

Cardiac massage

Note the linked fingers position used here when delivering cardiac massage. The thrust is delivered with the uppermost hand, and the lower hand provides a cushioning effect that reduces the risk of broken ribs.

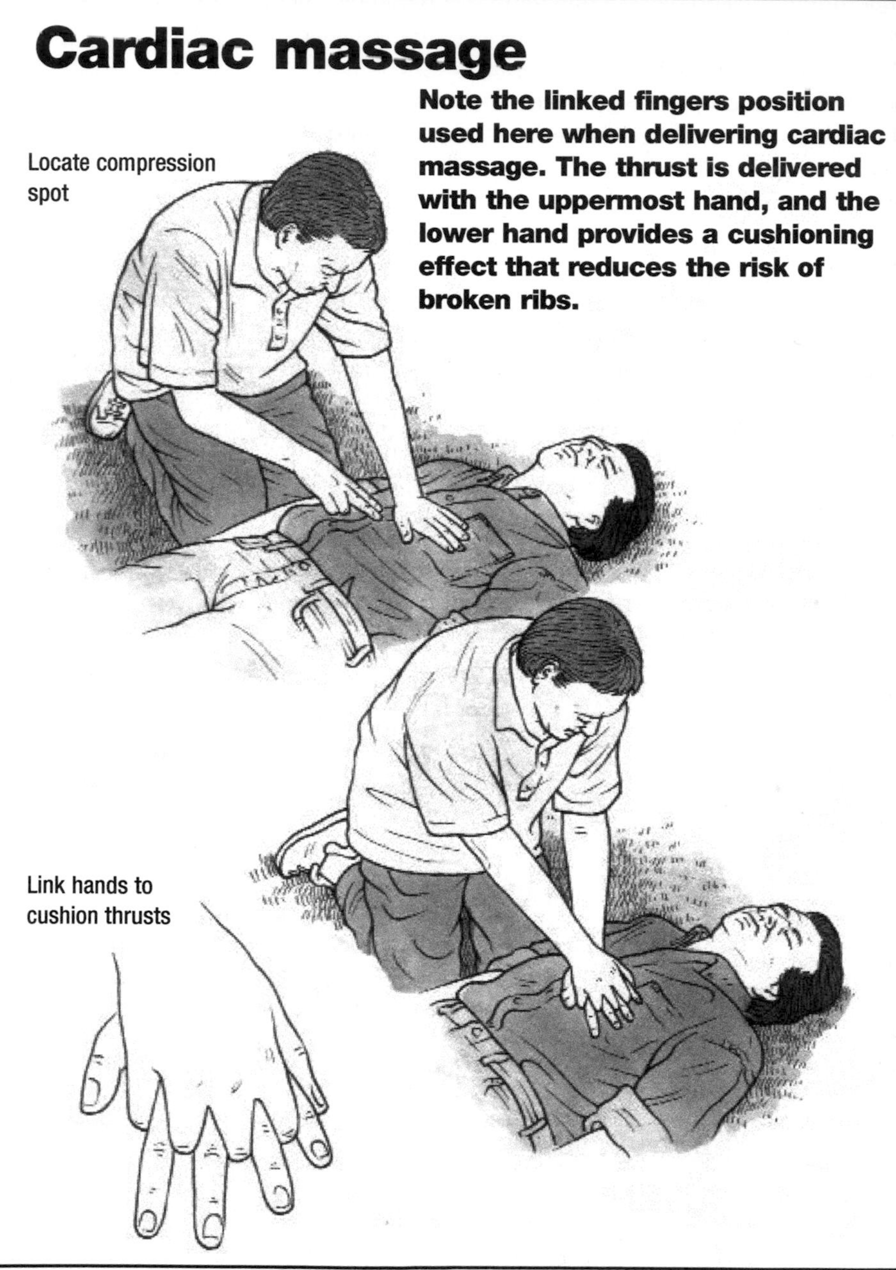

Locate compression spot

Link hands to cushion thrusts

trace the edge of their ribs up to where the ribs meet the bottom of the sternum – you will feel the fingers come to a stop in the middle lower chest. Keep a finger on this spot and measure two finger widths up. Hold these fingers in place and put the heel of your other hand just above them so that it is still touching the fingers.

The heel of the hand is now in the correct position, directly over the heart. Place your other hand over it, and knit your fingers together for stability. Lean over the casualty so that your shoulders are directly over their sternum. Push straight down to a depth of about 4cm (1.5in) with a strong, confident and rhythmic movement. Deliver about 80 compressions a minute and keep going, even though it is an exhausting process. Check for a pulse every minute.

When both breathing and heartbeat are arrested, you have to perform the artificial respiration and cardiac massage in a mutually-supporting sequence. Deliver 30 chest compressions at a speed of about 100 a minute, then give two breaths, and after four complete sets check for pulse and breathing. Repeat this sequence until, hopefully, the casualty's natural breathing and heartbeat take over. Note that if there are two of you able to treat the casualty, the process is made easier by one person doing the breaths and the other the chest compressions, switching over at regular intervals. Also note that for children and infants the above procedures need to be modified. On a baby or toddler, use only two fingers to make compressions to about 2.5cm (1in)

TIP: Recovery position

Unconscious or weak casualties should be placed into the recovery position following any other treatments, as long as the casualty does not have a spinal injury. First, roll the casualty onto their front with one leg bent up at a right angle to the body. The arm on the same side should be bent outwards (with the opposite arm running down the side of the body). The face should be lying naturally to the side with the head tilted back. This position allows drainage of any mucus and vomit out of the mouth to reduce the risk of choking.

Recovery position

The recovery position is designed to aid respiration in an unconsious person, allowing the tongue to hang forward and fluids to drain naturally outwards.

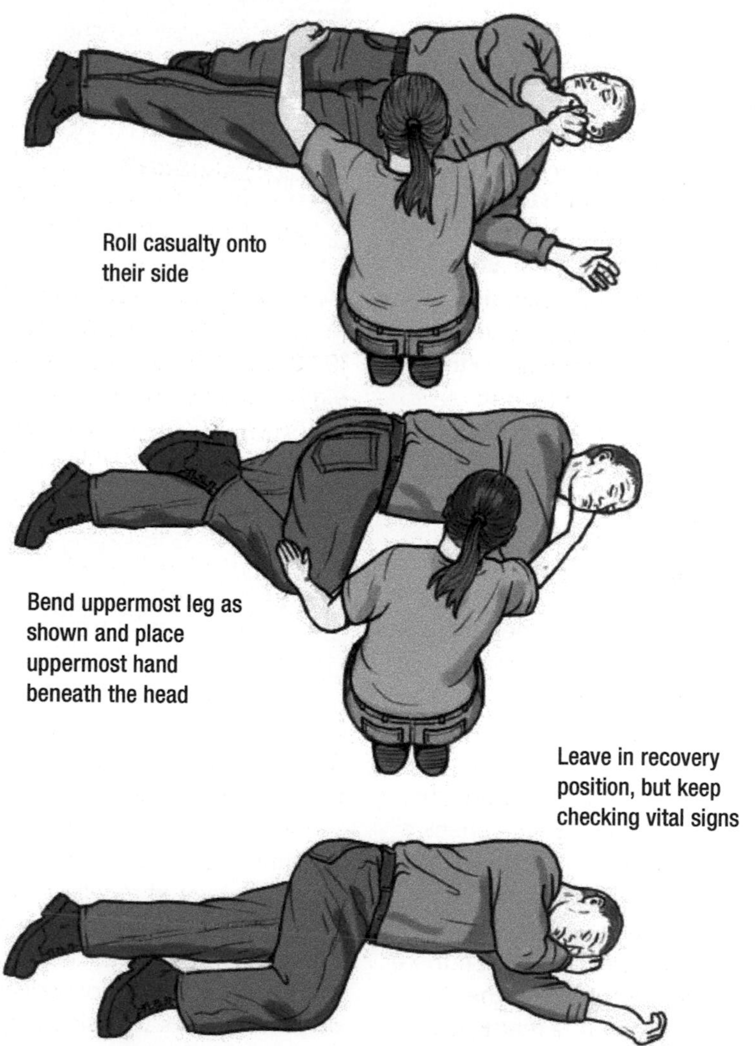

depth. For older children (up to 10 years), use the same heel method as with an adult but push to only about 3.5cm (1.4in) depth.

HEAT INJURIES

Heat injuries range from a simple case of light sunburn through to life-threatening heat-stroke. As we have already outlined in this book, prevention is far better than cure for such conditions. If you keep your body covered with proper clothing, stay hydrated and out of the sun, your chances of developing heat-related complications are much reduced.

Dehydration can be a precursor to all manner of other serious conditions. Symptoms to look out for include cramps, heavy sweating, chronic thirst, sickness and dizziness. The skin can also lose some of its elasticity – pinch the skin on the back of the hand, and if it stays upright in a ridge, then dehydration could be an explanation. Treatment for dehydration is, obviously, rehydration. Move the casualty into the shade, sit them down and loosen their clothing; give small sips of water very frequently until they feel rested and recovered. A more sophisticated rehydration liquid consists of 1 litre (1.8 pints) of water into which you dissolve about half a teaspoon of salt and about eight level teaspoons of sugar. This replaces some of the vital sugars and salts lost during dehydration.

Heat exhaustion and heat-stroke are both exacerbated or caused by dehydration, but can emerge simply from prolonged exposure to direct sunlight and heat, particularly if you are exerting yourself. The symptoms of heat exhaustion include acute headaches, pale and clammy skin, dizziness, nausea and confusion. Treat the casualty as for dehydration, but prolong the period of rest for at least 24 hours. Watch carefully for symptoms of shock developing.

Heat-stroke is a life-threatening condition in which the core temperature of the body climbs above its safe threshold of 36–38°C (97.8–100.4°F). Symptoms can be similar to those of heat exhaustion, but more severe in nature and complicated by breathing and circulation problems. Heat-stroke victims may develop a rapid, weak pulse and can start lapsing in and out of consciousness.

Your priority with a heat-stroke casualty is to cool the casualty's body and so reduce the core temperature to safe levels. Move them out of the sun to a cool, shaded area, such as a cave or under trees. Strip them down to their underclothes and soak their body with water to begin cooling. (Or, keep the casualty clothed and continually soak the clothes they are wearing with water to keep them cold.) You can also fan the wet body to accelerate heat loss through evaporation. For a conscious

Heat injuries: symptoms

This diagram illustrates some of the differences between heat exhaustion and the more serious heat-stroke. Both these conditions can be prevented by adequate hydration and rest in the shade.

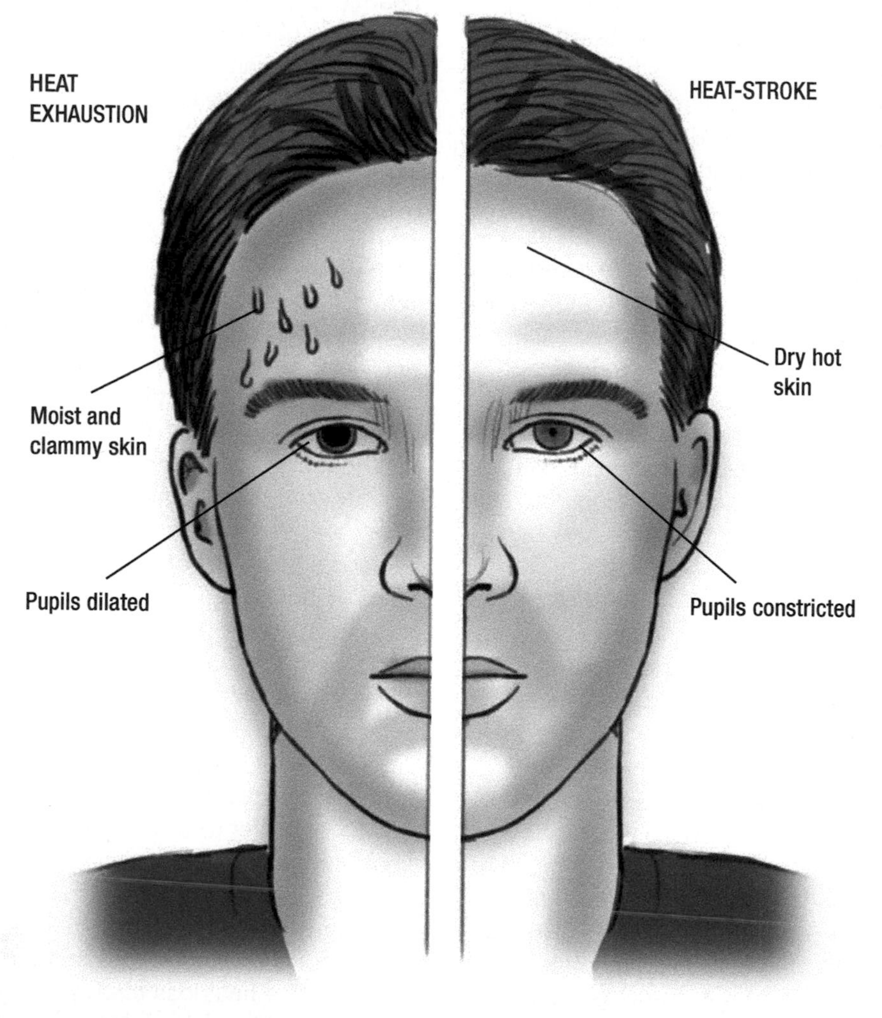

casualty, put in place rehydration treatments and monitor the casualty closely for symptoms of shock.

COLD INJURIES

We have already encountered some of the dangers of subzero environments in the previous chapter, and discussed how we can prevent such conditions occurring. When they do occur, however, professional medical help is the key, but as always, survival realities may require you to perform field treatments.

For frostbite, the objective is to thaw out any frozen parts and bring them progressively back up to body temperature. In moderate cases, this can be achieved by keeping the affected area warm and dry and preventing any further heat loss. (Frostbitten fingers can be placed between thighs or in armpits to warm them through.) Seriously frozen tissue, however, may require more substantial treatments. Heat a container of water until it is warm, but not uncomfortably so, and immerse the frozen body part in the water. (You will need to keep topping the water up to maintain its heat.) Steadily, this procedure will thaw out the frozen tissue, a process unfortunately accompanied by serious pain. Do not burst any blisters that have formed, and never let the body part refreeze once it has been warmed through – the resulting tissue damage would be

TIP: Reading body temperature

The healthy human body stays in a core temperature range of 36–38°C (97.8–100.4°F). Anything above or below this range can indicate a significant risk to the patient's health.

- To use a mercury thermometer, which you should have in your first aid kit, first shake it well, holding it at the opposite end to the silver mercury bulb, until the temperature reading drops below the 36°C (97.8°F) mark.
- Then place the thermometer, bulb end first, either under the tongue or under the armpit (use the latter if there is a danger of the patient biting, such as during a convulsion).
- Leave it there for three minutes to obtain a reading.

catastrophic and almost certainly lead to amputation.

Hypothermia is the real killer in subzero environments, and occurs when the core body temperature drops below its natural range. Early symptoms often appear to be psychological – dramatic mood swings (the casualty may become unusually angry or argumentative), lethargy, confusion and clumsiness. Physical symptoms progress to include icy-cold skin, drowsiness, shallow breathing, shivering coming in waves, a slow heart rate, and ultimately unconsciousness and even death.

Above all, warmth is the primary treatment. At the first signs of hypothermia, get the casualty to a

sheltered place, make a fire and change them out of their wet clothing. Wrap them up in clean, dry clothing or a sleeping bag, and you can also hug them to share body warmth. For mild or moderate cases (core temperature no lower than 33°C/92°F), give them hot food and hot drinks if you have them, but do this very slowly, as too much intake too quickly can overload their already weakened system. For a severely hypothermic casualty (temperature below 33°C/92°F), you should only give warm sugar water by mouth – don't give food, as by this stage the digestive system has shut down. You can apply more vigorous heat by warming stones over a fire, wrapping them in a towel or piece of thick material and placing them next to places where the blood flow is near the surface of the skin, such as between the thighs, the back of the neck, the pit of the stomach, the armpits and wrists. Be careful with this process, however – you don't want to add a burn to the casualty's problems. Keep the casualty still as their heart muscle will be weakened, and bring professional help in quickly.

Cooling down

One method of cooling down a person suffering from hyperthermia is to wrap them in a sheet and soak it with cool water. Refresh the water periodically as it warms up.

CHOKING

A distinctive type of respiratory emergency is choking, which usually occurs when the airway is blocked by an obstruction, typically food. Time is against you here, for the longer the casualty's breathing is restricted, the greater the danger that they will lapse into unconsciousness and eventually die from oxygen deprivation. As the oxygen level drops in their body, their face may at first go red, turning to blue in an unconscious patient. If the patient is coughing, however, it indicates that their body is attempting to clear the obstruction naturally. You therefore don't need to do anything, but watch carefully in case the symptoms suddenly worsen.

In a case of full choking, first see if you can manually clear the obstruction wlth your finger. Do not attempt to push your fingers against

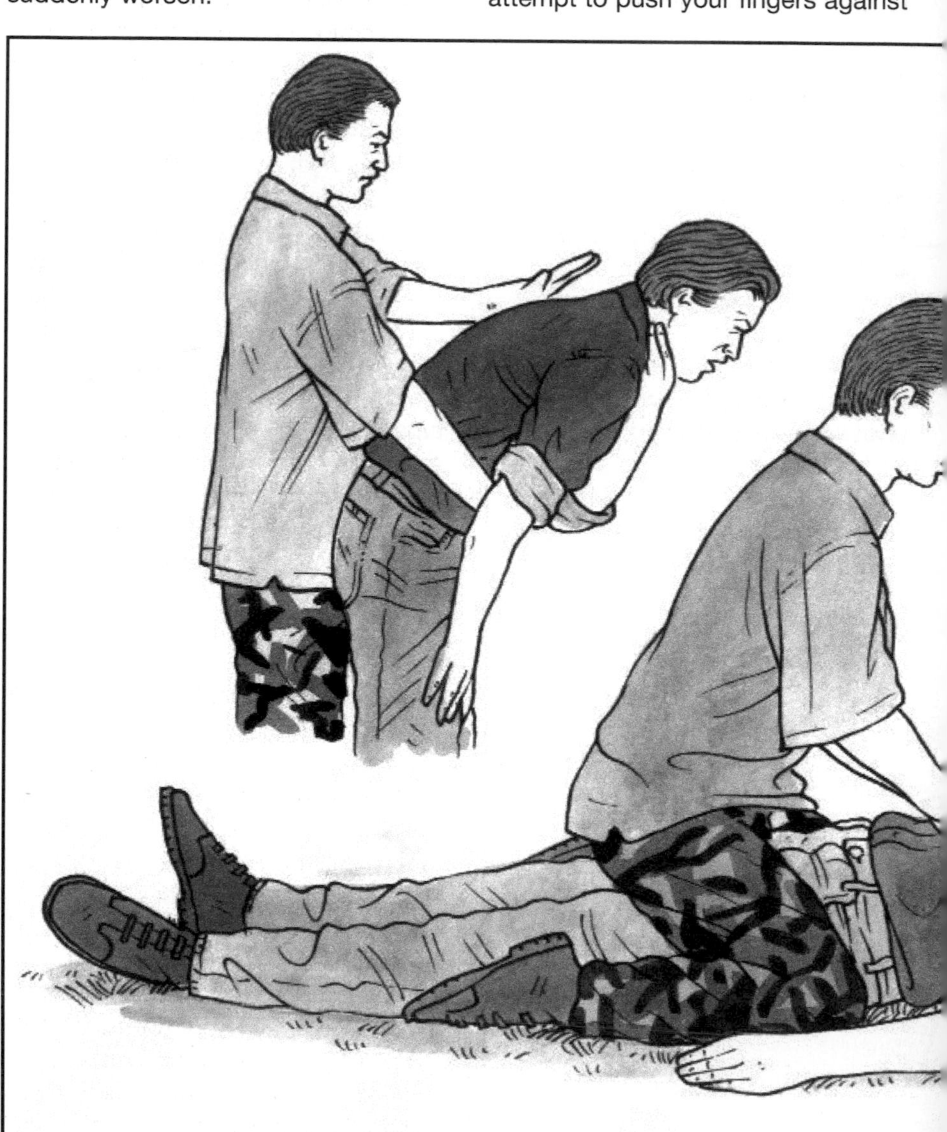

an object stuck at the back of the throat, as you might push it down further. If the obstruction can't be reached, stand behind the casualty and place their head lower than their chest. Now strike the back sharply five times between the shoulder blades with the palm of your hand. This action can help the casualty expel the obstruction. Repeat two or three times, checking the mouth between each set of blows.

If the sets of back blows don't work, you now need to try the famous Heimlich manoeuvre. (Note that this technique is not recommended for infants under the age of one.) Stand or kneel behind the casualty and wrap your arms around their waist. Make a fist of one hand and place it at the juncture of the ribs and the waist. Place your other hand over the fist and jerk the fist forcefully inwards and upwards four times.

The aim is to force the air in the lungs upwards, thus blowing out the obstruction like a cork from a bottle. Alternate this technique with four back blows until the obstruction is released. Should the casualty become unconscious, you can perform the back blows with the casualty lying on their side or by straddling them and making abdominal thrusts straight down with the heel of the hand.

Treating choking

The uppermost illustration here shows the classic back slap method of removing a throat obstruction. The other illustrates a variation of the Heimlich manoeuvre, suitable for performing on a person who is unconscious.

WOUNDS AND BLEEDING

Bleeding injuries vary in scale from minor cuts that will stop quickly and with little intervention, through to full amputation of limbs and massive

Heimlich manoeuvre

The Heimlich manoeuvre consists of an upward thrust against the upper abdomen, between the navel and the sternum. Repeat the thrust up to five times, and then return to other methods of removal if the manoeuvre is unsuccessful.

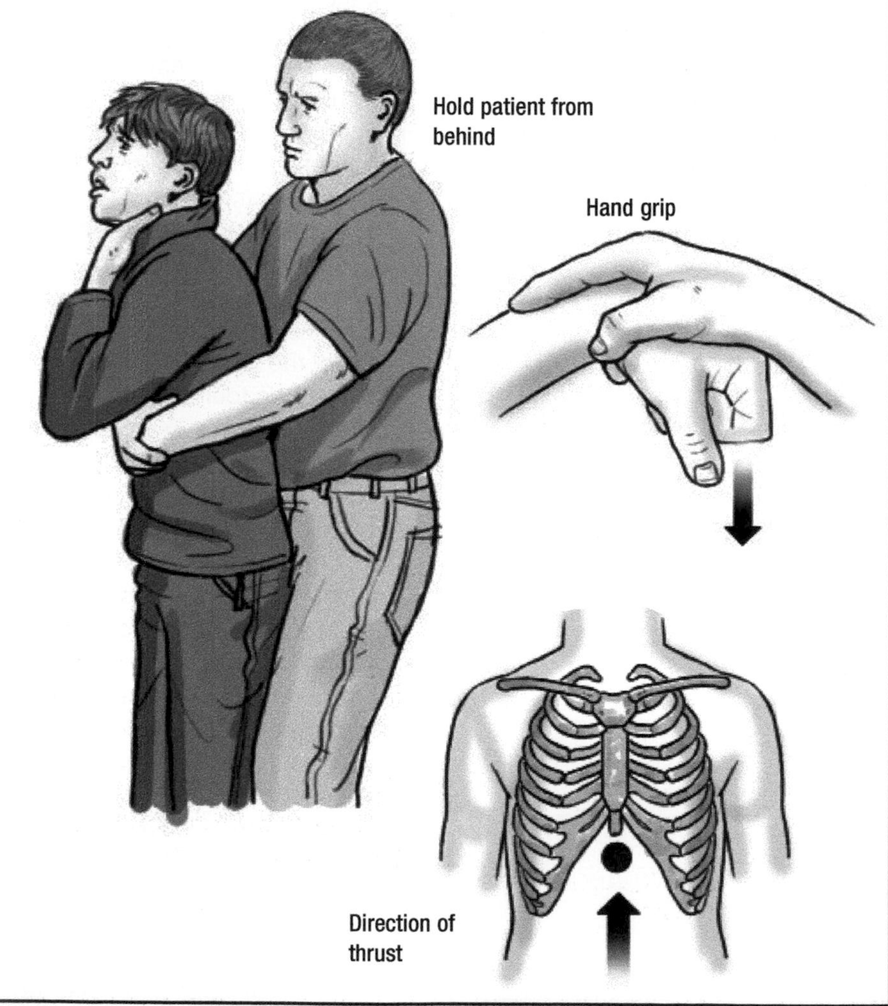

blood loss. An average-size adult can lose about 0.5 litres (0.9 pints) of blood with little danger, but loss of anything more than 1 litre (1.8 pints) of blood begins the process of sending the casualty into circulatory shock.

Controlling blood loss

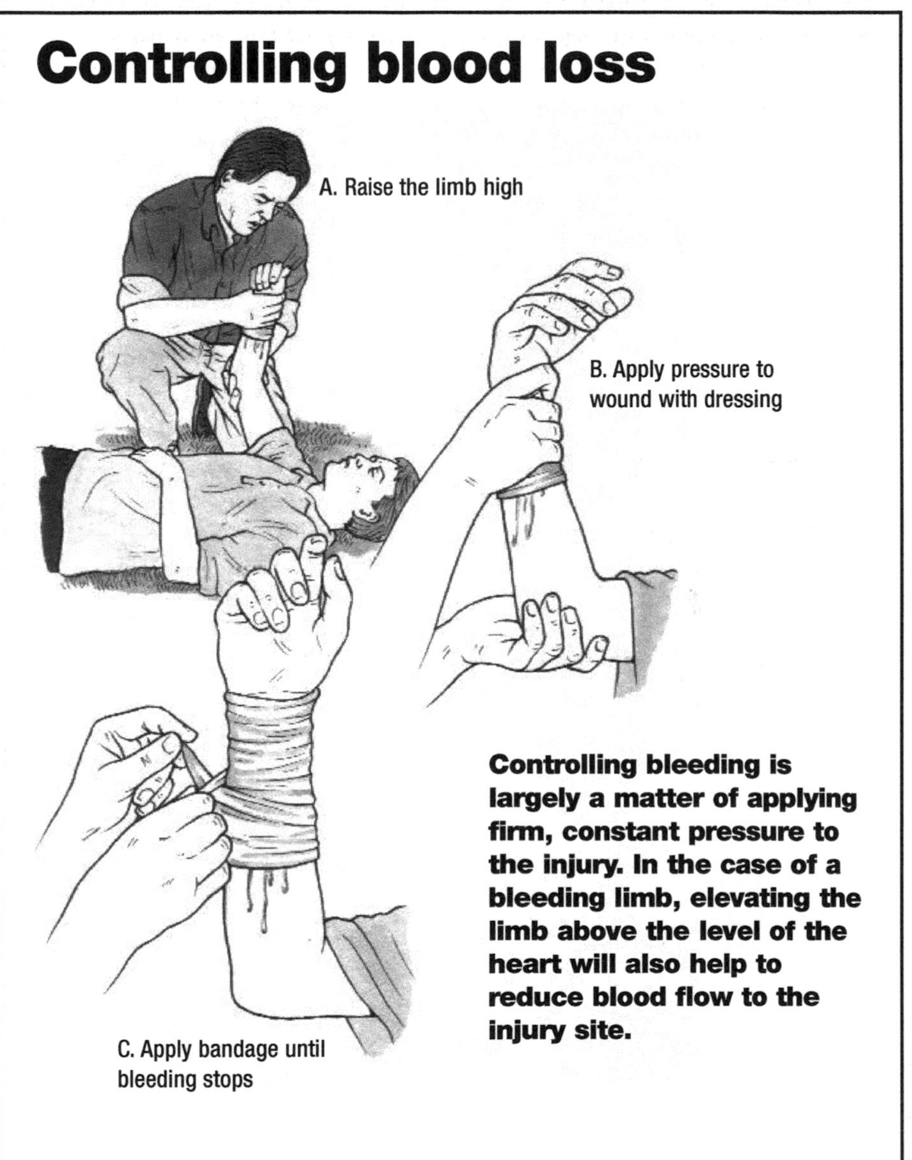

Controlling bleeding is largely a matter of applying firm, constant pressure to the injury. In the case of a bleeding limb, elevating the limb above the level of the heart will also help to reduce blood flow to the injury site.

Applying a roller bandage

Roller bandages are ideal for dressing injuries, although take great care that you don't cut off circulation to the limb by binding the bandage too tightly. Squeeze the fingernails – when you release them they should go pink again, indicating that the blood is still flowing to the extremities.

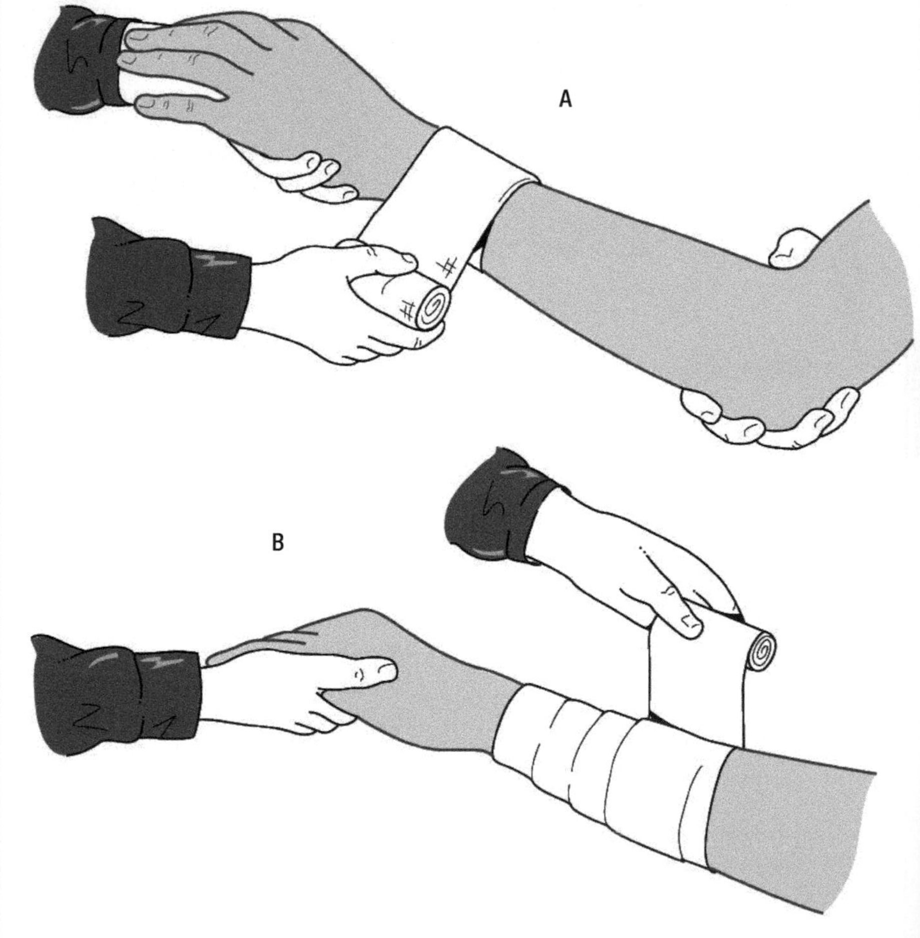

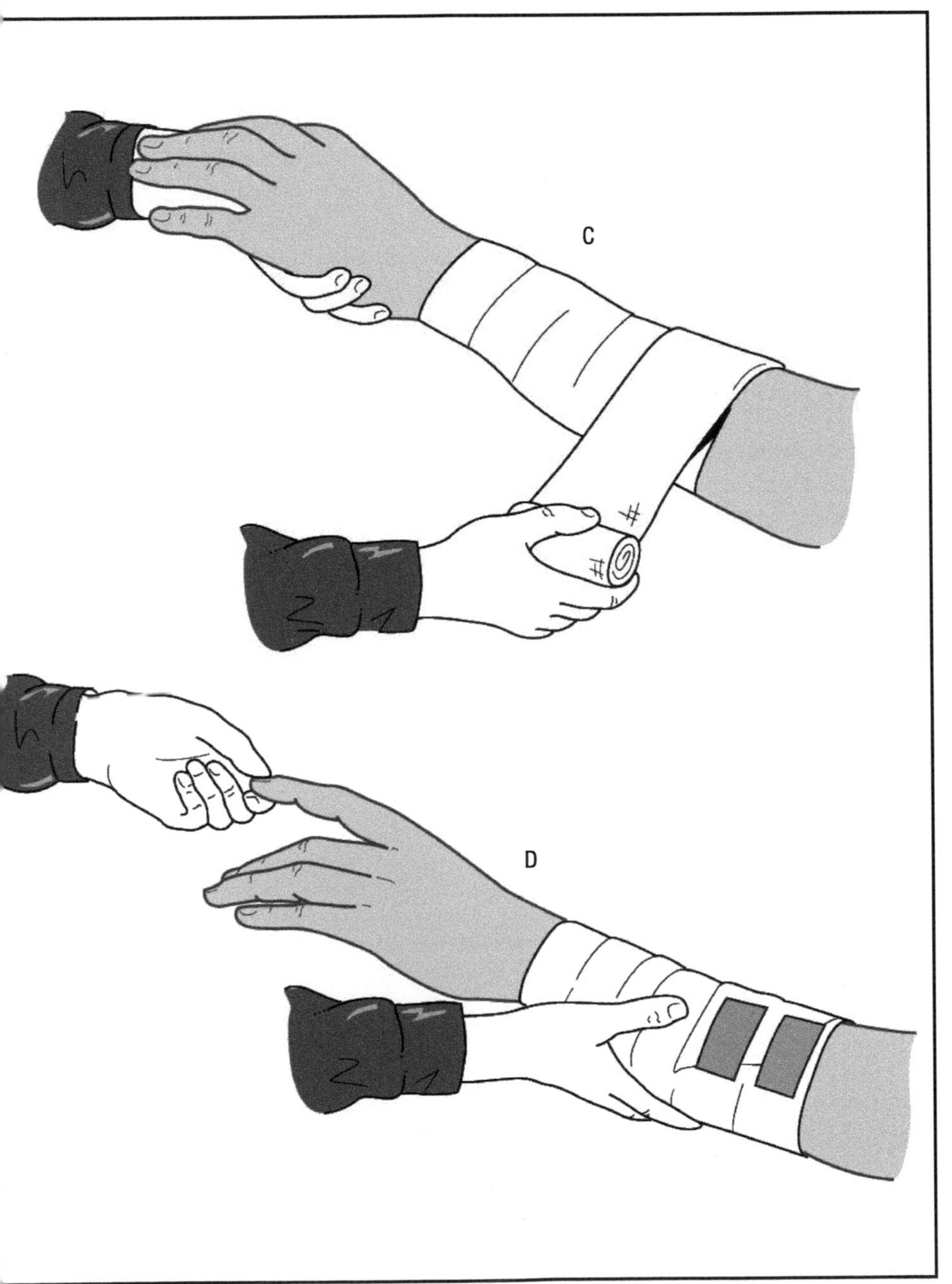
C
D

For this reason, bleeding needs to be controlled as quickly as possible.

To treat a localized bleeding injury, place a clean pad of material onto the wound, pressing down firmly. (If nothing else is available, use your hand to apply the pressure, but try to make sure it is clean to avoid giving the casualty blood poisoning.) Maintain the pressure, and don't remove the pad even if it becomes soaked in blood – leave it where it is and place another dressing on top of it. (Removing the pad can restart the bleeding.) By keeping pressure down on the wound, blood loss is reduced

Controlling bleeding by compression

Apply pressure to a bleeding injury directly downwards – don't push at an angle to the injury or you are likely to open it up further and make it worse. Maintain the pressure until blood is no longer soaking through the pad.

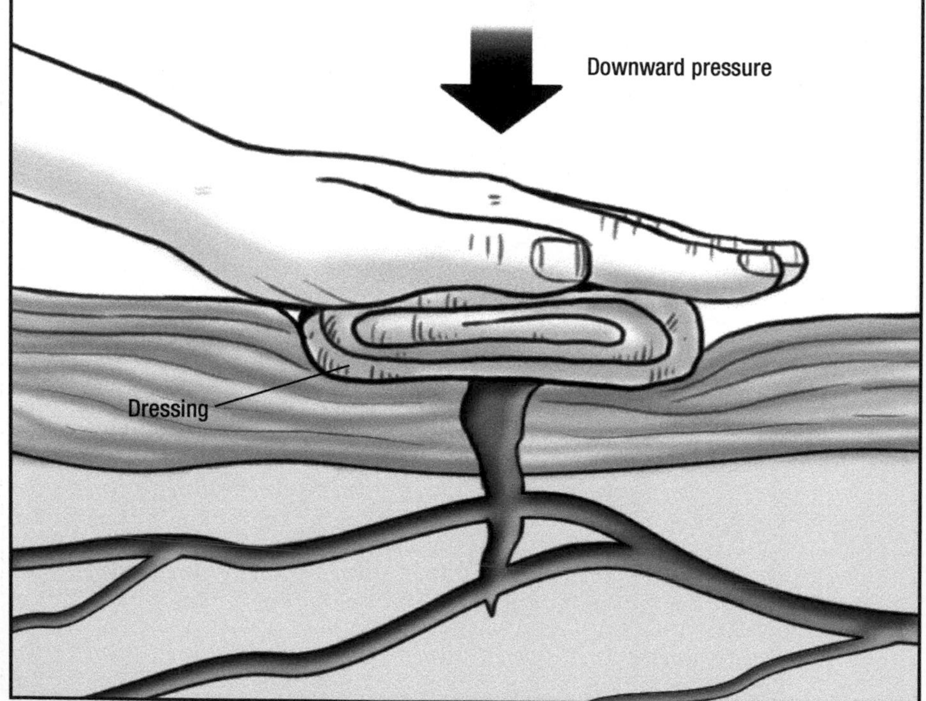

and eventually clotting occurs and the bleeding ceases.

Sometimes bleeding can be extremely severe, especially when an artery is severed (you will see bright red blood spurting into the air), and more drastic action is needed. If there is a real danger that the casualty is going to bleed to death quickly – such as occurs with the full amputation of a leg or arm – a tourniquet might be your last resort. Tourniquets are only of use to limb injuries – never apply them around a torso or, obviously, someone's neck. Yet even when applied appropriately, tourniquets can be dangerous to apply for two reasons. First, a

Tourniquets

Tourniquets can be extremely dangerous to the casualty, and should only be used if it looks like the casualty will bleed to death without drastic action. PROPER TRAINING IS ESSENTIAL IF YOU ARE TO USE TOURNIQUETS.

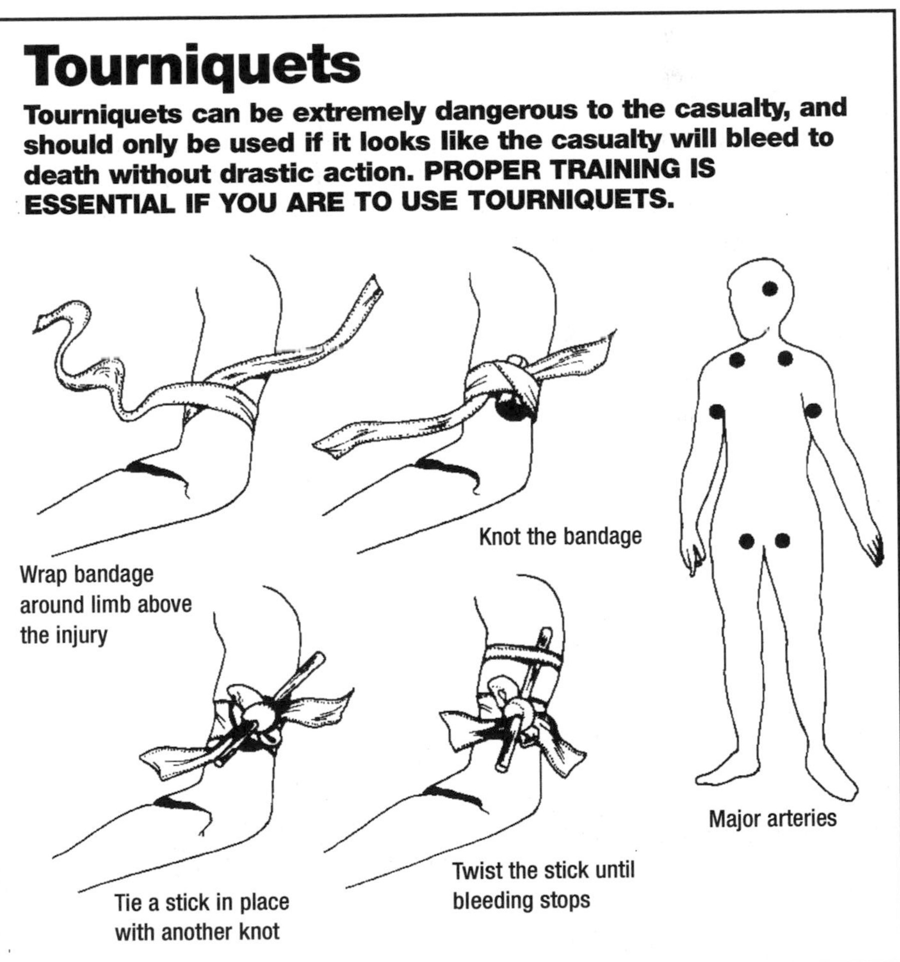

Stitching a wound

Stitching a wound is taught to special forces soldiers, but you should only attempt it if a) you have the skill; b) you have the right sterile equipment; and c) you can't get to a doctor or hospital for a long time.

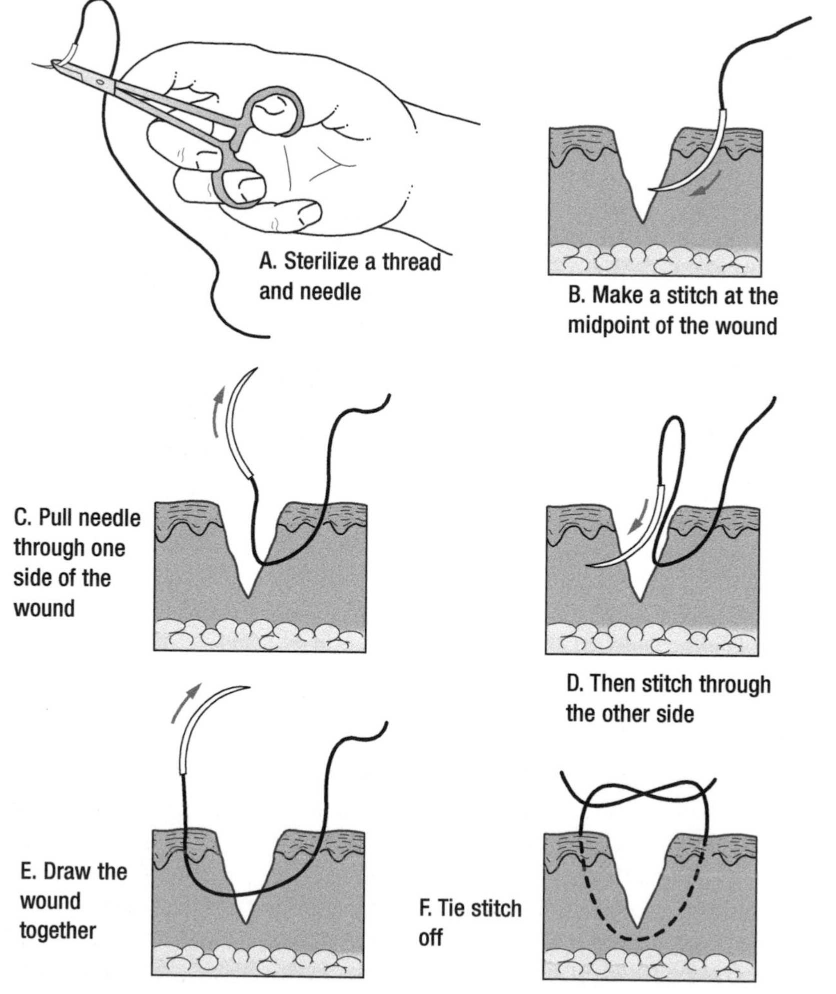

Arterial compression

Here the casualty is bleeding from a severe thigh injury. The first aider applies compression to the femoral artery to help reduce the blood flow to the injury. Only use this technique if direct pressure and elevation don't control the blood loss.

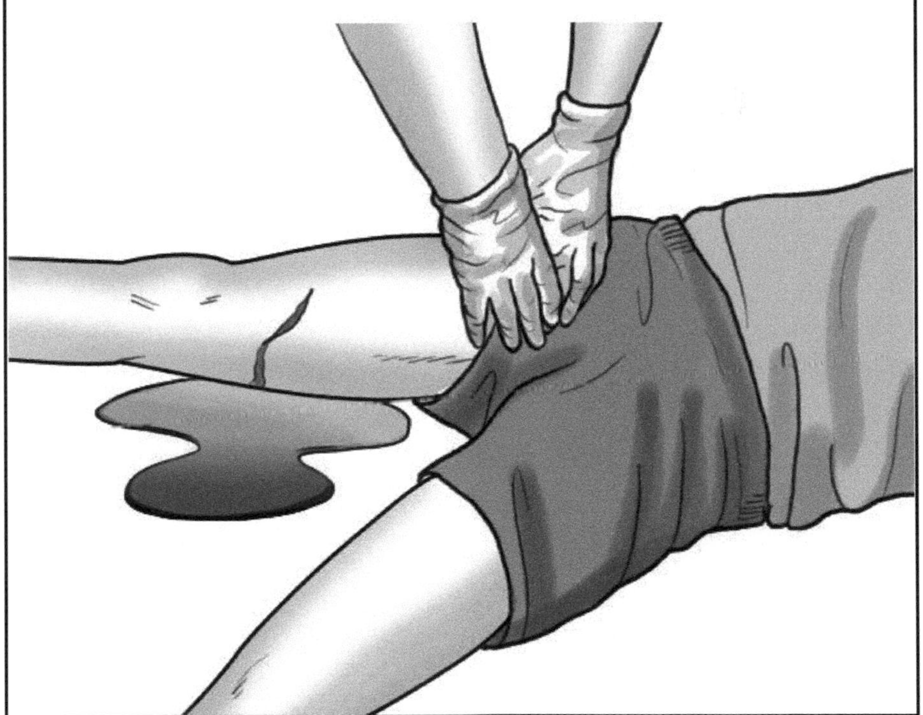

tourniquet works by cutting off blood flow to the limb below the wound, and this can result in tissue damage and the eventual loss of the limb. Second, if a tourniquet is kept on for a long period, when it is released, toxins that have built up in the injured limb flow into the blood stream where they can cause a potentially fatal systemic reaction. For this reason, always opt for the direct-pressure method first, which will be the best option in almost all cases. Furthermore, only use a tourniquet if you are confident you can reach professional medical assistance

TIP: Medium-term treatment of wounds

In dirty battlefield conditions, wounds present an ongoing danger through the risk of infection, even if the bleeding is stopped. In a survival situation, however, the following actions help to reduce this risk:

- Keep the wound clean and protected. Irrigate (don't rub or scrub) the wound with clean water, ideally containing some mild antibacterial soap. Note – only wash a wound once bleeding has been fully controlled.
- Gently pick out any foreign matter using tweezers. Again, do not do this if there is a danger of restarting the bleeding.
- Cover the wound with a sterile dressing (you can make your own by boiling improvised bandages for five minutes). Never reuse dirty dressings – clean them of matter then boil them for 15 minutes to sterilize them.
- Change the dressings every day.
- Signs of wound infection include: bad smells, discharges of pus, increased pain or heat at the wound site. In the case of infection, treat by wrapping hot rocks or boiled and mashed plant products in a cloth and applying to the injury site.

soon. (Author's note: The dangers of a tourniquet are such that you should only really attempt to use one after full first aid training – find a good local course near you.)

To make an emergency tourniquet, first take a piece of cloth about 5cm (2in) wide. Wrap the cloth several times around the limb, about 5cm (2in) above the site of the injury between the injury and the heart. Tie the two ends of the cloth together in a knot. Place a stick on top of the knot and then tie a double knot over the top of the stick. Now twist the tourniquet around and around, tightening the cloth until the bleeding stops. Once the bleeding has stopped, apply dressings to the wound to encourage clotting. If rapid medical assistance isn't available, you should release the pressure every 10 minutes to see if the bleeding has stopped and to save the limb.

Injuries caused by heavy impacts to the torso or thighs, particularly falls, can result in a special type of injury – internal bleeding. Internal bleeding is usually treated in hospital with surgery, which is beyond the realms of first aid. All you can do is treat the patient for shock, as described above, and try to get them to help as quickly as possible. For reference, the signs of internal bleeding can be:

- Faintness.
- Pale, cold, and clammy skin.
- Blood in the urine or stool (the stool will have a black, tarry appearance).
- Vomiting or coughing up blood.
- Symptoms of circulatory shock (see above).

BURN INJURIES

In a survival situation, burns typically come from accidents while making or

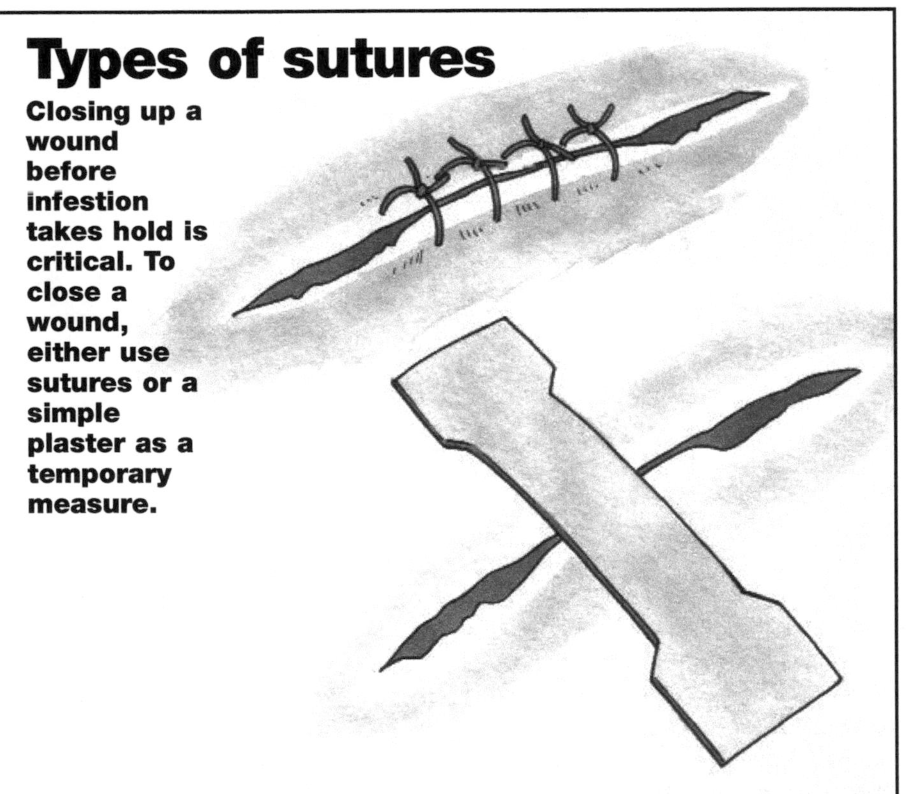

Types of sutures

Closing up a wound before infestion takes hold is critical. To close a wound, either use sutures or a simple plaster as a temporary measure.

Treating burns

To avoid continued tissue damage, apply cool water to a burn as soon as possible. Keep applying water for at least 10 minutes.

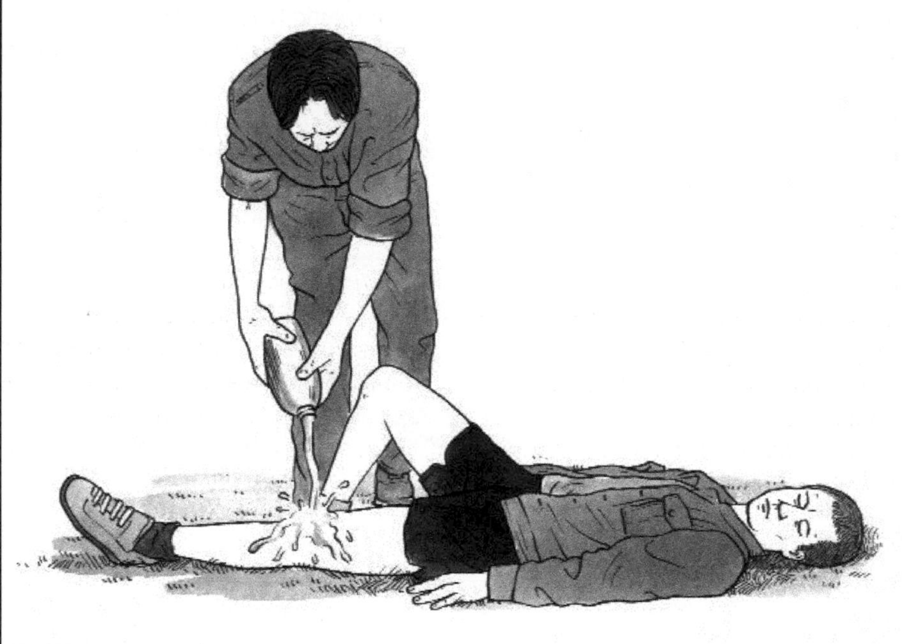

using campfires, or more rarely from forest fires. There are several other possibilities, however. Friction burns, for example, can occur when ropes run quickly through bare hands or between thighs, and are therefore a particularly common mountaineering accident. A far more common burn injury is sunburn, which in its extreme forms needs to be taken as seriously as other types of burn.

In the medical profession, burns are graded according to three degrees of severity:

- **First degree** – Only involves the outermost layer of skin. Minor, non-serious injuries.
- **Second degree** – Penetrates the second layer of skin, producing a red, blistered surface, which is intensely painful.
- **Third degree** – Destroys deep

tissues, even reaching the bones. Third-degree burns can produce horrifying open wounds that are charred black.

Severe burns are dangerous on many different levels. Not only do they destroy body tissue, they are also prone to infection and to inducing shock in the victim through loss of body fluids. Furthermore, the degree of burn can also be exacerbated by the percentage of the patient's body surface that has sustained injury. For example, a second-degree burn to a patient's entire front torso and legs will present a far more serious threat than a third-degree burn to a single finger.

The priority in treating burns is to cool the burn immediately. Even if the burn accident lasts less then a second – such as when touching a scalding-hot pan – the heat from the burn will continue to work into the tissue long after, inflicting more damage.

Treatment

A good first response, therefore, is to submerge or drench the wound in cold water for around 10 minutes. Note that if clothing has stuck to the burn, simply soak the clothing – do not attempt to pull it off the burn immediately, as this usually does nothing but pull off skin and increase the severity of later scarring.

Once the burn has been cooled down, usually indicated by no significant increase in pain when the injury is removed from the water, dress the wound with a sterile dressing. Do not put anything on the wound, including ointments. The old advice about applying butter or lard to a burn is actually dangerous to the patient. Change the dressing frequently, and clean the wound with water. Give the casualty plenty to drink to replace lost fluids, but reduce the intake if the urine output becomes unusually high. Watch out for signs of shock developing.

FRACTURES

Broken-bone injuries come in two types. An 'open' fracture occurs when the end of a broken bone pierces the skin, creating a bleeding wound. In a 'closed' fracture, the bone is broken but stays inside the flesh.

The symptoms of a broken bone are fairly clear:

- There is an audible sound of a bone breaking.
- The casualty feels the bone snap.
- There is a severe pain, followed by an acute tenderness around the injury site.
- A limb or joint may be noticeably deformed, and will have a partial or complete loss of movement.
- There may be a grating sound or sensation produced by the broken ends of the bone rubbing together.
- Muscles around the injury site may go into spasm.

Bone fractures

Bone fractures come in many different forms. Greenstick fractures tend to occur in young people, who have more flexible bones, while comminuted fractures are common in the elderly or as the result of a massive impact on the bone.

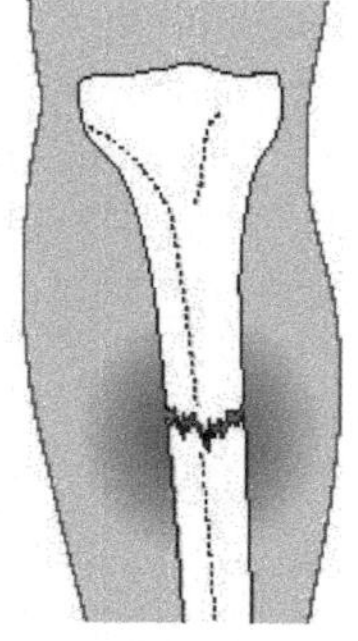

Simple fracture

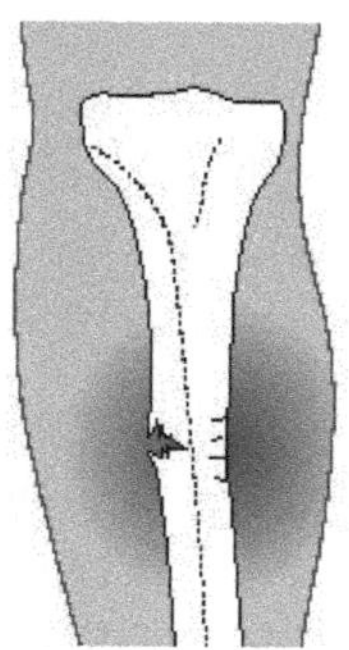

Greenstick fracture

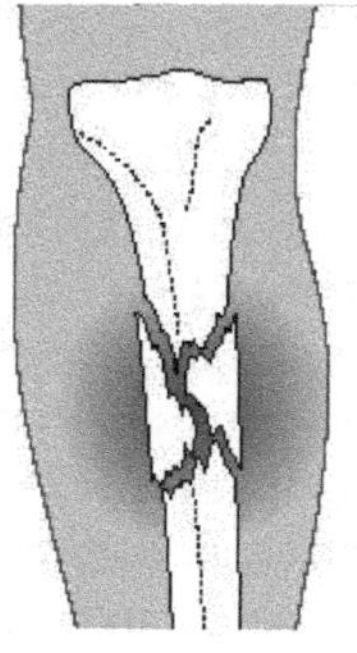

Comminuted fracture

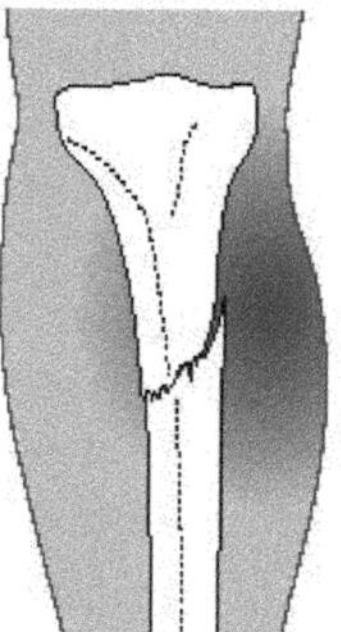

Closed fracture

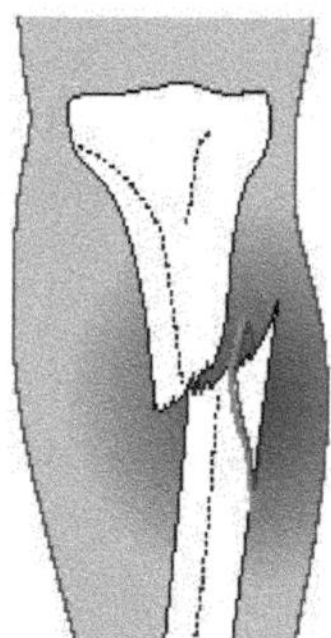

Open fracture

Open fractures require careful treatment, as you need both to stop the bleeding and prevent subsequent movement of the bone. To stop the bleeding, follow the guidelines described above, but apply pressure around the exposed bones, not directly on top of them. Use tweezers to clean out any fragments of bone from the wound.

Fractures of both types can press against nerves and blood vessels, resulting – if left untreated – in nerve or circulatory damage that in extreme cases can result in the eventual loss of limbs. In the case of limb fractures, check for circulatory damage by looking for a pulse at the wrist (in the case of an arm break) or see if the extremities are unusually cold or have gone pink or blue (although there are other conditions that could account for these). Pinch the toe or fingernails hard, then release them and see if they go pink again, which would indicate that blood flow is still functioning. Check for nerve damage by pinching or scratching the toe or hand. If the casualty can feel this, nerve impulses are operating.

TIP: Sprains

Sprains are a common complaint among soldiers in training. Treat as follows:

- Put a cold compress on the sprain area to reduce swelling.
- Bandage the injured area and elevate the affected limb.
- Give the injured limb complete rest.
- If you sprain an ankle but have to keep walking, keep your boot on to brace the injury and to help reduce swelling.

Realigning bones

Circulatory or nerve problems should really only be treated by medical professionals. If you are confident that you can reach assistance quickly, simply stabilize the injury with bandages and splints and get to help as swiftly as possible. Yet if professional treatment is not likely for some time, you should try to release pressure on nerves and blood vessels by realigning the bones into their natural configuration via traction. (Do not apply traction to fractures directly on joints. These are best protected by being placed and supported in the midpoint of their normal range of movement.)

To perform traction, have the casualty lie down and try to relax the muscles in the affected area. Pull gently but firmly on the broken limb, drawing it outwards, then angling it back towards the original line of the bone. This process can take around 10–15 minutes, as you are drawing against the resistance of the muscle, and you may have to obtain extra leverage by placing the casualty against a tree or other stable feature against which you

R.I.C.E.

Rest, Ice, Compression, Elevation – R.I.C.E. – is an easily memorable sequence for treating sprained joints. The last three stages of the sequence all work to reduce the blood flow to the injury, and hence alleviate swelling.

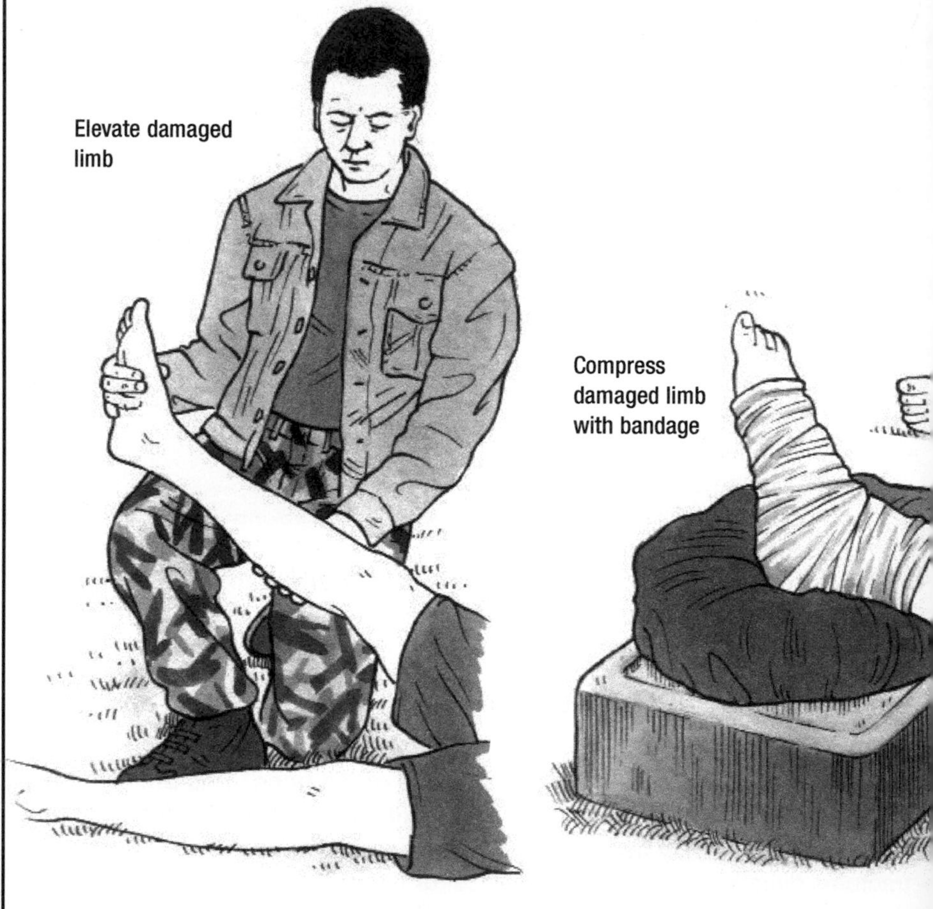

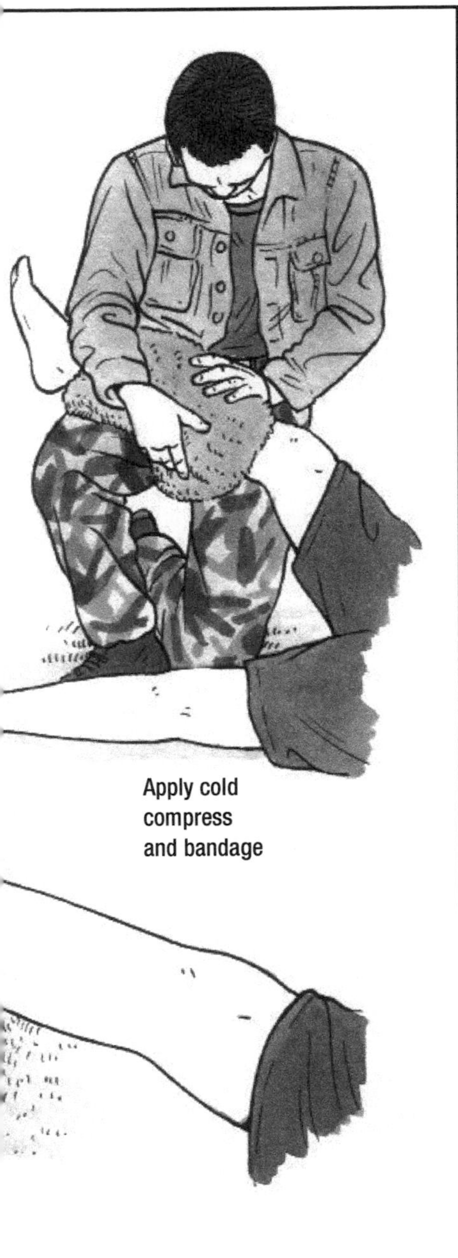
Apply cold compress and bandage

can push while performing the traction. For open fractures, clean the exposed bone and wound first before applying traction, and take care that you don't trap any skin as the bone is moved back under the flesh.

When the traction has been performed properly, the broken limb should be in a natural alignment and nerve signals and blood flow should be restored. You should now splint the injury to prevent its moving.

Splinting

Splinting essentially means setting the limb in a rigid position using an external brace. Straight, strong sticks and branches, walking or ski poles or even rolled-up newspapers can all be used for splints, just so long as they are long enough to reach significantly above and below the fracture site.

For an injured limb, use two splints, one on each side, tying the limb and splints together at four points, two above and two below the fracture. Place thick padding between the splint and bony or uncomfortable parts of the injured limb.

For additional stability, you can tie the injured and splinted limb to an uninjured part of the body, such as a wounded leg to its healthy counterpart. After tying on the splint, check the circulation and nerve impulses in the extremities to ensure that the bandages are not too tight.

Arm bandage

This simple triangular bandage will keep a fractured arm or damaged elbow stable while moving around. You can add a cross bandage around the torso, main bandage and upper arm to provide extra stability if required.

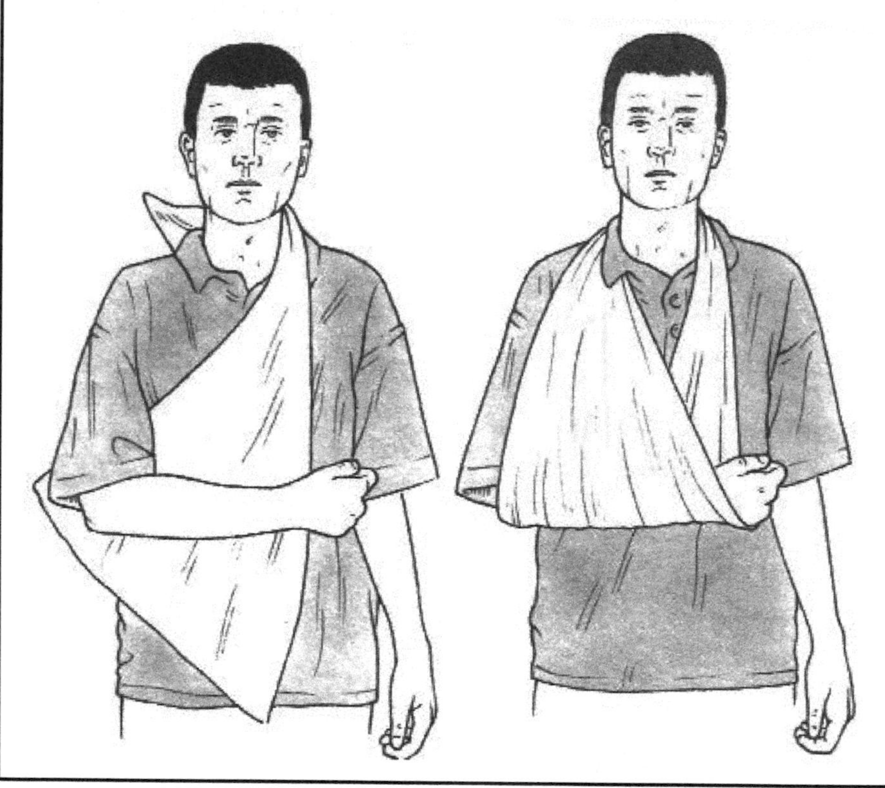

DISLOCATIONS

Dislocations in many ways present similar challenges to fractures. They occur when a joint is wrenched out of its normal alignment, most commonly a shoulder or hip joint having the 'ball' of the humerus or femur pulled out of the socket. Typically, such injuries occur from a heavy impact or jolt, often as the result of a fall. Dislocations can be serious injuries. Not only are they excruciatingly painful, but like fractures they can also trap nerves

Splinting an arm and leg

Splints can be improvised by using bandages and any rigid materials. Note, however, that professional splint tape can be purchased from medical suppliers. This is made from padded aluminium alloy, and is cut to shape to make a supportive frame or binding around the fracture.

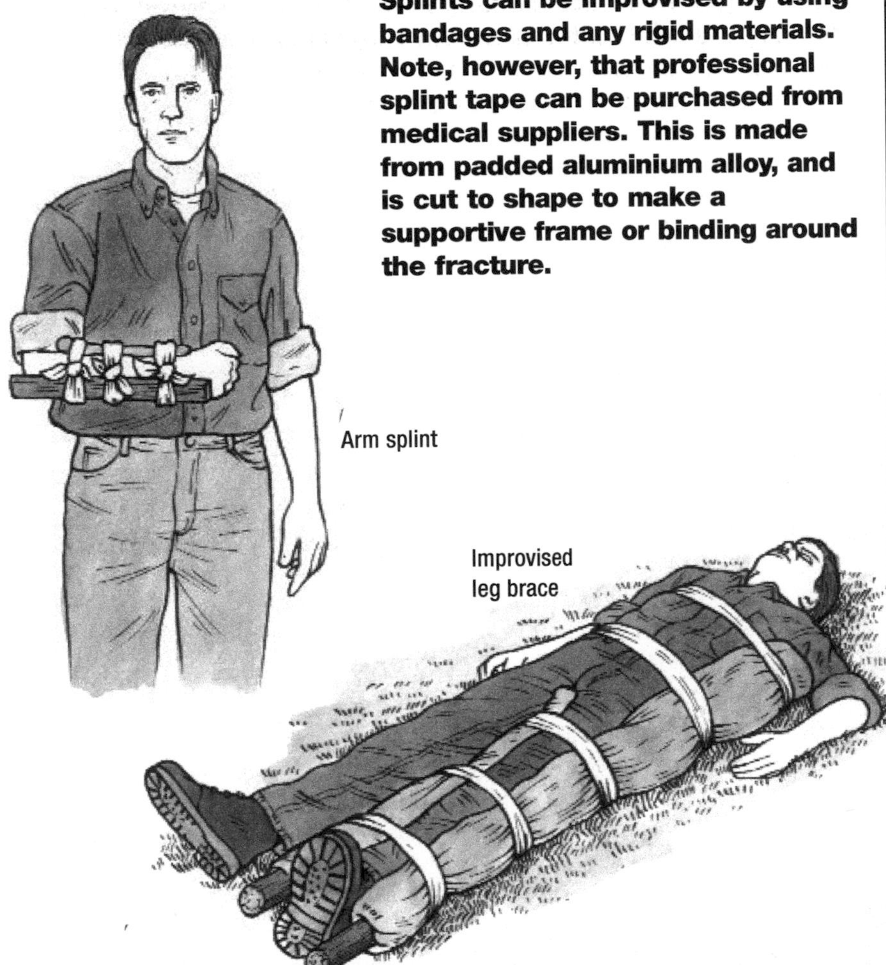

and blood vessels, and thereby do longer-term damage, including developing gangrene or a deformity.

In almost all cases of dislocations, your primary treatment should be to splint and stabilize the injury and get the casualty to a hospital. If professional medical help won't be available for the immediate future, however, your first objective should be to relocate the joint through traction. Important: traction is a difficult and technical skill, and not one to be attempted lightly. As with realigning fractures, only attempt it if there is no possibility of medical help within a long period, such as more than 24 hours, and if you have attended a professional training course in these techniques. Also, only apply traction if you are 100 per cent sure that you are dealing with a dislocation.

The skin, particularly in the case of the shoulder, may show unusual contours from the displaced bones; the joint will be very painful and unable to move; and there will probably be swelling and discoloration.

Traction

Traction the joints slowly but with force, pulling the limb outwards smoothly and progressively until you can lower the joint back into its normal configuration. Repeat this until the joint is stable and nerve function and circulation is confirmed. To aid recovery after relocation, apply cold packs to the injured joint, then bandage the joint into a stable position, but still take the casualty to a hospital as soon as possible.

SPINAL INJURIES

Spinal injuries are well beyond any treatment that a first aider can deliver. The best that can be done is to stabilize the injury and bring medical help to the casualty as fast as possible. Such injuries tend to occur either from heavy impacts or from the spine being twisted or wrenched suddenly. Symptoms can include the following:

- Chronic pain in the back regardless of movement.
- A noticeably deformed spinal column.
- Heavy bruising or other injury over the spinal area.
- Extreme tenderness over the spine.
- Loss of bladder control; in men the penis may be persistently erect.
- A tingling or numb sensation in the limbs.
- Paralysis, or a lack of response to stimulus (try scratching the palms of the hands or the soles of the feet and ask if the casualty can feel it).

The priority for the first aider is to keep the casualty immobile – any movement can worsen the injury, potentially with lethal consequences. Stabilize the casualty's neck by improvising a collar out of something like a towel or magazine. Bend it around the neck, but do not move the head while doing this, nor restrict the casualty's throat.

If the casualty is on their back, place a rolled-up blanket, boots or anything else you can find around the sides of the head and neck to stop

Aligning a broken leg

Aligning a broken leg serves to release the pressure of broken bones on nerves and blood vessels, but should only be attempted if professional medical help will not be forthcoming, or if you need to splint the leg in a stable position.

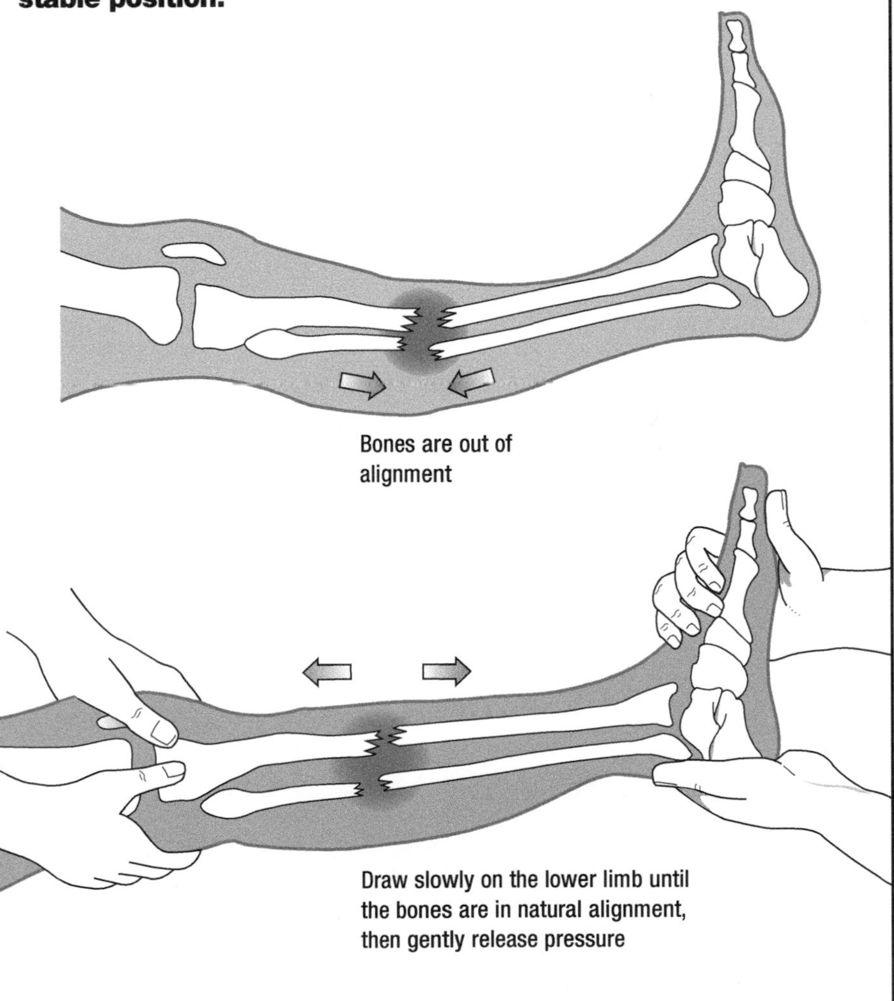

Neck brace

Apply a neck brace to any casualty suspected of having a spinal or neck injury (and, of course, if medical help isn't forthcoming). The brace should prevent lateral and forward movement, but must not apply any pressure to the throat or the arteries in the neck.

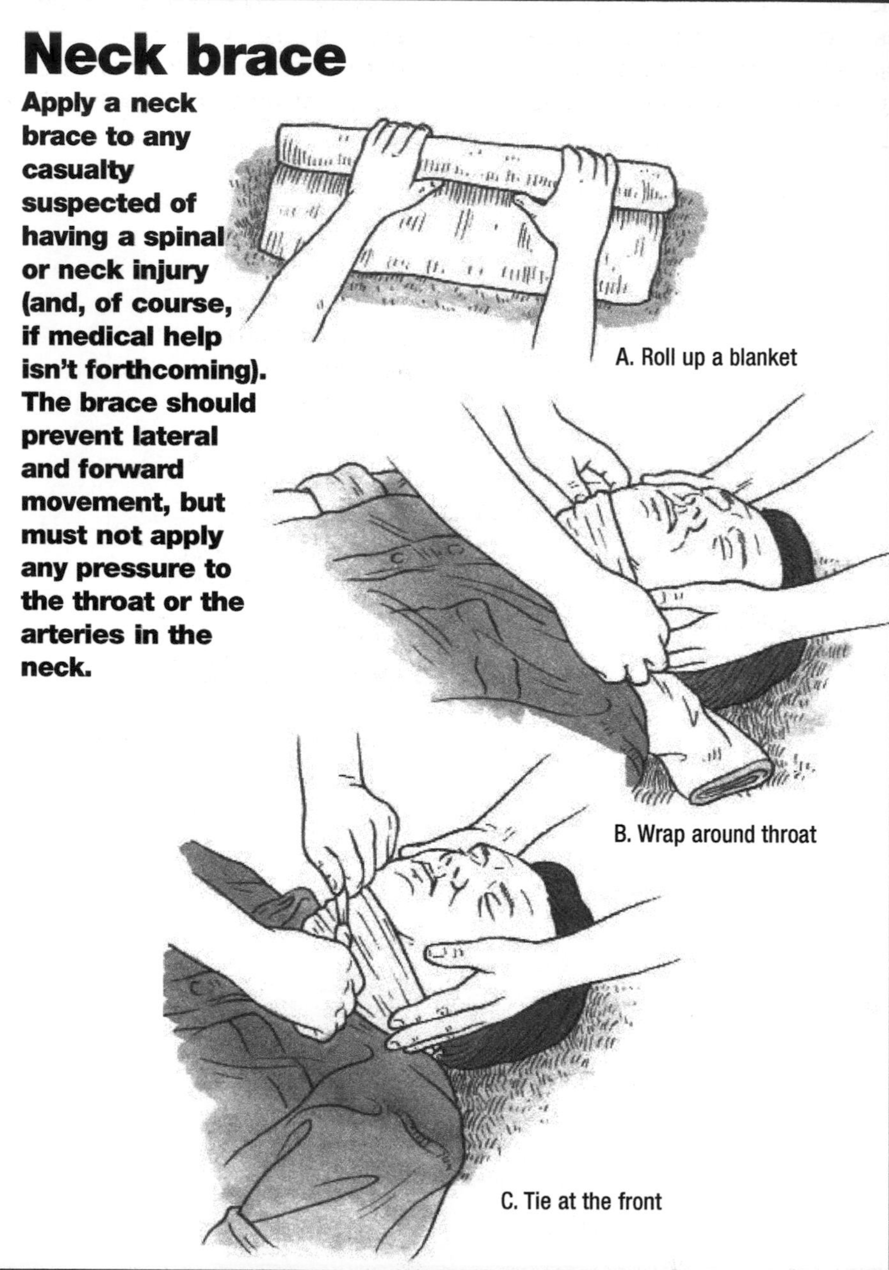

A. Roll up a blanket

B. Wrap around throat

C. Tie at the front

sideways movement. Check the casualty's breathing and heartbeat regularly – both can be affected by spinal injuries – and be prepared to deliver CPR if necessary. In some instances, there is no choice but to move the casualty. This procedure isn't recommended, but if there is a

Lifting a casualty

Here is a method of lifting a casualty by using a rolled-up blanket. If the casualty has a suspected spinal injury, keep their posture straight throughout the procedure.

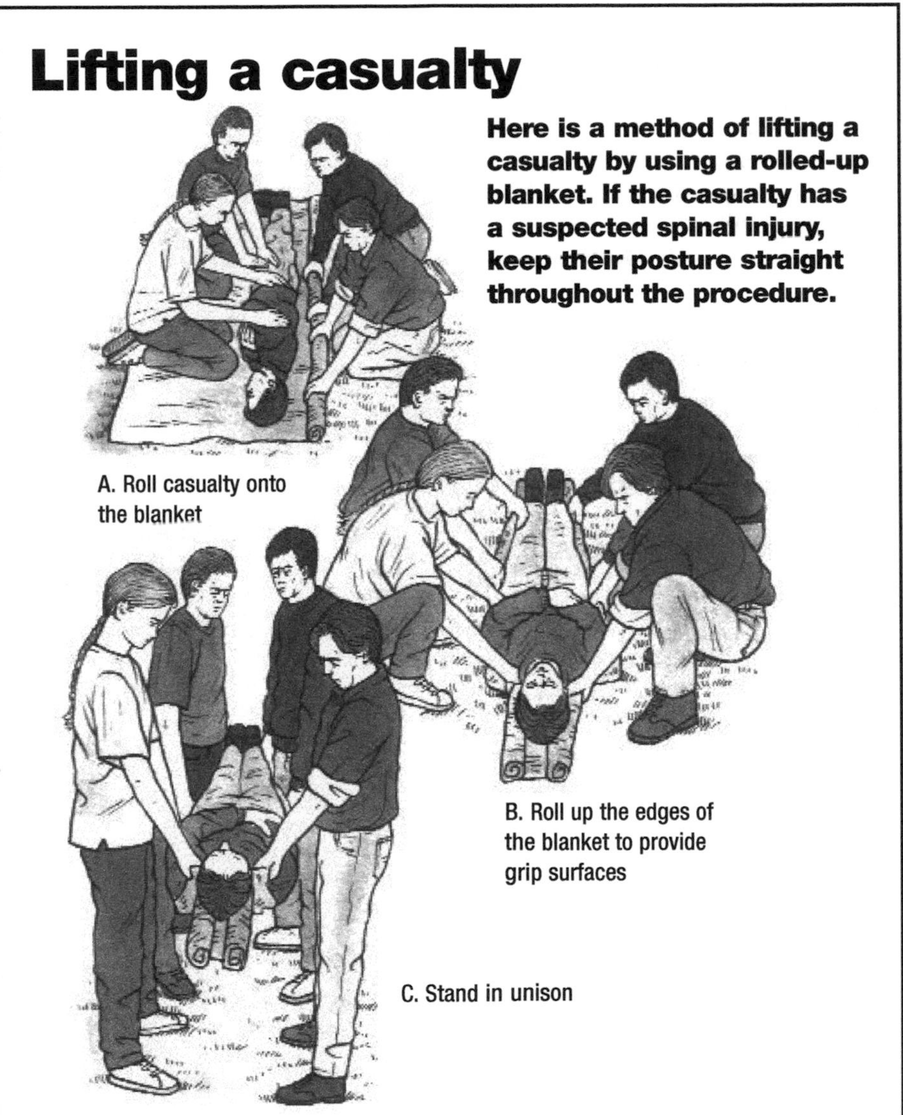

A. Roll casualty onto the blanket

B. Roll up the edges of the blanket to provide grip surfaces

C. Stand in unison

continuing risk from, say, rockfall or avalanche, then there is no choice. You can only attempt this if there are multiple helpers, ideally five people in total, to position themselves along the length of the casualty's body and slowly lift them onto a rigid litter or board. One person should have

Fireman's carry

This classic lift technique, much used by soldiers, is useful if you have to move a casualty quickly from continuing danger. It is obviously not suitable for spinal-injury casualties.

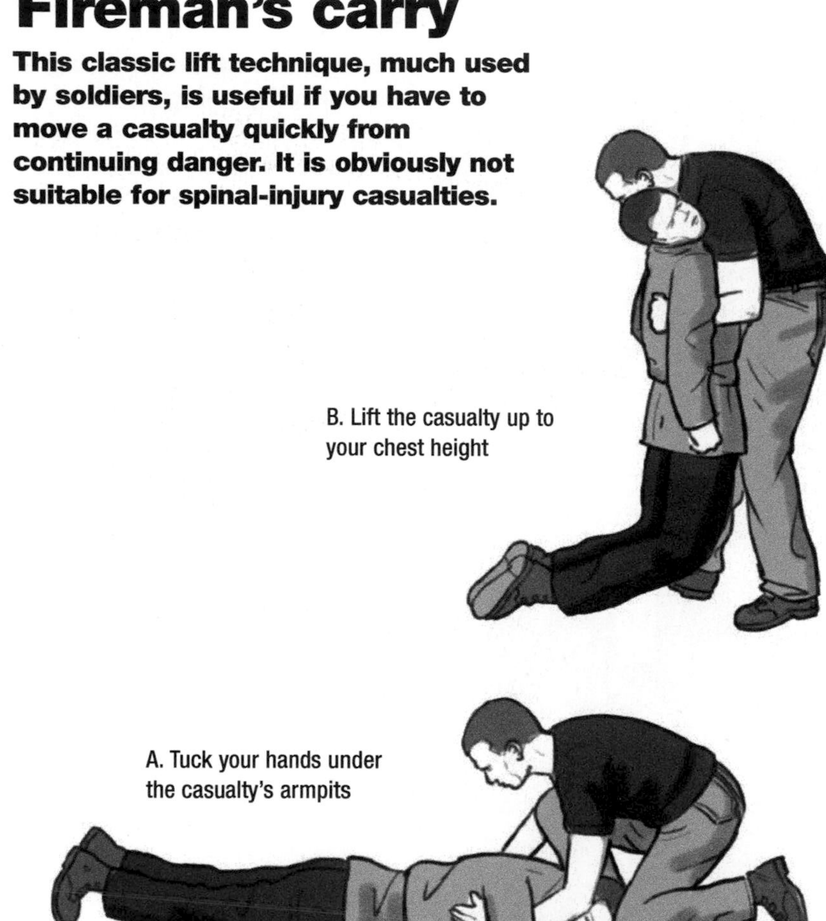

B. Lift the casualty up to your chest height

A. Tuck your hands under the casualty's armpits

the dedicated job of keeping the head facing forward and naturally aligned with the shoulders. If the head is not in this position before movement, place your hands firmly over the casualty's ears and turn the head very slowly to the front without any jerking movements.

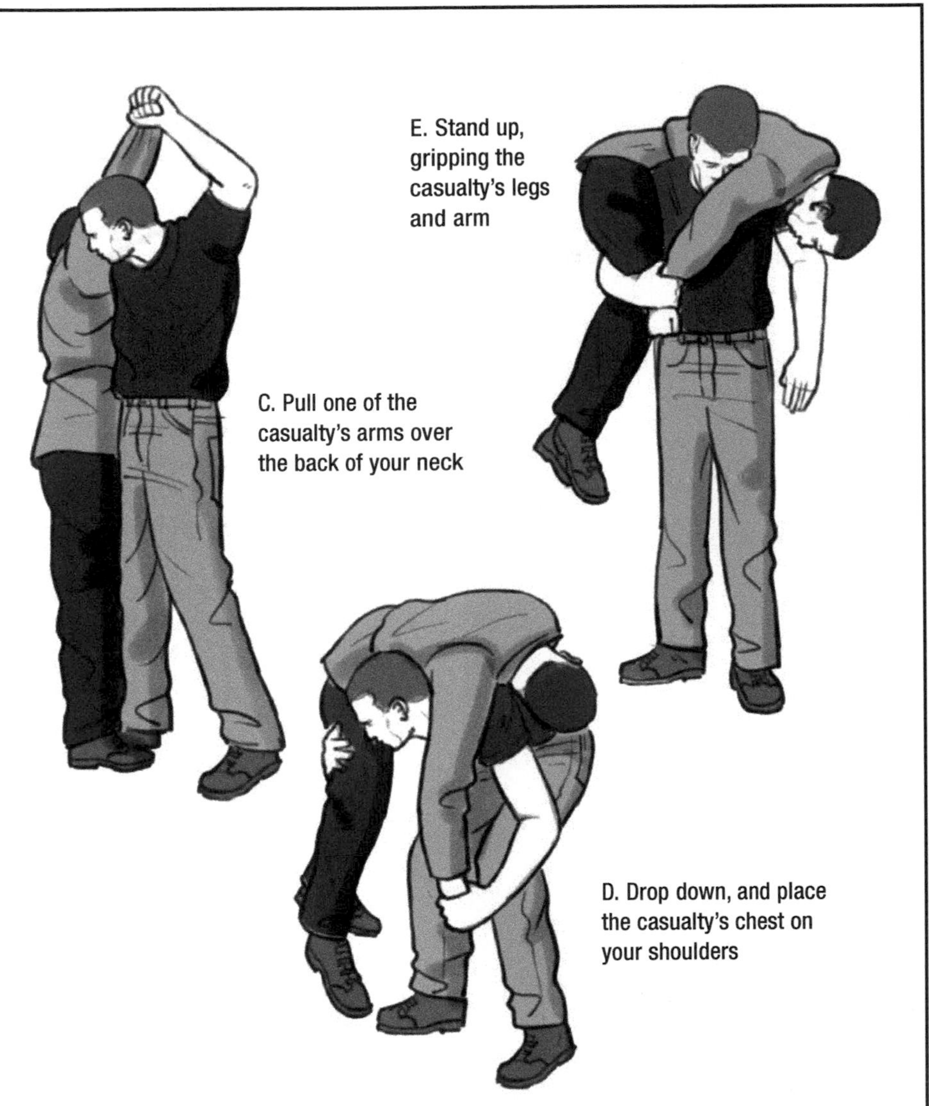

Visual mapping

Utilize high vantage points to make a visual map of the terrain that you are about to cross. Note salient features of the landscape and their relationship to one another, and if possible make a sketch of the terrain to guide your subsequent movements.

Herringbone step

The herringbone step – in which the feet are turned distinctly outwards – is useful for making an ascent of steep slopes, particularly if they consist of loose or frangible material.

Aiming off

When returning to camp, the hiker deliberately set a compass course that would lead him to the river upstream of his tent, even if he made an error of up to five degrees in following the compass course. By 'aiming off' in this manner, he could be sure of which way to turn when he reached the river.

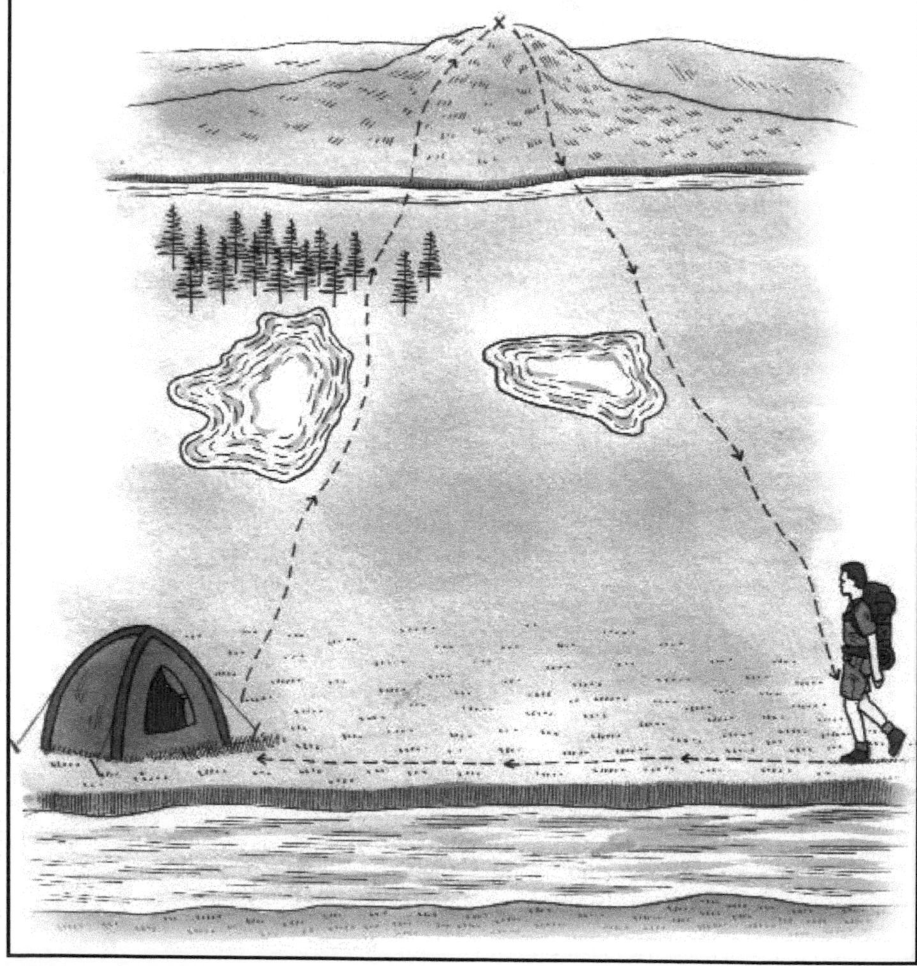

ascend it using a traversing pattern – a zig-zag movement up the slope that allows the legs to avoid the full stress of the incline. When descending similar slopes, keep your back straight, knees bent and your weight centred, and again adopt a traverse route if a direct descent feels uncontrollable or stressful.

Walking poles

Walking poles can relieve tons of pressure on the legs for every hour walked. They can, however, increase strain on wrists, arms and shoulders, so only use them as your body dictates.

Climbing cam

Spring-loaded climbing cams can be inserted into cracks in rocks. Once downward pressure is applied to the cam, from attached ropes, the cams are forced outwards to grip the rock, and provide a stable anchor.

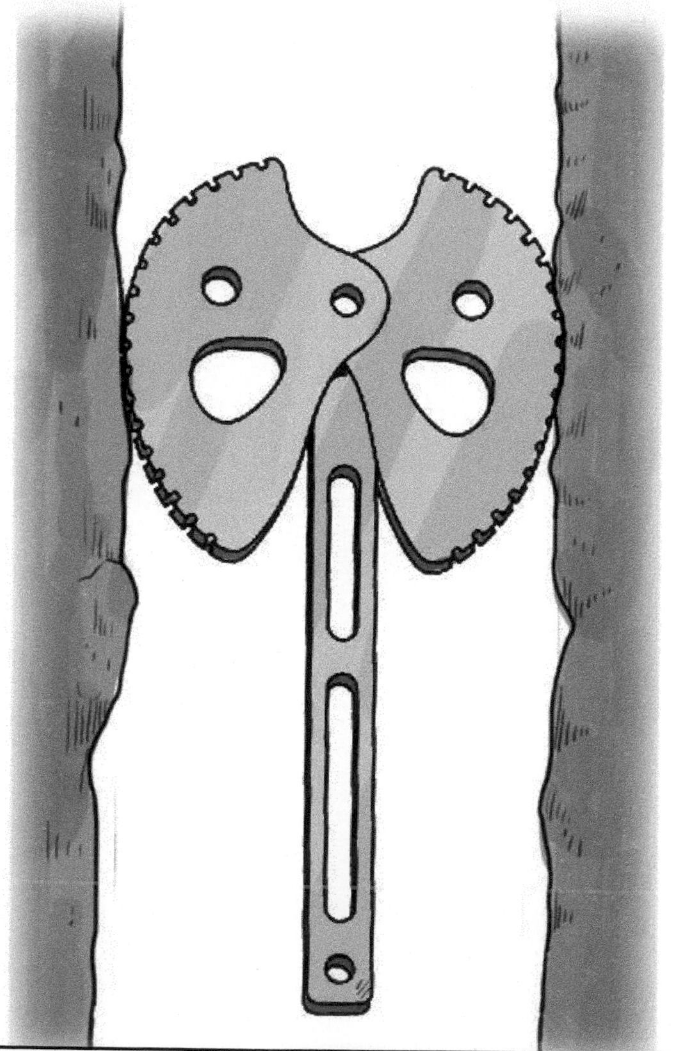

Belaying

Belaying is a way of climbing for two or more people using ropes. The belayer (the person who feeds out the rope) should be firmly anchored to a solid structure and must lay the rope out to run freely through the braking knot.

When negotiating rocky slopes, step with care so that you don't dislodge large rocks or inadvertently start a rockfall or landslide. Always step on top of and on the uphill side of each rock; if you slip, the rock might brace your foot and arrest your slide. For ascending scree slopes, kick in with the toes to gain purchase. When descending, walk

Abseiling

When abseiling, make sure you lean out from the rockface at a 45-degree angle and keep the legs spread about shoulder width apart for stability. Brake by leaning back and facing straight into the rockface.

down the slope with your feet in a slightly pigeon-toed position.

Waterways

Streams and rivers are practical obstacles in almost all wilderness environments, not just mountains. If at any point you need to cross a waterway, first choose an entry point away from rapid, rocky or deep waters, and a place where the current is at its least threatening.

Crossing a river

Using a looped rope as a lifeline in case the man in the water stumbles, this three-man team makes a safe river crossing.

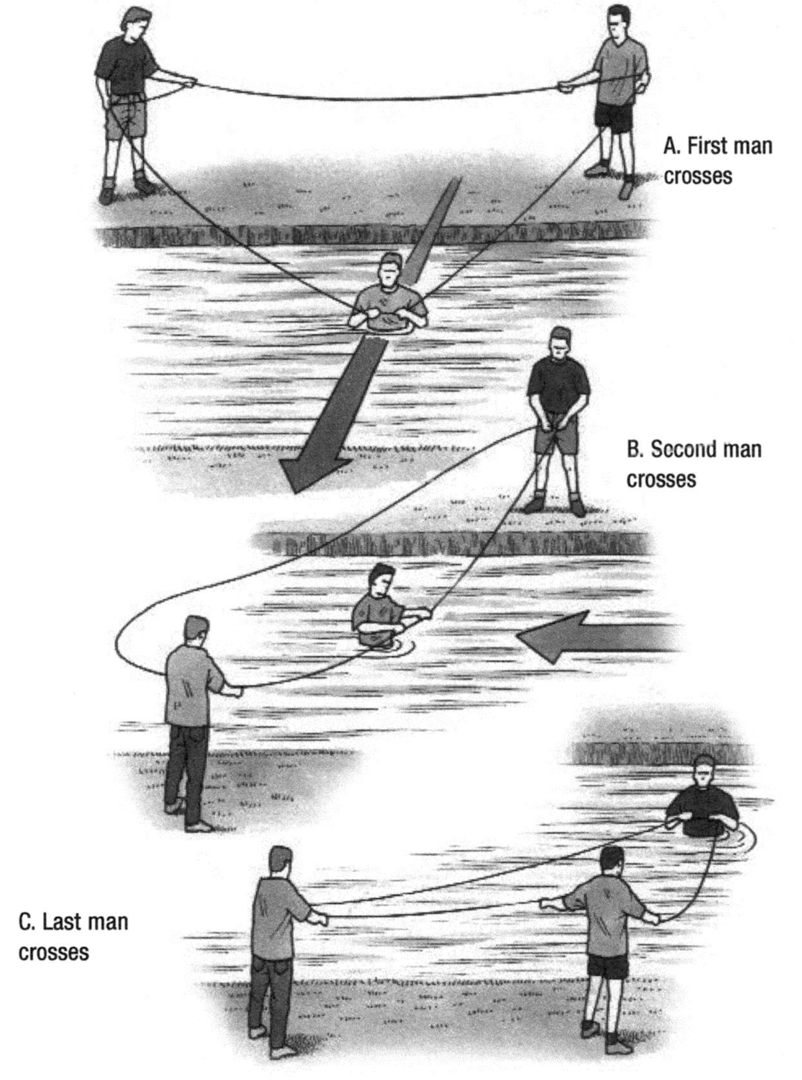

Log raft

Log rafts are a good means of travel down relatively calm rivers with manageable currents. Note here how the cross-members sit in grooves cut into the main platform logs, and are squeezed by a self-tightening knot.

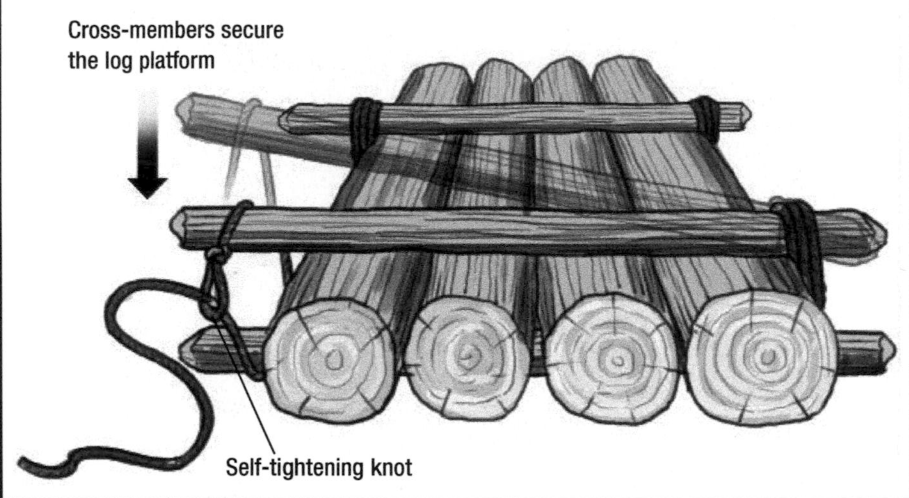

Look across to the opposite bank – make sure that it is solid, free from large patches of sucking mud or dense foliage, and shallow enough for you to climb out.

If crossing a river on your own, you should move at a 45-degree angle to the current, to lessen its impact, so pick your exit point accordingly. Take a thick stick with you into the water, one longer than you are tall, to use as a brace against the riverbed. Position the stick upstream of your body – as well as providing extra stability, it will also help break the current's impact against your body.

Never cross a river with a pack strapped to your back – it will make movement more difficult and could drag you down like a stone if you fall at any point. If necessary, make a small raft of sticks and float the backpack across. (See illustration on page 271 for techniques for crossing a river if there are two or more of you.)

Riverbed routes

Rivers – even dry rivers like the one here – are good paths to follow, as human habitation is likely to occur along the banks. If the going on the bank is too hard, follow roughly parallel to the river at a distance.

TIP: Rules for crossing glaciers

Glaciers are expansive rivers or sheets of ice that move across a mountain or through a valley. They are dangerous geological features, with brittle and weak surfaces, crevasses, and glacial streams running just beneath the ice. The streams may run on the surface, creating a lethal and almost frictionless surface. Moraines (accumulations of rocky debris) are also dangerous, the material being loose and difficult to cross. When crossing a glacier, therefore, observe the following rules practised by mountain troops:

- All group members should be roped together and walking in single file, stepping in the leader's footsteps.
- Early-morning crossings are best – higher temperatures later in the day will turn more ice to meltwater.
- In especially icy conditions, or if a glacier is heavily crevassed, lateral and medial moraines can provide the best routes of travel, particularly if composed of larger blocks of stone.
- Exercise extreme care when crossing a glacial surface stream because the bed and undercut banks are usually made up of hard, smooth ice that offers no secure footing.
- Watch out for areas where the glacier gets steeper or bends, as these are often unstable locations.

Snow and ice

Of all terrains, snow and ice are amongst the most arduous to negotiate, being both exhausting and dangerous. Fresh, daytime snowfall makes for particularly hard going, whereas early-morning snow is the most stable, after low night-time temperatures have hardened it.

When travelling across deep snow fields, snowshoes are an essential if you are to make convincing progress. Snowshoes work by distributing your weight over a wider area than your normal footprints, thus enabling you to walk across the snow rather than sink into it. Improvised snowshoes basically consist of an oval outer frame, much larger than your foot, constructed from a strong green sapling or twisted bush material. (Tie the cut ends together to create the shape.) To this frame you then tie numerous 'struts' made from strong sticks, creating a platform for your foot. Strap this platform directly to your boot.

In areas of heavy snowfall, low visibility or in a mountainous environment, rope all members of the group together for safety, moving in a single-file formation. When you leave your camp, however, make an indicator of your direction for rescue crews or any other members of your party that are following later. To do this, fashion a large arrow in the snow, making it as high as you can so that it throws a shadow visible from the air. Build further signals along your route as you change direction – these will also help you to get back to camp if you get lost, which is all too easy in disorientating polar conditions.

In mountainous snowscapes, keep a sharp eye out for crevasses, which are often snow-covered and virtually invisible to the naked eye. (Look for irregularities in the snow, such as dark patches or dips, which indicate a crevasse beneath.) Try to avoid crossing crevasses if at all possible, but if you have to do so, take off any bulky clothing and equipment first and throw it across before you jump. Pack down the snow at the edge of the crevasse to make a solid take-off point, and identify a clear, solid landing point.

Jungle terrain

Jungle terrain is obviously very different to subzero landscapes, but it is equally demanding to travel through. Progress is constantly hampered by thick vegetation, which not only restricts your route of travel but also reduces long-range visibility, making navigation problematic.

For these reasons, and on account of increased activity of many dangerous animals at night, only travel through the jungle during the daytime, sticking to clear trails if possible. Obviously avoid going straight through dense vegetation, but if you have to, you will need a machete to make progress (see feature on page 276). When moving through thick vegetation, press it aside with your body (another good reason to stay covered up in the tropics) and resist the temptation to grab hold of plants, which might potentially be thorny or emit poisons and irritants. Furthermore, you don't want to grab hold of biting insects, spiders or snakes that live in the foliage. Other places to avoid in the jungle are swamplands, which are exhausting to traverse and typically contain a wide range of threats, from leeches through to crocodiles and alligators.

TIP: Using a machete

For soldiers on jungle ops, a machete is essential. It can be used to cut through vegetation, make shelters, collect firewood, build rafts and prepare food. When hacking at vegetation, cut at an oblique angle to the stems of the plants, leading with your elbow and giving a flick of the wrist just as the blade makes contact. (Cutting at right angles can result in the blade getting stuck in the foliage.) Ensure that the machete is very sharp before using it, and it will need honing on a daily basis if used heavily.

Riverbanks can provide better options for travelling through the jungle, as the vegetation around them may be less dense. Furthermore, civilization tends to cluster around rivers, so following one downstream increases your chances of finding human assistance, a lesson that holds good in most environments. You will often find trails (human and animal) that largely run parallel to the flow of the river, although try to avoid using such trails at night, when they will be frequented by wild animals. Indeed, when using any jungle trail, watch out for snare, deadfall, pit and spear traps set by the locals. If the banks of the river are overgrown, however, your best option might be to raft down the river, as long as the current is gentle.

Ridgelines are also good options for jungle travel, as their altitude gives you better visibility over the jungle canopy, and therefore makes navigation easier. Tropical ridges, however, can be crumbly in nature, and many run alongside dangerous ravines, crevices and cliffs, so exercise caution. Make sure that if you start to descend into a ravine or valley, you are confident you can get out again – don't make any jumps or drops that you can't reverse.

Desert terrain

The challenge of moving around deserts is the frequently featureless terrain, which complicates many aspects of navigation. Distances are particularly hard to judge, as the heat haze often makes landmarks appear closer than they are. As a general rule, multiply your distance estimation by three to get an accurate picture of how far you will need to travel. Also, the barren nature of deserts means that it is easy to lose your bearings, imagining you are walking in a straight line whereas you are actually describing a large circle. In short, don't walk without purpose, and be very clear about where you are going and what you are trying to achieve. Move between clearly identified landmarks, and check your compass regularly (if you have one) to ensure that you are still on the right bearing.

Another peril of desert movement is a sandstorm, in which high winds fill the air with whipped-up sand, forming a choking and opaque environment. Naturally, don't attempt to move during a sandstorm. Ideally, as soon as you spot one approaching (you will see sand massing in the sky), get into shelter and sit it out. If you are caught in the open, sit with your back to the wind and cover your face with a cloth. If you have a chance before the sandstorm strikes, mark your direction of travel with a long stick, a pile of stones or by any other means. When the sandstorm is over, you will be able to use this sign to pick up your bearing, even though the sand deposits from the storm are likely to have altered the landscape around you.

NATURAL NAVIGATION

While this chapter will move on to look at the technicalities of map and compass navigation, the fact remains that these resources might not be available. In those instances, nature provides you with some navigational tools, although the value of these can depend on many factors, such as the season and the time of day.

The first tool for 'natural navigation' is the sun, useful because wherever you are it rises predictably in the east and sets in the west. At midday in the Northern Hemisphere the sun is due south, and due north in the Southern Hemisphere. (If you are almost on the equator, the midday sun will be straight above you.) As long as you have a clear sense of where the sun is in the sky, therefore, you have a basic navigational aid.

First, you can use the shadows cast by the sun to create an elementary form of compass. Push a long stick into a patch of flat, even ground so that it stands a good height – about 1m (3ft 3in) – above the earth (the longer the stick, the better the results). If the sun is strong enough, the stick will throw a dark shadow onto the ground. Mark the tip of the shadow with a stone, wait about 15 minutes, then mark the tip of the shadow again with another stone. Scrape a straight mark in the soil between the two stones and you have your east–west line. Bisecting this line will give you north–south orientation. Repeating this process at regular intervals can help you maintain a specific bearing, and avoid aimless wandering.

If you are wearing an analogue watch (i.e. one with hands), then it

Movement and tracking

Here are four instances of what soldiers know as 'sign' – indicators of the past presence of people or animals. Also look for indications of age when judging the usefulness of sign – footprints, for example, will become dry, crumbly and filled with debris with the passage of time.

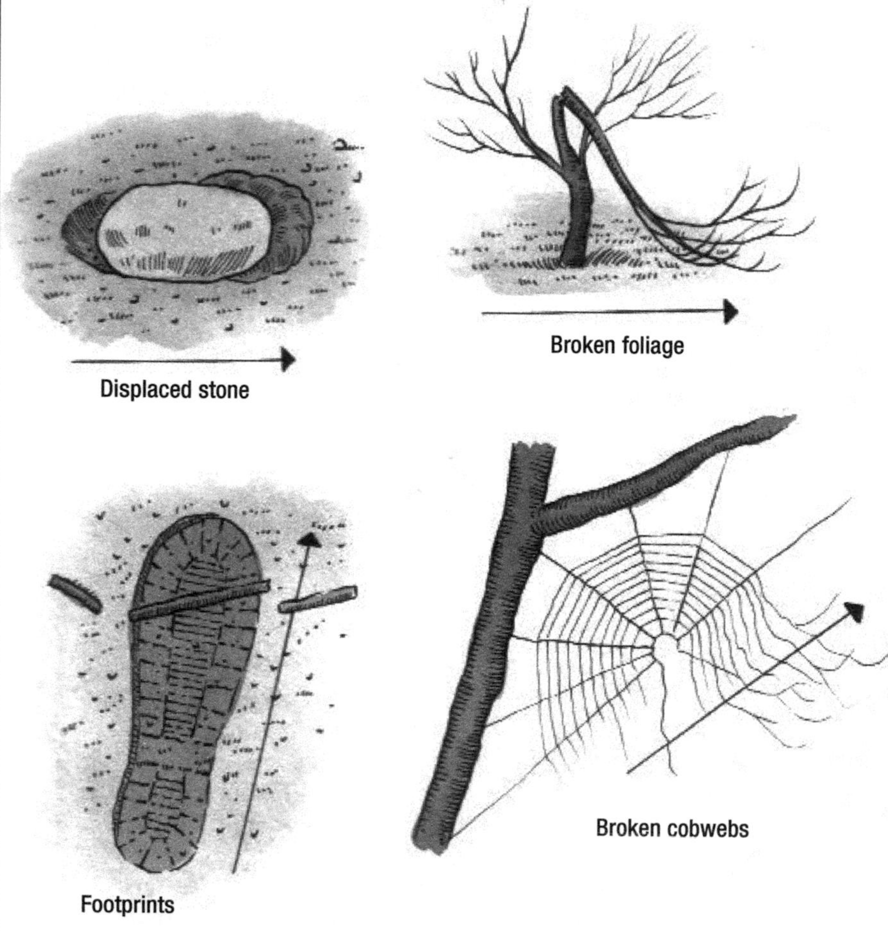

A transit

A transit is the extension of a straight line joining two features that you can identify on your map. Keep your eyes open for naturally-occurring transits, as they provide excellent position lines.

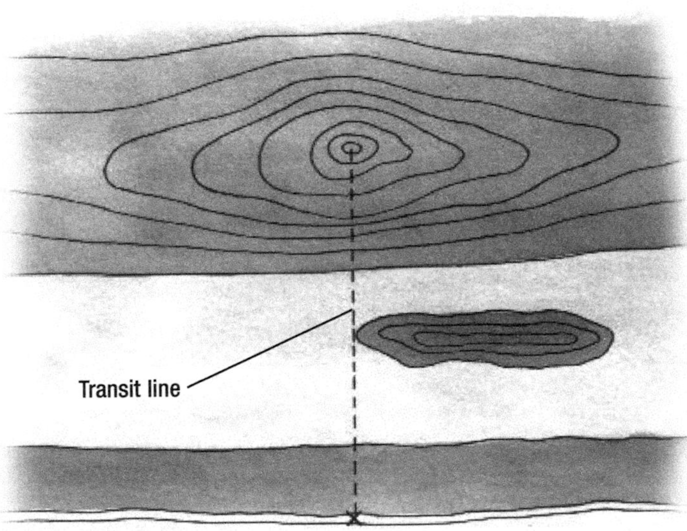

Draw the transit line on your map, connecting your position with where you aim to be

Bracketing

Bracketing is a useful technique for finding your way back to a fixed point. Take note of features that lie on either side of your chosen destination. When you reach one of the bracketing features, you will know which way to turn.

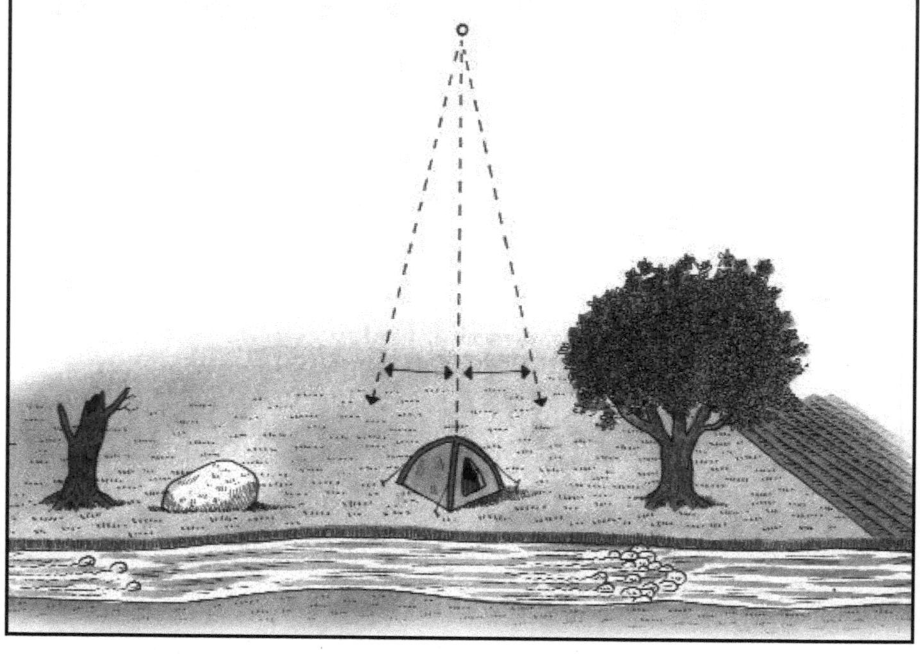

can be another tool for helio-navigation. Note, however, that the technique of reading direction using a watch varies slightly according to whether you are in the Northern or Southern Hemisphere. For both, set the watch to true local time – do not incorporate any daylight-saving additions or subtractions. Now hold the watch face flat. If in the Northern Hemisphere, point the hour hand towards the sun and bisect the angle between the hour hand and the 12 o'clock mark on the watch face. This direction is south, except before 06:00 and after 18:00, when it will indicate north. To make a reading in the Southern Hemisphere, point the 12 o'clock mark itself at the sun, and then bisect the angle between the mark and the hour hand to find north, or south before 06:00 and after

Marking a trail

The following are markers you can use to send messages to either a search party or other members of your group. Make the signs prominent, away from concealing vegetation.

Navigation by shadow

The diagrams here illustrate how you can use the sun to plot an east–west line on the ground. Once you have this line, then you will be able to draw the north–south line and create a basic directional guide.

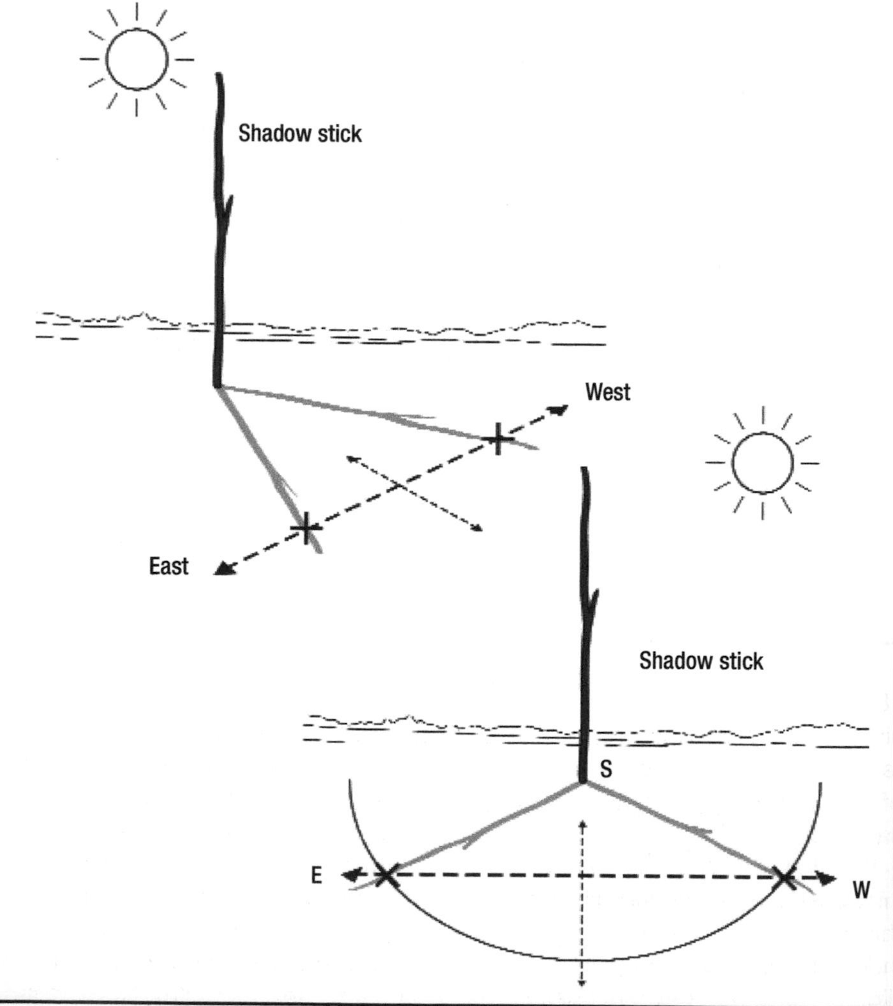

Watch navigation

Analogue watches can be used to indicate either north or south (see main text). You can use this technique at sunrise or sunset, but usually the position of the sun on the horizon will give you the directional information you need, based on the sun rising in the east and setting in the west.

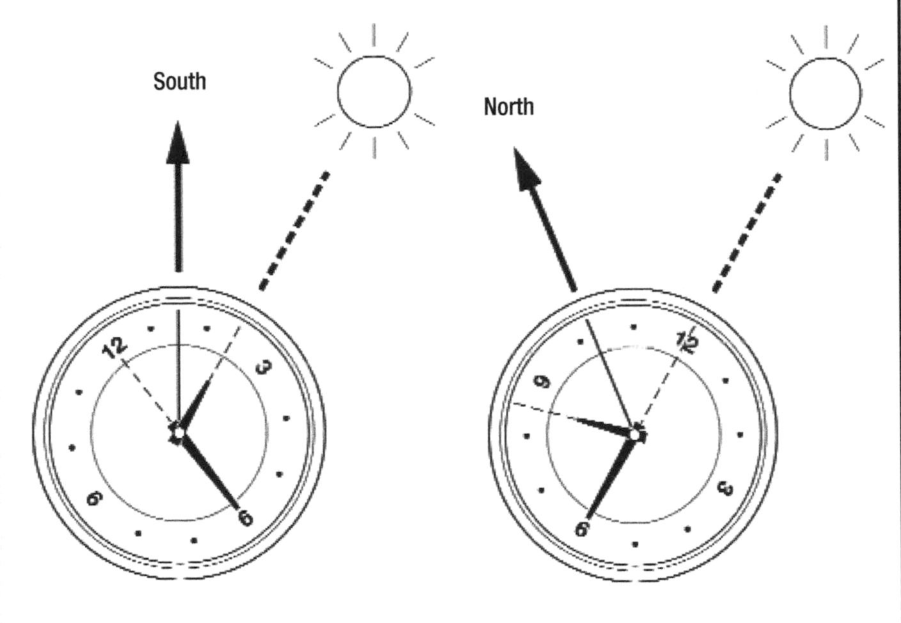

18:00. If you have a digital watch simply draw out an analogue representation of the time on a piece of paper or the ground, and make the same calculation.

Prevailing winds are other indicators of direction, albeit ones that can change periodically. Indicators of the prevailing wind direction include trees and bushes bent in a common direction, particularly around coastal areas, or snowfalls or sand dunes sculpted into common patterns. Transverse dunes, which occur in areas with a large amount of sand, set themselves perpendicular to the wind, with a long, gentle slope facing into the wind, and a steep downwind slope. In arid areas with thin sand, the dunes tend to align themselves parallel to the prevailing wind. Used in association with other natural signs, therefore, wind direction can at least give you a rough sense of orientation.

Plants are also of some navigational assistance. Most plants and trees strain towards the strongest source of sunlight, so will often lean to the south (in the Northern Hemisphere) or north (in the Southern Hemisphere). Trees tend to have their densest foliage on the sunward side, and in the Northern Hemisphere, mountains generally display more vegetation on the lower slopes of their southern faces. (Note also that in springtime the north-facing slopes tend to be the last ones to keep the remnants of winter snow and ice.) The reverse principles are true in the Southern Hemisphere. As with all natural navigation, however, be careful when reading plant signs. Many factors affect plant growth, including soil conditions and competition from surrounding flora, so they are a fallible method of navigation. Used in combination with other natural signs, however, they can be useful for adding to your sense of direction.

Night-time navigation

Celestial bodies have been used for accurate navigation for centuries, and they remain an excellent guide as long as you have the clear skies through which to view them. In the Northern Hemisphere, for example, the Big Dipper (known as the Plough in the UK), part of the constellation

Navigating by the Southern Cross

The Southern Cross is accompanied by two bright 'trailing' stars to its east. The 'coalsack', a dark nebula, forms a starless area immediately southeast of the cross. As the diagram at bottom right illustrates, when the Southern Cross appears upright in the night sky, its long axis points down at geographic south on the horizon.

called Ursa Major, and the constellation Cassiopeia can both direct you to Polaris, the Pole Star. By locating Polaris, you can either follow it directly or choose another star on the bearing you want and

The Southern Cross consists of four primary stars plus two 'trailing stars' out to the east. A dark nebula colours the sky just off to the side of the cross.

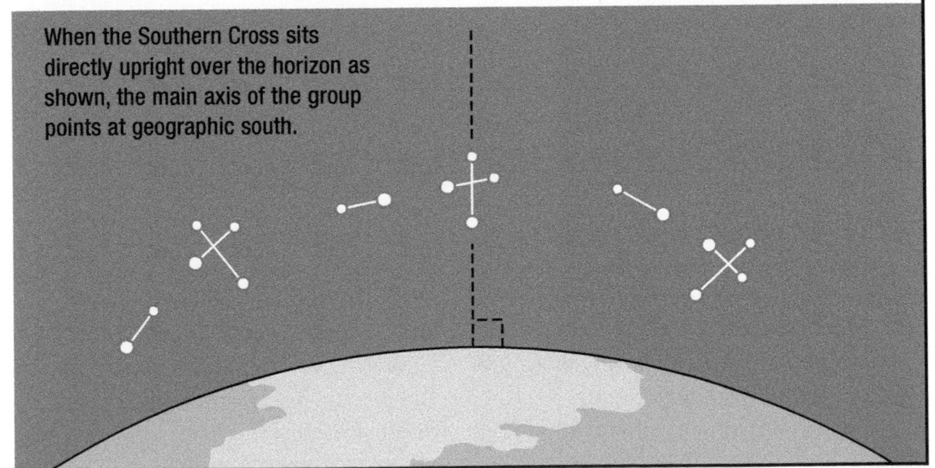

When the Southern Cross sits directly upright over the horizon as shown, the main axis of the group points at geographic south.

Pole Star

The Pole Star, North Star, or Polaris (to use its three most popular names) is a sure indicator of north. Extending lines out from the Plough or from Cassiopeia, as shown, will help you correctly identify the Pole Star, which sits in a relatively isolated aspect in the night sky.

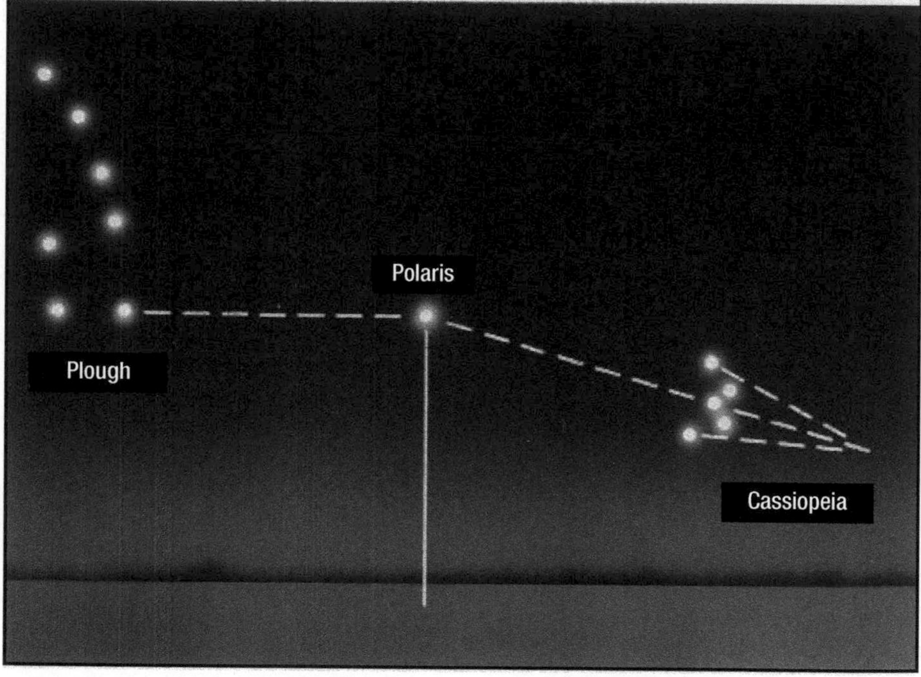

follow that instead. If you do the latter, check your course every 20–30 minutes, as other stars are rotating around the Pole Star at 15 degrees per hour. Keep selecting new stars to guide you on the right course.

Another distinctive constellation is Orion, the most noticeable feature of which is its straight 'belt' of three stars, which are spaced evenly in a line. Like the sun, Orion rises almost exactly due east and sets almost exactly due west. As Orion sets below the horizon, the point at which the belt disappears out of sight is due west.

For those in the Southern Hemisphere, the Southern Cross stands out – when it is standing vertically in the sky, south is directly below the bottom star. If the Cross is at an angle, multiply the longest axis of the cross by 4.5, which brings you to an imaginary point above the horizon. Direct south will be immediately below that point.

MAP AND COMPASS NAVIGATION

Even in the age of GPS, map and compass navigation remains at the core of special forces navigation skills. While a GPS receiver is undoubtedly an excellent navigational tool, the fact remains that technology can and does fail. Furthermore, map and compass navigation arguably gives you a deeper understanding of the terrain around you, and compels you to think more about the safety considerations in your navigational choices.

Map reading

Maps are the bread and butter of military and survival navigation, and understanding their principles is vital. First, select the appropriate scale. A typical outdoor map scale is 1:50,000, which means that one unit of measurement on the map represents 50,000 of the same unit on the ground (this equation is known as a representative fraction). To aid quick distance measurement, a map

TIP: Star orientation

Any star can give you a useful point of reference for navigation. To achieve this, you need to sit still for about 15 to 20 minutes – excessive movement will spoil the results of the exercise. Note two fixed points on the ground in the distance, then pick a star and monitor its movement in relation to these points. The direction of the star will, according to the following rules, tell you in which direction you are facing:

Northern Hemisphere:
Rising – the star is in the east
Falling – the star is in the west
Left – the star is in the north
Right – the star is in the south

Southern Hemisphere:
Rising – the star is in the west
Falling – the star is in the east
Left – the star is in the south
Right – the star is in the north

TIP: GPS receivers

The following are some guidelines to observe when buying a GPS receiver for wilderness use:

- Make sure that it is sturdy. Check that the receiver is impact-resistant, waterproof and will function in both extremely low and extremely high temperatures.
- Ensure that it has a large map-type screen (as opposed to a purely numerical type), and that you can purchase and upload extra maps as required.
- Choose a 12-channel parallel receiver system, which has greater accuracy than sequential or multiplexing receivers, particularly in complex terrain such as a forest.
- Get a receiver with a transreflective screen, which is easier to read in direct sunlight than other screen types.
- Buy a unit that can store at least 500 waypoints and 20 routes.
- Ensure that the unit has good battery life, and utilizes automatic power-saving modes.

is often also provided with a bar scale, a line marked off in units of easily understandable distance, such as kilometres and miles. The bar scale will give you a quick understanding of the practical distances shown on the map.

Wilderness maps represent the elevation of land through contour lines, imaginary lines that join up points of equal elevation. They not only indicate the elevation of terrain above sea level, but they also provide information about gradient – the ratio of vertical to horizontal distance. If contour lines are widely spaced, for example, the slope is gentle. If narrow, the slope is steep.

The map will have distinct grid lines superimposed over the landscape. The lines running vertically (north–south) are called northings, while the lines running horizontally (east–west) are called eastings. Your position on the map

Map details

Study your map and its legend closely to become aware of all the natural and man-made features around you. Having visual contact with two or more of these features at the same time will ensure that you stay on the right route.

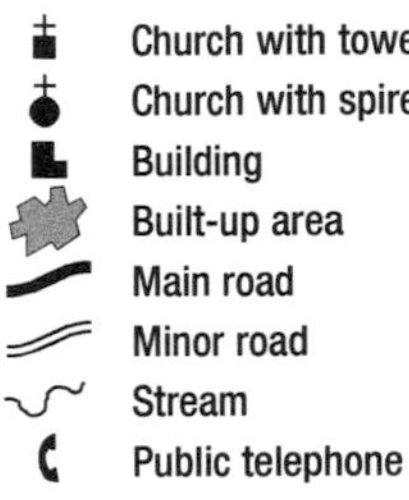

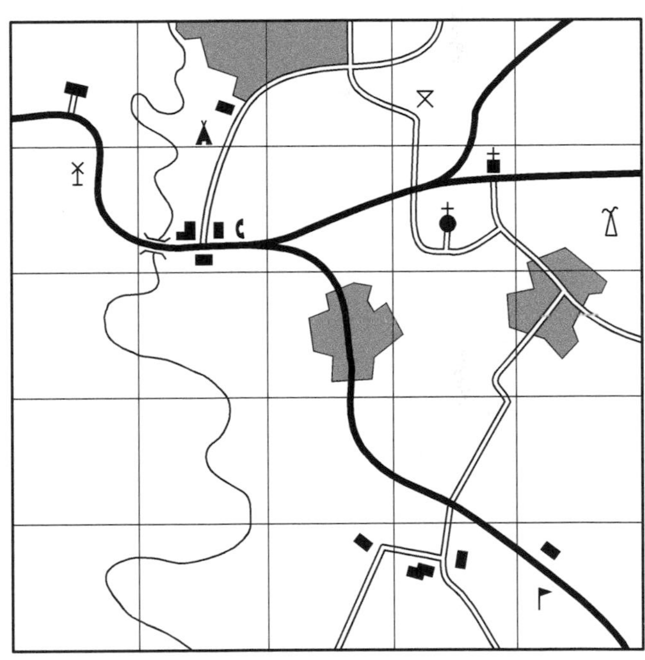

is plotted using the grid lines to produce a six-figure number, first quoting the eastings, then the northings. This can be slightly confusing, as it is the other way round when using latitude and longitude, where latitude (the equivalent of northings) comes first. If it helps, just remember that E comes before N in the alphabet.

To provide a six-figure grid reference, first find your position on the map, and then identify the nearest north–south grid line to its left (west). The number of this line provides the first two digits of your

Types of contours

Contour lines may look innocuous enough on a printed map, but they can indicate very severe terrain. Remember that the more tightly packed the lines are, the steeper the ground is, while widely spaced lines indicate gentle slopes.

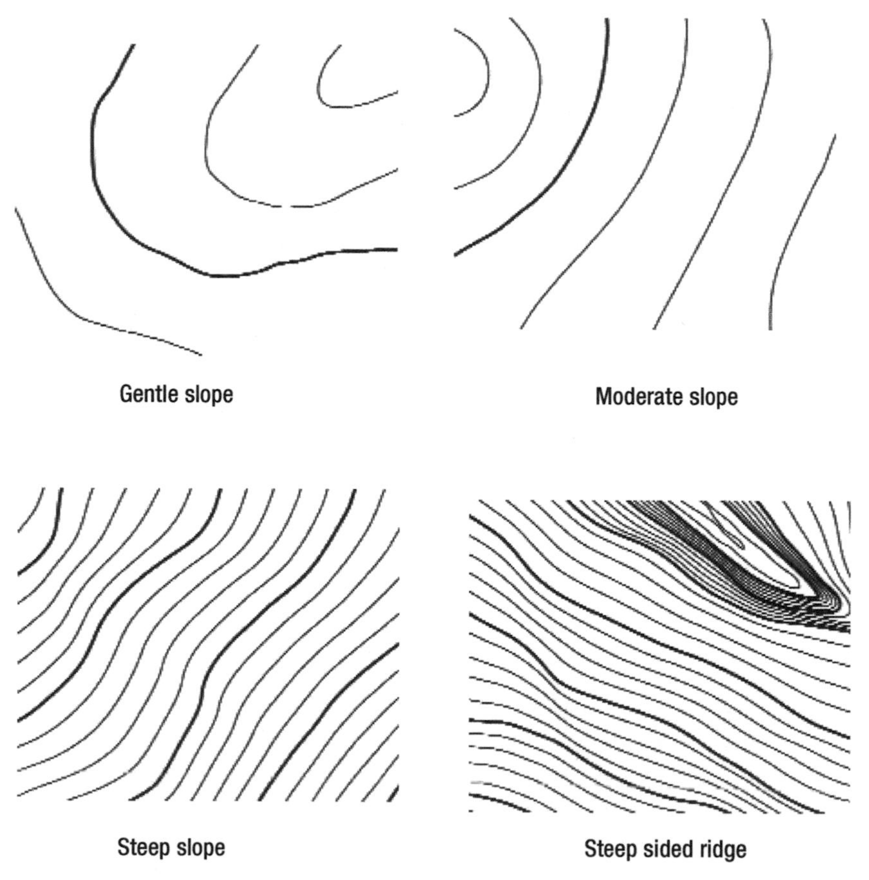

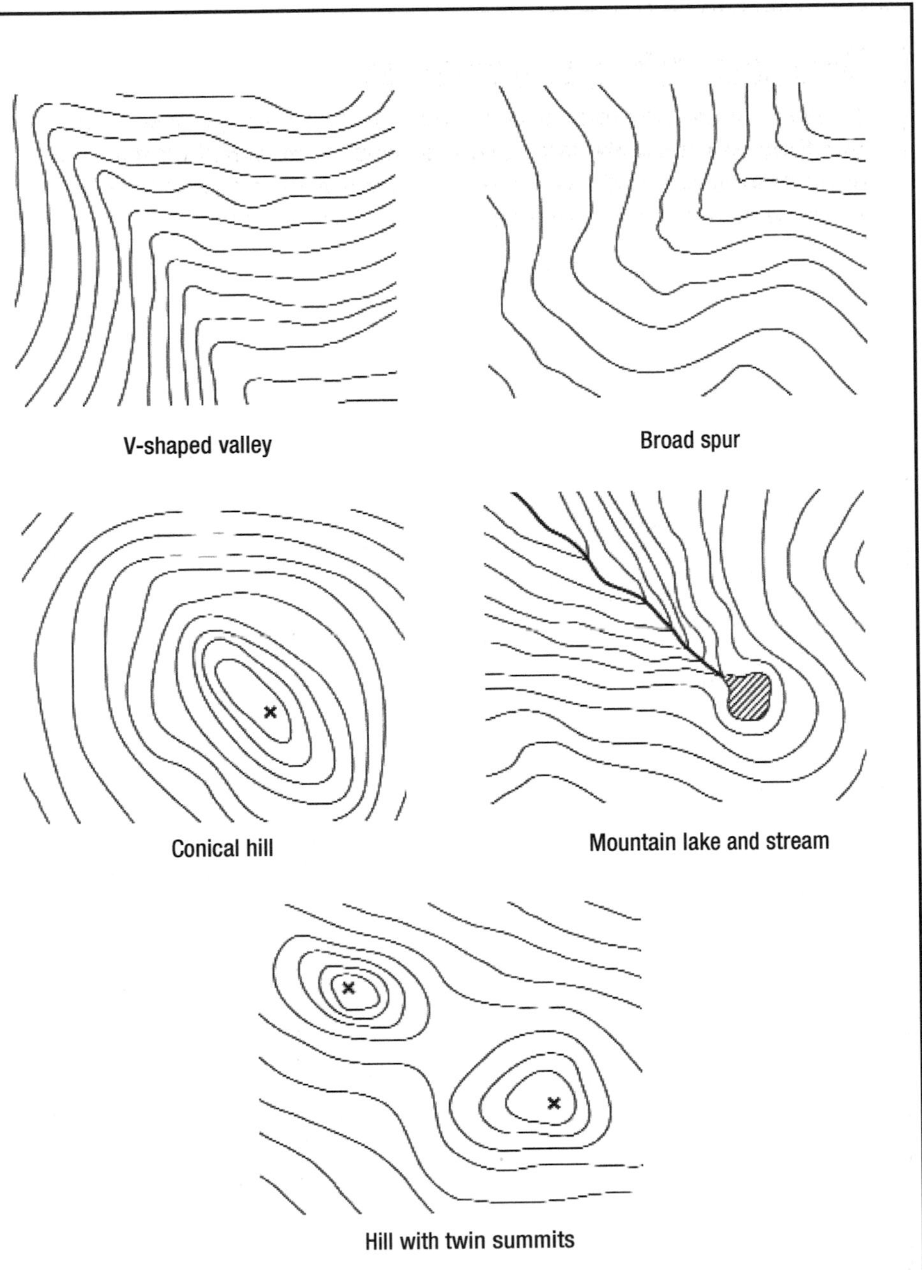
V-shaped valley
Broad spur
Conical hill
Mountain lake and stream
Hill with twin summits

Maps and the landscape

A map is a two-dimensional visualization of a three-dimensional reality. Learn to see maps with a three-dimensional eye, and also take account of difficult features when planning your routes of travel.

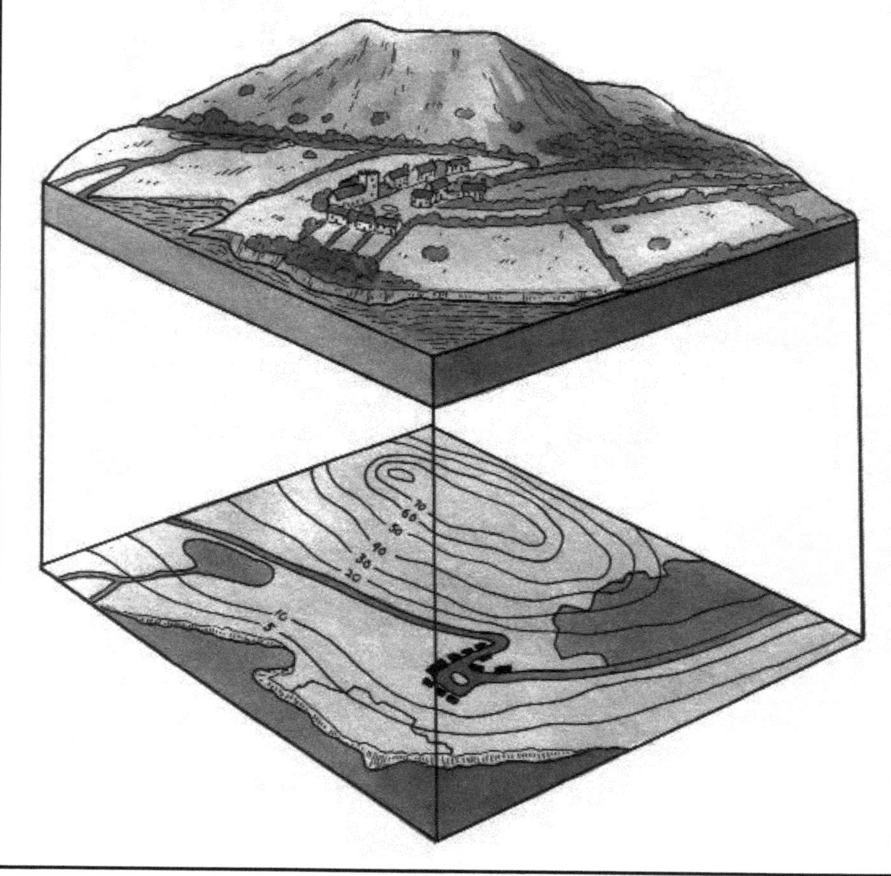

eastings. Estimate the distance between the grid line and your position in tenths of a kilometre/mile (that is, tenths of the distance between two adjacent grid lines); this gives you the third digit of your eastings. Repeat the process for northings, finding the nearest grid line below (south of) your position and estimating how far north of this line you are. The full six-digit grid reference specifies your position on that particular map to the nearest 100m (328ft).

Compasses

Compasses are devices that point to magnetic north, with a circular, rotating dial divided into a 360-degree scale. They constitute a fundamental piece of all soldiers' equipment. Note, however, that there is a difference in bearing between true north (the direction of the geographic North Pole) and magnetic north, this difference being known as 'declination'. More confusingly, magnetic declination also varies with place and with time. Declination is described as so many degrees east or west, depending on whether the compass points to the east or west of true north. We will say more about declination when we look at the practicalities of compass navigation below, but note that good outdoor

Magnetizing a needle

The US Army 'Survival' manual notes that 'You can magnetize or polarize [a needle] by slowly stroking it in one direction on a piece of silk or carefully through your hair using deliberate strokes.' You can also achieve the same effect with another magnet or a piece of leather.

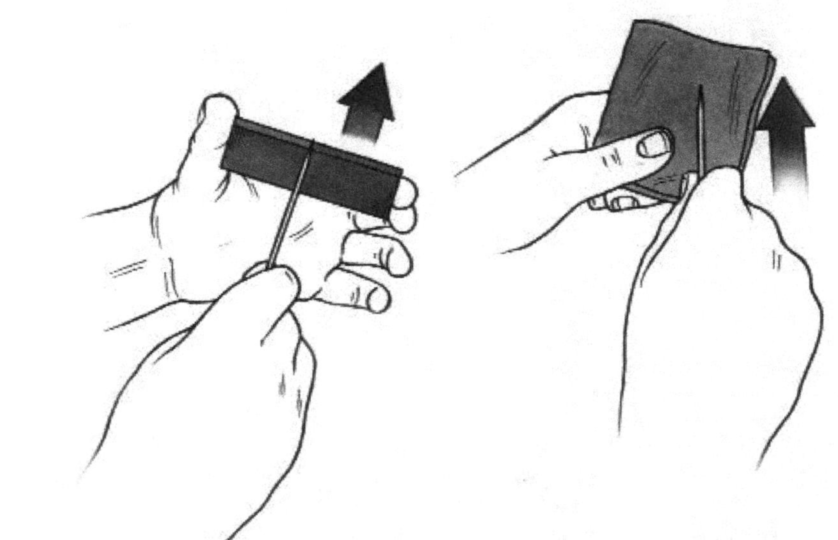

Types of compass

There are numerous different types of compass. Electronic compasses have become increasingly sophisticated, and can store bearings and routes in their memory banks, but manual compasses are never dependent on batteries.

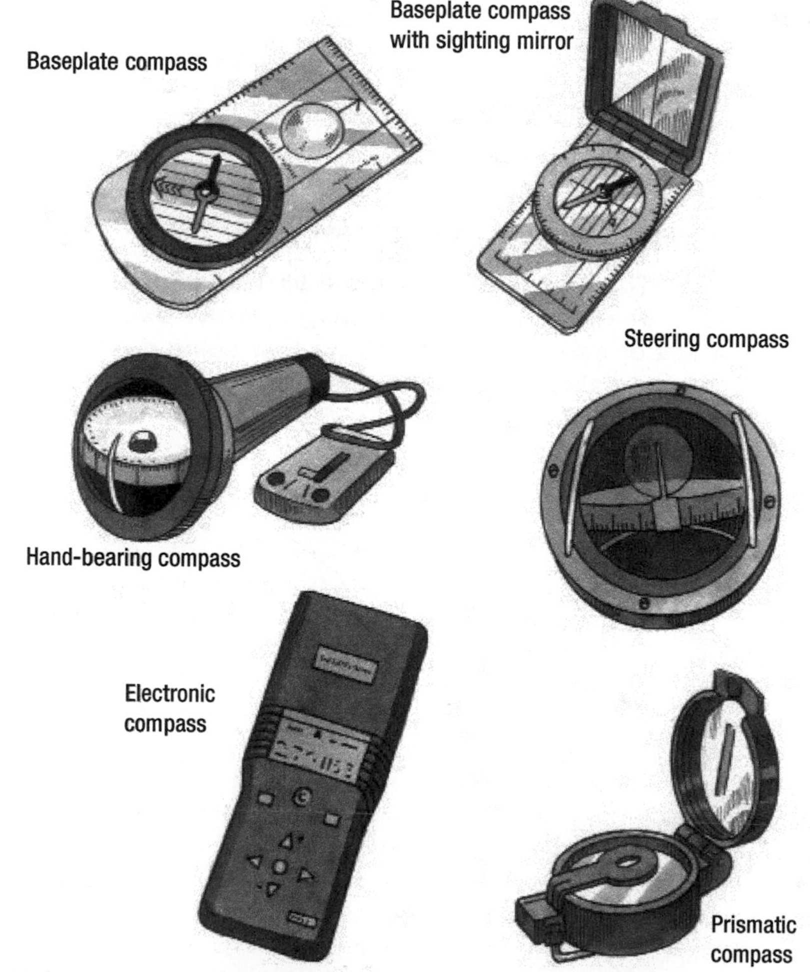

Improvised compass

This improvised compass consists of nothing more than a magnetized needle (see p.295) balanced on a cork in water. The water must be absolutely still, as tiny currents can affect the compass reading.

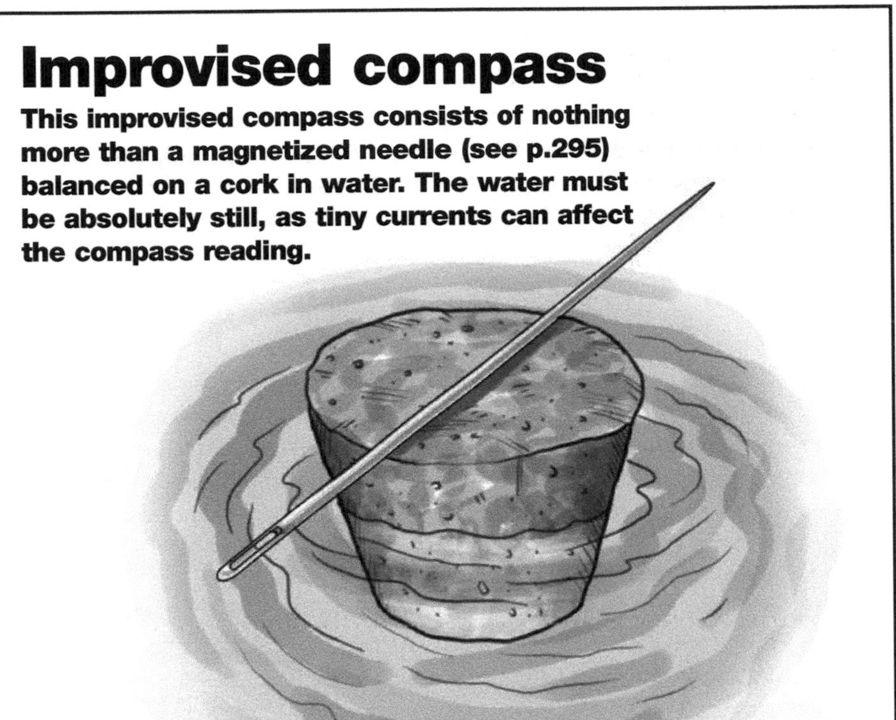

navigation maps should provide declination information, such as follows: 'The direction of magnetic north is estimated at 4° 22' west of grid north in July 2000. Annual change is about 13' east.'

There are many different types of compass, but the baseplate variety (classically made by Silva) is the type most commonly used by hikers and mountaineers, and it will hence form the basis of our discussion here – you will need one in front of you to understand the following instructions. The most basic thing you can do with a compass is to find magnetic north. Rotate the compass housing until the dial reads N (000°). Now hold the compass level and allow the needle to settle. The red end of the needle points to magnetic north.

If you now rotate the entire compass so that the needle is aligned with the orienting arrow, the direction-of-travel arrow will be pointing towards magnetic north.

To find true north using a baseplate

compass, first rotate the compass housing so that north on the dial lies over the index mark for the direction-of-travel arrow. Then, adjust for declination. For example, if declination is 10° W, set the dial to 010°; if declination is 15° E, set the dial to 345°. Next, rotate the whole compass until the north (red) end of the compass needle is aligned with the orienting arrow. The direction-of-travel arrow will now be pointing to true north.

To confuse matters, there is another type of north, called grid north, which is represented by the top ends of the vertical grid lines on your map. It is not the same as true north or magnetic north, but is important because it allows you to orientate your map easily using a baseplate compass, and simplifies the process of plotting and reading compass bearings. Finding grid north uses exactly the same procedure as for true north, except that the declination correction should be made using the difference between magnetic north and grid north. This is usually slightly different from the declination between magnetic and true north – you can find the appropriate value in the map legend.

Using your compass

Before using your compass, first align your map with the features on the ground, with the map's north point pointing towards true north indicated by your compass. Taking a bearing from the map, and then following the resulting compass course, is the most commonly used procedure in navigation. (A bearing is the angular direction of a point, line or course measured in relation to true, grid or magnetic north, and is usually expressed in degrees.) This method is useful simply for finding your way to an objective that you cannot see, and consists of the following steps:

1. Place your compass on the map, with the edge of the baseplate along your intended line of travel. The direction-of-travel arrow should point in the direction you want to go.
2. Rotate the compass housing so that the orienting lines are parallel to the grid lines on the map, with the N on the dial pointing to the north edge of the map.
3. If necessary, correct the bearing for declination by rotating the dial the appropriate number of degrees clockwise or anticlockwise, respectively.
4. Hold the compass in front of you, with the direction-of-travel arrow pointing away from you. Turn around until the compass needle is aligned with the orienting arrow, with the north (red) end of the needle pointing to the north end of the arrow. You are now facing the direction in which you want to travel.

To transfer a bearing from the real

Following a compass course

When following a compass course, hold the compass in front of you and rotate your whole body to left or right until the needle is correctly aligned with the orienting arrow.

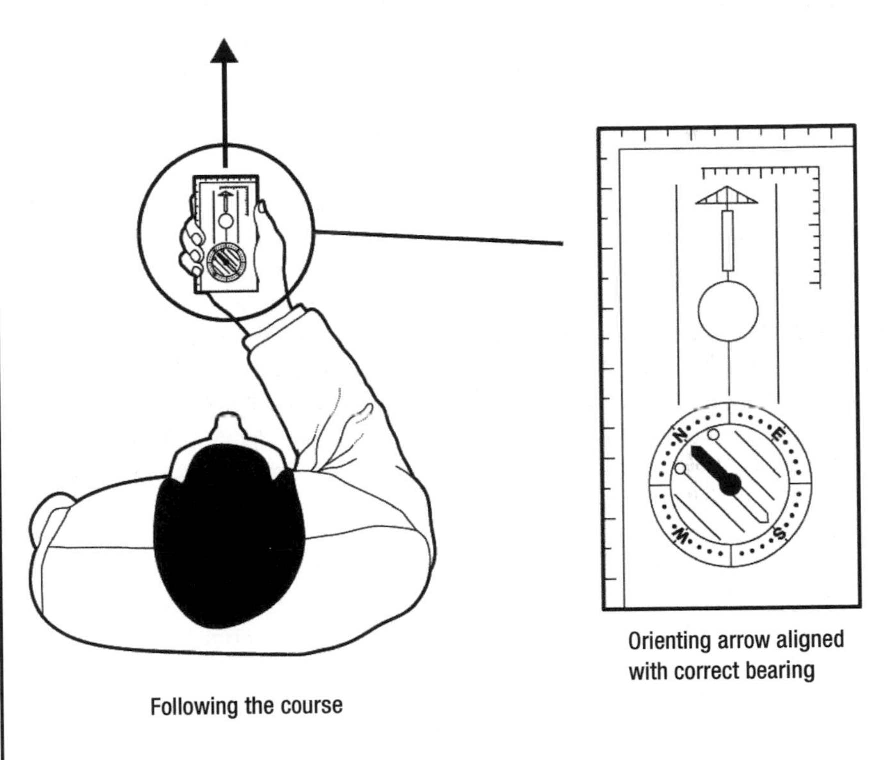

Orienting arrow aligned with correct bearing

Following the course

world to a map, you simply reverse the previous procedure. This method can be used to plot the bearing of a landmark on the map, either to create a position line (see below), or to help identify an unknown landmark.

However, there is one vital difference. What you want to measure is a back bearing (i.e. the bearing *from* the landmark *to* your position):

1. Hold the compass in front of you, and point the direction-of-travel arrow directly at the object or feature whose bearing you

wish to take. For greater accuracy, try sighting along one edge of the baseplate.

2. Keeping the baseplate steady, rotate the compass housing until the orienting arrow is aligned with the compass needle, but with the north end of the arrow under the south (white) end of the needle; this gives you a back bearing instead of a direct bearing.
3. If necessary, correct the bearing for declination by rotating the dial the appropriate number of degrees anticlockwise or clockwise.
4. Place the compass on the map, and lay the edge of the baseplate over the feature whose bearing you have taken – you can now ignore the compass needle. Move the compass until the orienting lines are parallel to the north–south grid lines on the map, and the north end of the orienting arrow is pointing to the north edge of the map.
5. Draw a line from the feature towards the direction-of-travel arrow – this is the back bearing, and your position lies somewhere along this line. Aligning the south end of the compass needle with the orienting arrow is simply a way of saving you the trouble of measuring the direct bearing of the object and then subtracting 180 degrees.

Fixing your position

Taking a bearing of a mapped object provides you with a position line – you know that your position lies somewhere along that line. In order to fix your position precisely, you need to have at least two intersecting position lines, in a technique known as resection.

To perform resection with two bearings, simply use your compass to record the bearings of two or more landmarks, correct the bearings for declination, and then plot the bearings on your map. Where the two lines intersect is your position.

If you use three bearings in your resection, the three lines are unlikely to meet at a single point. Instead, you are more likely to produce a small triangle, so you would generally assume that the centre of the triangle is your position. Note that actually following a compass course is naturally complicated by the terrain. Rough terrain, obstacles, gradients and any irregularities in your step are just some of the factors that will affect your faithful pursuit of a bearing. For this reason, make regular checks of your location and also use your common sense – don't slavishly follow a bearing if is going to lead you into trouble.

SIGNALLING

Survival navigation is about moving *yourself* to rescue or safety. Signalling, by contrast, is about bringing *others* to wherever you are, essential if you want to attract the attention of rescue parties or search-and-rescue aircraft. Signalling is essentially the process of advertising your location over long distances by either visible or auditory means. The wilderness is a huge place, and even with modern technologies it is hard to spot someone lost in thousands of square kilometres of landscape, particularly if that landscape is covered in trees or snow. Here, therefore, are a selection of useful ways to make yourself stand out and be seen.

In terms of visual means, professional signal flares are obviously ideal, but make sure that you follow the instructions about their operation extremely carefully, and don't waste them unnecessarily in a short period of time – fire them when you have reason to believe they will be seen by someone. In the absence of flares, bright fire (at night) and smoke (in the daytime) are excellent alternative means of signalling. A smoky fire can be made by adding green boughs, fresh leaves, damp wood, rubber or oil to a regular cooking fire.

Make the colour of smoke appropriate to the colour of the landscape background. The white smoke produced by smouldering green vegetation stands out well against a jungle or forest landscape, for example, while the black smoke

TIP: Accurate resection

When judging the accuracy of a position obtained using resection, you should take into account any potential sources of error. When you record the bearing of a landmark using an ordinary baseplate compass, it is unlikely that you will be able to measure it more precisely than to the nearest two degrees. If you have a more advanced compass with sighting aids, or a prismatic compass, you might be able to read a bearing to the nearest degree. An error of two degrees in a bearing will introduce an error of around 30m (100ft) for every 1km (0.6 miles) between you and the landmark. For this reason, when choosing landmarks to fix your position, it is best to select two objects that are roughly 90 degrees apart, as these will produce a smaller area of potential error than objects that are closer together.

Body signals

The following are internationally-recognized body signals, typically used to communicate with helicopter-rescue or search-party personnel. Make the actions bold, as large as possible, and clearly defined from one another.

Receiver is operating

Affirmative (Yes)

Can proceed shortly, wait if possible

Need mechanical help or parts, long delay

Do not attempt to land here

Pick us up, aircraft abandoned

Use drop message

All OK, do not wait

Negative (No)

Land here (point in direction)

Need urgent medical help

emitted by burning oil or rubber is good to use against snowscapes. Whatever fire you make, ensure that it is sited in open, prominent terrain for maximum visibility.

Also, don't light fires randomly in the hope they will be spotted. Instead, if you aren't using a fire already for cooking and heat, build an unlit fire at the ready, ideally treated with some sort of accelerant (such as large bundles of dry grass, oil, petrol or gunpowder) and get ready to light it as soon as you spot rescuers in the distance or hear the drone of an approaching aircraft.

Smoke signals

An important consideration with smoke signals is to generate smoke that contrasts with the background. Here white smoke is highly visible against a green coniferous forest.

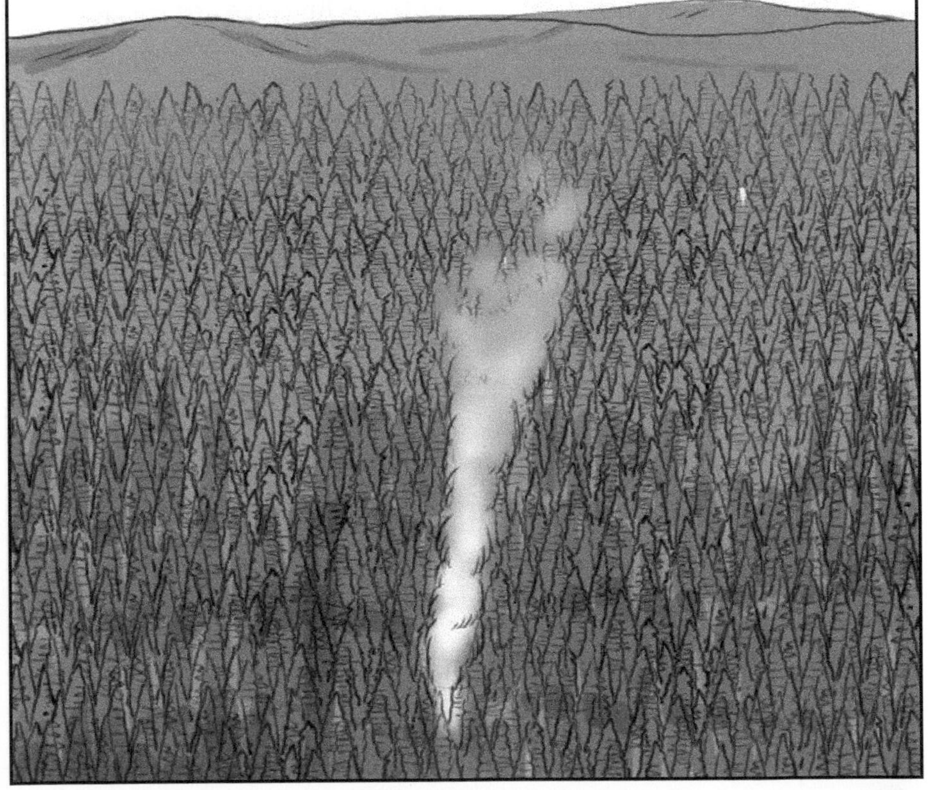

Note that there are a range of internationally-recognized ground-to-air signals that you can construct from natural materials. The actual signals are illustrated in this chapter, but the most important points in their construction are: 1) make them big, so they can be seen from high altitude; and 2) make them contrast visually with the ground on which they sit. In terms of size, you want each bar of a letter or symbol to be about 10m (33ft) long and 3m (10ft) wide, although smaller structures will still be useful and meaningful to ground search parties. To create contrasting signals, use every material you can find, plus some innovation. Bright clothing, sheets and backpacks can be good

Helicopter landing zone

A helicopter landing zone must be at least 35m (115ft) wide for the aircraft's body and have at least 50m (164ft) for the main rotor clearance. Also, ideally allow a landing strip approach of several hundred metres (bottom).

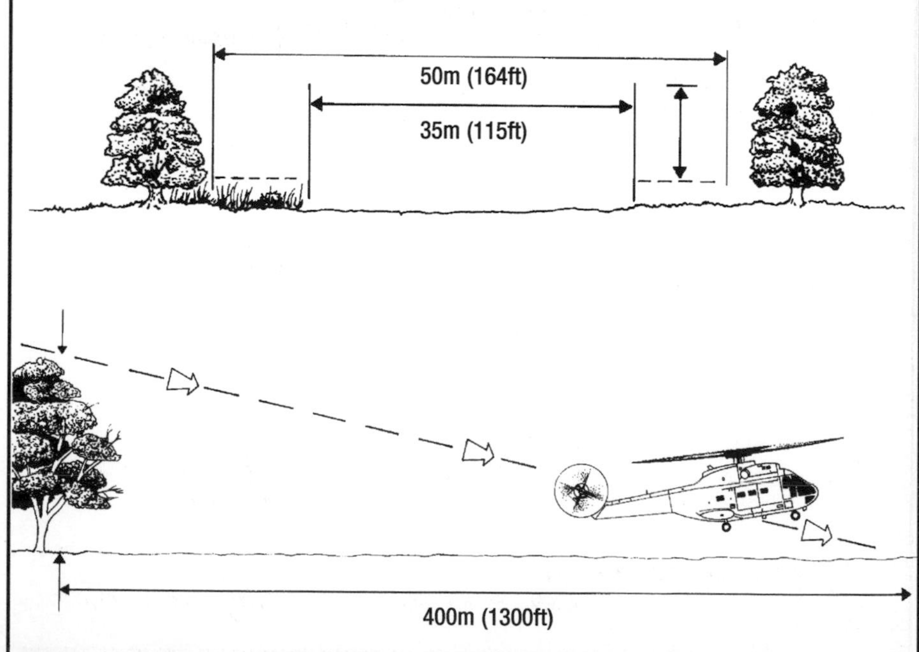

signalling materials, for example, and in snowy conditions black twigs and branches will stand out in stark relief. Alternatively, you can pile up snow blocks which, if you have some direct sunlight, will throw out deep, black shadows. Boulders, vegetation and seaweed can be used to form symbols in sand, and in brush-covered areas you can flatten down grasses with rocks to create the images. In short, do whatever stands out, but obviously don't make your process too labour-intensive.

In sunny conditions, signalling mirrors are effective at broadcasting your presence over very long distances – tests have revealed that a flash of bright sunshine from a mirror can be seen more than 32km (20

Ground-to-air signals

Communicate with aircraft using the following signals, which can be constructed from branches, rocks, earth, grasses or any other suitable natural material.

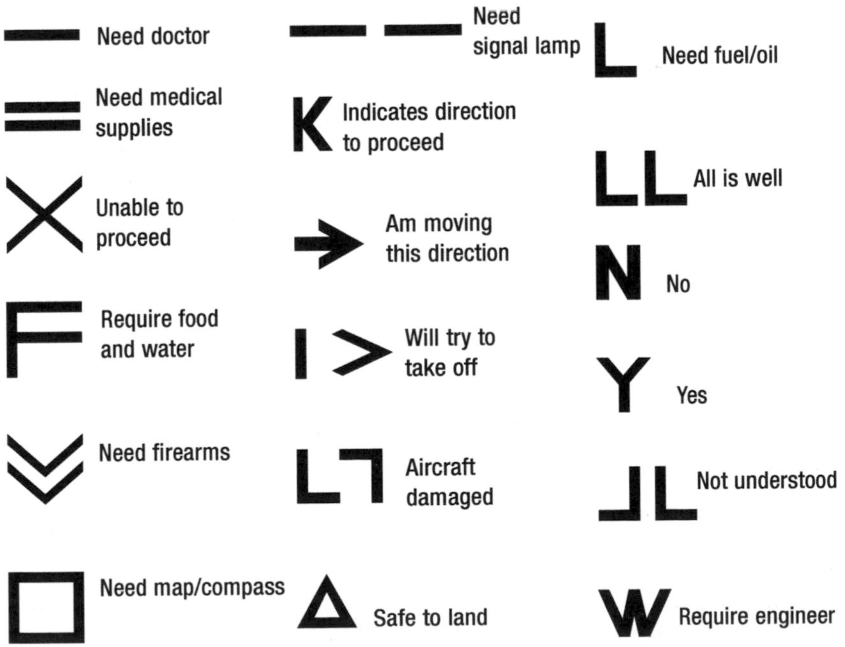

miles) away. Heliographs, meanwhile, include features that make them highly accurate in terms of directing light towards an observer. Yet any hand-held mirror will work, and if that isn't available, CD/DVDs or polished pieces of metal will suffice. Basic reflector technique is as follows:

- Catch the sunlight on your reflector, and direct it onto the ground in front of you.
- Look at your target (say a rescue party or distant aircraft).

Mirror signalling

Using this signal mirror, the man first catches the sun, indicated by the sunlight passing through the hole in the middle of the mirror and striking his right hand. He then turns the mirror towards the target object to project a bright flash.

- Flash the patch of light up from the ground directly at the target. Don't aim for a steady, blinding beam of light, but create a flashing pattern of signals – these will attract more attention and don't require you to be so accurate with your signalling.

Another method is to hold the reflector in one hand near your face, with your other hand outstretched in front of you and aimed at the target like a gunsight. Illuminate the back of this hand with the light from the reflector, then drop the hand so that the beam continues out to the target. A good torch can take the place of a reflector if available, but make sure that you have a clear signalling objective before you use up some of the power in your precious batteries.

Visual means of signalling can be rendered ineffective by the time of day – your signalling options at night are obviously limited to a bright fire or flares – or on account of severe weather conditions. At these times, auditory signalling can be an alternative or accompaniment to visual means. Shouting, whistles and foghorns can, in the right conditions, be heard over considerable distances. For example, six long blasts on a whistle or foghorn evenly spread over one minute, followed by a minute of silence and then repeated, is an international distress signal.

Morse code

Morse code is still taught today to special forces soldiers. Using a flashlight or whistle, you can broadcast morse messages over long distances, and they will be internationally understood.

A .–	M ––	Y –.––
B –...	N –.	Z ––..–
C –.–.	O –––	1 .––––
D –..	P .––.	2 ..––
E .	Q ––.–	3 ...––
F ..–.	R .–.	4 ....–
G ––.	S ...	5 .....
H	T –	6 –....
I ..	U ..–	7 ––...
J .–––	V ...–	8 –––..
K –.–	W .––	9 ––––.
L .–..	X –..–	0 –––––

GLOSSARY OF SURVIVAL TERMS

ABC—a mnemonic for remembering immediate first aid priorities: Airway, Breathing, Circulation.

bearing—the compass direction from your position to a landmark or destination.

bergen—a large backpack for carrying survival supplies.

bivi-bag—a portable low-profile, one-man tunnel tent.

bola—a weapon consisting of multiple weights bound together by rope and thrown to bring down prey.

calorie—the amount of heat required to raise the temperature of 1 gram of water by 1° Celsius.

carbohydrate—an organic compound of carbon, hydrogen and oxygen found in many foods. When ingested, carbohydrates are broken down to provide energy.

chlorine—a chemical element that may be added to water as a purifying agent.

circulatory shock—a medical emergency caused by a casualty's blood pressure dropping below safe levels.

compass—a navigational instrument that uses the Earth's magnetic field to indicate direction, with an indicator pointing to magnetic north.

coniferous—denotes an evergreen tree with cones and needle-like leaves.

contour—a line on a map joining points of equal elevation.

coordinates—a pair of numbers and/or letters that describe a unique position.

CPR—cardio-pulmonary resuscitation; a first aid term referring to methods of articifically maintaining blood circulation and breathing.

cyclone—a large-scale, atmospheric wind-and-pressure system characterized

by low pressure at its centre and by circular wind motion, counterclockwise in the Northern Hemisphere, clockwise in the Southern Hemisphere.

datum—a reference point used by cartographers, from which all elevations or positions on a map or chart are measured.

deadfall trap—a trap designed to kill an animal by dropping a heavy weight on it.

declination—in navigation, the difference between magnetic north and true north.

degree (or °)—the unit of measurement of an angle. A full circle is divided into 360°; each degree is divided into 60 minutes, and each minute into 60 seconds.

dehydration—in a person, a significant loss of body fluids that are not replaced by fluid intake.

dysentery—a chronic diarrhoeal illness that can lead to severe dehydration and, ultimately, death.

elevation—height above mean sea level.

fats—natural oily substances which, in humans, are derived from food and deposited in subcutaneous layers and around some major organs.

GPS—Global Positioning Satellite; refers to the navigational satellites orbiting the Earth, which a GPS receiver utilizes to determine its exact position of longitude and latitude.

grid—the horizontal and vertical lines on a map that enable you to describe position; on a map they have a north–south and east–west orientation.

grid reference—a position defined in relation to a cartographic grid.

hearth—in survival firelighting, the piece of wood on which you generate heat sufficient to ignite tinder.

Hobo stove—an improvised stove made from an empty metal can.

hyperthermia—a condition in which the body temperature rises to a dangerously high level. Also known as heat-stroke.

hypothermia—a condition in which the body temperature falls to a dangerously low level. Also known as exposure.

iodine—a chemical element that has a use in water purification.

kindling—small pieces of dry material, usually thin twigs, added to ignited tinder to develop a fire.

latitude—a measure of distance north or south of the equator.

layering—in survival clothing, refers to the principle of wearing multiple thin layers of clothing to control heat retention.

longitude—a measure of distance east or west of the prime meridian.

lure—anything used in fishing or hunting that tempts prey into a trap or particular location.

magnetic north—the direction of the magnetic North Pole.

minerals—inorganic substances that the human body requires to maintain health.

monsoon—a period of intense rainfall and wind in India and Southeast Asia between May and September annually.

potassium permanganate—a chemical that can be used to sterilize water.

proteins—organic compounds that form an essential part of living organisms. Among other things, they are integral to the function of body tissue, muscle and antibodies.

quarry—in tracking, the animal or human that is being hunted or pursued.

savannah—grassy plains of tropical and subtropical regions with flat terrain and very few trees.

sign—a term used by trackers to denote any disturbance in the environment that indicates the previous passing of a human or animal.

smoking—the process of drying out food over a smoky fire, to increase the food's storage life.

solar still—a device that traps moisture from the soil under a plastic sheet, this condensing out into drinkable water.

stalking—in tracking, the art of moving silently and stealthily so as not to alert the quarry to your presence.

temperate—any climate characterized by mild temperatures.

tinder—small pieces of light and dry material that are very easily ignited and are used to initiate a fire.

track—a line of sign that indicates the route of an animal or human quarry through the environment.

tracking—the pursuit of an animal or human quarry by observing and following the sign they have left behind. See also sign.

transit—an imaginary straight line extended through two landmarks and used as a position line.

transpiration bag—a plastic bag tied around vegetation to trap water vapour emitted by the plant and condense it out into drinking water.

tropical—denotes the latitudes 23° 26′ north or south of the equator.

true north—the direction of the geographic North Pole.

UET—Universal Edibility Test; a test to determine whether unidentified plants (not fungi) are safe for consumption.

vitamins—a group of organic compounds that are an essential part of human nutrition, though they are required in only very small doses.

Yukon stove—an advanced survival stove consisting of a chimney of mud-packed stones over a cooking pit.

INDEX

Page numbers in italics refer to illustrations

T

Y